HISTORY BEGINS AT SUMER

DR. SAMUEL NOAH KRAMER was born in Russia in 1897 and came to the United States at the age of nine. After graduating from the University of Pennsylvania, he went with a group from that university to excavate in Iraq in 1930. A Fellow of the American Council of Learned Societies, Dr. Kramer was also a Fulbright Research Professor in Turkey and was an annual professor of the American Schools of Oriental Research. Now one of the foremost Sumerologists in the United States, Dr. Kramer became the first American to breach the wall dividing scholarship in the Iron Curtain countries from the West when he received permission to study the tablet collection at the Friedrich-Schiller University in Jena, in East Germany. He is at present Clark Research Professor of Assyriology at the University of Pennsylvania and Curator of the tablet collections at the University Museum there.

HISTORY BEGINS AT
SUMER

Samuel Noah Kramer

Doubleday Anchor Books
Doubleday & Company, Inc.
Garden City, New York

COVER AND TYPOGRAPHY BY EDWARD GOREY

History Begins at Sumer was originally published by The Falcon's Wing Press in 1956. The Anchor Books edition is published by arrangement with The Falcon's Wing Press.

Anchor Books edition: 1959

To the memory of
The master of Sumerological method
my teacher and colleague
Arno Poebel
(1881–1958)

PREFACE

For the past twenty-six years I have been active in Sumerological research, particularly in the field of Sumerian literature. The ensuing studies have appeared primarily in the form of highly specialized books, monographs, and articles scattered in a number of scholarly journals. The present book brings together—for the layman, humanist, and scholar—some of the significant results embodied in those Sumerological researches and publications.

The book consists of twenty-seven essays strung on a common thread: they all treat of "firsts" in man's recorded history. They are thus of no little significance for the history of ideas and the study of cultural origins. But this is only secondary and accidental, a by-product, as it were, of all Sumerological research. The main purpose of the essays is to present a cross section of the spiritual and cultural achievements of one of man's earliest and most creative civilizations. All the major fields of human endeavor are represented: government and politics, education and literature, philosophy and ethics, law and justice, even agriculture and medicine. The available evidence is sketched in what, it is hoped, is clear and unambiguous language. Above all, the ancient documents themselves are put before the reader either in full or in the form of essential excerpts, so that he can sample their mood and flavor as well as follow the main threads of the argument.

The greater part of the material gathered in this volume

is seasoned with my "blood, toil, tears, and sweat"; hence the rather personal note throughout its pages. The text of most of the documents was first pieced together and translated by me, and in not a few cases I actually identified the tablets on which they are based and even prepared the hand copies of their inscriptions.

Sumerology, however, is but a branch of cuneiform studies, and these began more than a century ago. In the course of these years, scores of scholars have made innumerable contributions which the present-day cuneiformist utilizes and builds on, consciously and unconsciously. Most of these scholars are now long dead, and today's Sumerologist can do no more than bow his head in simple gratitude as he uses the results of his unnamed predecessors' labors. Soon his days, too, will come to an end, and his more fruitful findings will become part of the collective stream of cuneiform progress.

Among the more recent dead, there are four to whom I feel especially indebted: to the eminent French savant, François Thureau-Dangin, who dominated the cuneiform scene for half a century and who exemplified my ideal of a scholar—productive, lucid, aware of the significant, and ever prepared to admit ignorance rather than overtheorize; to Anton Deimel, the Vatican scholar with a keen sense of lexicographical order and organization, whose monumental *Schumerisches Lexikon* proved highly useful in spite of its numerous drawbacks; and to Edward Chiera, whose vision and diligence helped pave the way for my own researches in Sumerian literature.

But it is to Arno Poebel, the leading Sumerologist of the past half century, that my researches owe the heaviest debt. In the early thirties, as a member of the Assyrian Dictionary Staff of the Oriental Institute, I sat at his feet and drank in his words. In those days, when Sumerology was practically an unknown discipline in America, Poebel, a master of Sumerological method, gave me generously of his time and knowledge.

Among the living cuneiformists whose work I have found most valuable, especially from the point of view of Sumerian lexicography, are Adam Falkenstein of Heidelberg, and

Thorkild Jacobsen of the Oriental Institute of the University of Chicago. Their names and works will appear frequently in the text of this book. In the case of Jacobsen, moreover, a rather close collaboration has developed as a result of the tablet finds of the joint Oriental Institute-University Museum expedition to Nippur in the years 1948–52. The stimulating and suggestive works of Benno Landsberger, one of the most creative minds in cuneiform studies, proved to be a constant source of information and guidance; his more recent works in particular are crowded treasure-houses of cuneiform lexicography.

Sumerology, as the reader may surmise, is not reckoned among the essential disciplines even in the largest American universities, and my chosen path was hardly paved with gold. The climb to a relatively stable and more or less comfortable professorial chair was marked by a constant financial struggle. The years 1937–42 were particularly critical for my scholarly career, and had it not been for a series of grants from the John Simon Guggenheim Memorial Foundation and the American Philosophical Society, it might well have come to a premature end. In recent years, the Bollingen Foundation and the Barth Foundation have made it possible for me to secure at least a minimum of clerical and scientific help for my Sumerological researches, as well as to travel abroad in connection with them.

To the Board of Managers of the University Museum, and to its Director, F. G. Rainey, I am most thankful for the unwavering support and encouragement which they have given to my researches, even when these took me abroad for many months. To my colleagues in the Department of Oriental Studies and in the Department of Anthropology, I am deeply indebted for providing the intellectual stimulation so essential to fruitful scholarly research. The "Interconnections" seminar of the Department of Oriental Studies served as a sounding-board for not a few of the translations and interpretations presented in this book, and the interest and enthusiasm of the participating students and colleagues were of no little spiritual support to me in my Sumerological efforts. I would also like to express my warm thanks to the members of the technical and administrative staffs of the University Museum for their expert practical aid over the years.

To the Department of Antiquities of the Republic of Turkey and to the Director of the Archaeological Museums in Istanbul, I am deeply grateful for generous cooperation. They made it possible for me to benefit from the use of the Sumerian literary tablets in the Museum of the Ancient Orient, whose two curators of the Tablet Collection—Muazzez Cig and Hatice Kizilyay—have been a constant source of very real help, particularly by copying several hundred fragments inscribed with portions of the Sumerian literary works. I am also deeply indebted to the Directorate of Antiquities of the Republic of Iraq for their generous scholarly cooperation on many occasions. For the photographs of the Louvre pieces, I owe a debt of thanks to M. André Parrot, Chief Curator of the Department of Oriental Antiquities, and the members of his staff.

Finally, I wish to express my heartfelt thanks to Mrs. Gertrude Silver, who helped prepare the typescript for this book.

SAMUEL NOAH KRAMER

Philadelphia, Pa.

PHOTOGRAPHIC SOURCES

Reuben Goldberg (staff photographer of the University Museum, University of Pennsylvania): Figures 1, 2, and 3; and Plates 1, 2, 5, 10, and 13.

Audrain: Plates 3, 8, 15, and 17.

Franceschi: Plates 6, 7, 9, 14, and 16.

Antran Evan (staff photographer of the Iraqi Directorate of Antiquities, Baghdad): Plates 4 and 12.

Museum of the Ancient Orient, Istanbul: Plate 11.

Photographic Institute of the Friedrich-Schiller University, Jena: Figure 4.

CONTENTS

ILLUSTRATIONS

Line Drawings

Halftone Plates

Following 92

Following 132

ILLUSTRATIONS

INTRODUCTION

The Sumerologist is one of the narrowest of specialists in the highly specialized academic halls of learning, a well-nigh perfect example of the man who "knows mostest about the leastest." He cuts his world down to that small part of it known as the Middle East, and limits his history to what happened before the days of Alexander the Great. He confines his researches to the written documents discovered in Mesopotamia, primarily clay tablets inscribed in the cuneiform script, and restricts his contributions to texts written in the Sumerian language. He writes and publishes articles and monographs bearing such stimulating titles as "The Be- and Bi-Prefix in the Times of the Early Princes of Lagash," "Lamentation over the Destruction of Ur," "Gilgamesh and Agga of Kish," "Enmerkar and the Lord of Aratta." After twenty to thirty years of these and similar world-shaking researches, he gets his reward: he is a Sumerologist. At least that is how it all happened to me.

Incredible as it may seem, however, this pinpoint historian, this Toynbee in reverse, has something of unusual interest (an "ace in the hole," as it were) to offer to the general reader. The Sumerologist, more than most other scholars and specialists, is in a position to satisfy man's universal quest for origins—for "firsts" in the history of civilization.

What, for example, were man's first recorded ethical ideals and religious ideas—his first political, social, and philosophical rationale? What did the first histories, myths, epics, and hymns sound like? How were the first legal contracts worded? Who was the first social reformer? When did the first tax reduction take place? Who was the first lawgiver? When did the first bicameral congress meet, and for what purpose? What were man's first schools like—their curriculum, faculty, and student body?

These and many similar "firsts" in man's recorded history are the Sumerologist's "meat." He can give the correct answer to many of the questions concerning cultural origins. Not, of course, because he is particularly profound or clairvoyant, unusually sagacious or erudite. Actually, the Sumerologist is a very limited fellow indeed, who rates "way down," even among the lowly academicians. Credit for the high number of cultural "firsts" goes not to the Sumerologist but to the Sumerians—that gifted and practical people who, as far as is known today, were the first to invent and develop a usable and effective system of writing.

One remarkable fact is that only a century ago nothing was known even of the existence of these Sumerians in ancient days. The archaeologists and scholars who, some hundred years ago, began excavating in that part of the Middle East known as Mesopotamia were looking not for Sumerians but for Assyrians and Babylonians. On these peoples and their civilizations they had considerable information from Greek and Hebrew sources, but of Sumer and the Sumerians they had no inkling. There was no recognizable trace either of the land or of its people in the entire literature available to the modern scholar. The very name Sumer had been erased from the mind and memory of man for more than two thousand years.

Yet today the Sumerians are one of the best-known peoples of the ancient Near East. We know what they looked like from their own statues and steles scattered throughout several of the more important museums in this country and abroad. Here, too, will be found an excellent representative cross section of their material culture—the columns and bricks with which they built their temples and palaces, their tools and weapons, pots and vases, harps and lyres, jewels and ornaments. Moreover, Sumerian clay tablets by the tens of thousands (literally), inscribed with their business, legal, and administrative documents, crowd the collections of these same museums, giving us much information about the social structure and administrative organization of the ancient Sumerians. Indeed—and this is where archaeology, because of its mute and static character, is usually least productive—we can even penetrate to a certain extent into their hearts and souls. We actually have a large number of Sumerian clay documents on which are inscribed the literary creations revealing Sumerian religion, ethics, and philosophy. And all this because the Sumerians were one of the very few peoples who not only probably invented a system of writing, but also developed it into a vital and effective instrument of communication.

It was probably toward the end of the *fourth* millennium B.C., about five thousand years ago, that the Sumerians, as a result of their economic and administrative needs, came upon the idea of writing on clay. Their first attempts were crude and pictographic; they could be used only for the simplest administrative notations. But in the centuries that followed, the Sumerian scribes and teachers gradually so modified and molded their system of writing that it completely lost its pictographic character and became a highly conventionalized and purely phonetic system of writing. In the second half of the third millennium B.C., the Sumerian writing technique had become sufficiently plastic and flexible to express without difficulty the most complicated historical and literary compositions. There is little doubt that sometime before the end of the third millennium B.C. the Sumerian men of letters actually wrote down—on clay tablets, prisms, and cylinders—many of their literary creations which until then had been current in oral form only. However, owing to archaeological accident, only a few literary documents from this earlier period have as yet been excavated, although this same period has yielded tens of thousands of economic and administrative tablets and hundreds of votive inscriptions.

It is not until we come to the first half of the *second* millennium B.C. that we find a group of several thousand tablets and fragments inscribed with the Sumerian literary works. The great majority of these were excavated between 1889 and 1900 at Nippur, an ancient Sumerian site not much more than a hundred miles from modern Baghdad. They are now located primarily in the University Museum of Philadelphia and the Museum of the Ancient Orient at Istanbul. Most of the other tablets and fragments were obtained from dealers rather than through excavations, and are now largely in the collections of the British Museum, the Louvre, the Berlin Museum, and Yale University. The documents range in size from large twelve-column tablets, inscribed with hundreds of compactly written lines of text, to tiny fragments containing no more than a few broken lines.

The literary compositions inscribed on these tablets and fragments run into the hundreds. They vary in length from hymns of less than fifty lines to myths of close to a thousand lines. From the point of view of form and content, they display a variety of types and genres which, considering their age, is both startling and revealing. In Sumer, a good millennium before the Hebrews wrote down their Bible and the Greeks their Iliad and Odyssey, we find a rich and mature literature consisting of myths and epic tales, hymns and lamentations, and numerous collections of proverbs, fables, and essays. It is not too unrealistic to predict that the recovery and restoration of this ancient and long-forgotten literature will turn out to be a major contribution of our century to the humanities.

Now, the accomplishment of this task is no simple matter. It will demand the concentrated efforts of numerous Sumerologists over a period of years—especially in view of the fact that most of the sun-baked clay tablets came out of the ground broken and fragmentary, so that only a small part of their original contents is preserved on each piece. Offsetting this disadvantage is the fact that the ancient Sumerian "professors" and their students prepared many copies of each literary work. The breaks and lacunae of one tablet or fragment can therefore frequently be restored from duplicating pieces, which may themselves be in a fragmentary condition. To take full advantage of these text-restoring duplications, however, it is necessary to have the source

Fig. 1. *The Origin and Development of the Cuneiform System of Writing. A table showing the forms
of eighteen representative signs from about 3000 B.C.
to about 600 B.C.*

material available in published form. This frequently en-
tails copying by hand hundreds and hundreds of minutely
inscribed tablets and fragments—a tedious, wearisome, time-
consuming task.

But let us take those rare instances where this particular
hurdle no longer blocks the way—where the complete text
of the Sumerian composition has been satisfactorily restored. All that remains in those instances is to translate the
ancient document and get at its essential meaning, which
is easier said than done. To be sure, the grammar of the
long-dead Sumerian language is now fairly well known, as
a result of the cumulative contributions of scholars over the
past hundred years. But the vocabulary is something else
again. In the matter of semantics, the uncomfortable Sumerologist finds himself time and again "chasing his own
tail." Very often he can only guess the meaning of a word
from the sense of the surrounding context, which itself may
depend on the meaning of the word—a rather frustrating
state of affairs. Nevertheless, in spite of textual difficulties
and lexical perplexities, a number of reasonably trustworthy
translations of the Sumerian literary works have appeared
in recent years. Based on the contributions of various scholars, living and dead, the translations vividly illustrate the
cumulative, cooperative, and international character of productive scholarship. The fact is that, in the decades following the excavations of the Sumerian literary tablets from
Nippur, more than one scholar, realizing the value and importance of their contents for Oriental studies, examined
and copied some of them. Among them were George Barton,
Leon Legrain, Henry Lutz, and David Myhrman, all of
whom contributed to this task.

Hugo Radau, the first to devote much time and energy
to the Sumerian literary material, prepared careful and
trustworthy copies of more than forty pieces in the University Museum at Philadelphia. Though the time was not
ripe, he worked diligently on the translation and interpretation of the texts and made some progress in this direction.
The well-known Anglo-American Orientalist, Stephen Langdon, picked up, in a sense, where Radau left off. He copied
close to a hundred pieces from the Nippur collections of

both the Istanbul Museum of the Ancient Orient and our own University Museum. Langdon had a tendency to copy too rapidly, and not a few errors crept into his work. Moreover, his attempted translations and interpretations have failed to stand the test of time. On the other hand, he did succeed in making available, in one form or another, a number of very important Sumerian literary texts that might otherwise have remained stored away in the museum cupboards. By his zest and enthusiasm he helped to make his fellow cuneiformists realize the significance of their contents.

At the same time the European museums were gradually making available the Sumerian literary tablets in their collections. As early as 1902, when Sumerology was still in its infancy, the British cuneiformist and historian L. W. King published sixteen excellently preserved tablets from the British Museum. Some ten years later, Heinrich Zimmern of Leipzig published copies of some two hundred pieces in the Berlin Museum. In 1921, Cyril Gadd, then a Keeper in the British Museum, published copies of ten unusual pieces. In 1930, the late Henri de Genouillac, French excavator, made available ninety-eight copies of unusually well-preserved tablets which the Louvre had acquired. One of the outstanding contributors to the field of Sumerian literature and to Sumerological studies as a whole is Arno Poebel, the scholar who put Sumerology on a scientific basis with his publication of a detailed Sumerian grammar in 1923. In his monumental and invaluable *Historical and Grammatical Texts*, which contains superb copies of more than 150 tablets and fragments from the Nippur collection of the University Museum in Philadelphia, there are close to forty that are inscribed with parts of Sumerian literary works.

But it is the name of Edward Chiera, for many years a member of the faculty of the University of Pennsylvania, which is pre-eminent in the field of Sumerian literary research. He had a clearer idea than any of his predecessors of the scope and character of the Sumerian literary works. Aware of the fundamental need for copying and publishing the pertinent Nippur material in Istanbul and Philadelphia, he traveled to Istanbul in 1924 and copied some fifty pieces from the Nippur collection. A number of these were large and well-preserved tablets, and their contents gave scholars a fresh insight into Sumerian literary works. In the years that followed, he copied more than two hundred literary tablets and fragments from the Nippur collection of the University Museum. Thus he made available to his fellow cuneiformists more of these texts than all his predecessors put together. It is largely as a result of his patient and far-sighted spadework that the true nature of Sumerian belles-lettres finally began to be appreciated.

My own interest in this highly specialized field of research stemmed directly from Edward Chiera's contributions, though I actually owe my Sumerological training to Arno Poebel, with whom I was privileged to work closely for a number of years in the early thirties. When Chiera was called to the Oriental Institute of the University of Chicago, as head of its Assyrian Dictionary project, he took with him his copies of the Nippur literary tablets, and the Oriental Institute undertook to publish them in two volumes. Upon Chiera's death in 1933, the editorial department of the Oriental Institute entrusted me with the preparation of these two volumes for posthumous (under Chiera's authorship) publication. It was in the course of carrying out this task that the significance of the Sumerian literary documents dawned on me, as well as the realization that all efforts to translate and interpret the documents would remain largely futile and barren until many more of the uncopied Nippur tablets and fragments in Istanbul and Philadelphia had been made available.

In the two decades that followed I have devoted most of my scientific efforts to the copying, piecing together, translation, and interpretation of the Sumerian literary compositions. In 1937 I traveled to Istanbul as a Guggenheim Fellow, and, with the full cooperation of the Turkish Directorate of Antiquities and of its authorized museum officials, I copied from the Nippur collection of its museum more than 170 tablets and fragments inscribed with portions of Sumerian literary works. These copies have now been published with a detailed introduction in Turkish and English. The succeeding years were spent largely at the Uni-

versity Museum in Philadelphia. Here, with the help of
several generous grants from the American Philosophical
Society, I studied and catalogued the hundreds of unpublished Sumerian literary documents, identifying the contents of most of them so that they could be attributed to
one or another of the numerous Sumerian compositions, and
I copied a number of them. In 1946 I traveled once again
to Istanbul and copied another hundred-odd pieces, practically all inscribed with portions of myths and epic tales;
these are now being prepared for publication. But this still
left, as I knew only too well, hundreds of pieces in the Istanbul museum uncopied and unutilizable. It was for the purpose of continuing this task that I was awarded a Fulbright
research professorship to Turkey for the academic year
1951–52. In this period, three of us—the ladies Hatice
Kizilyay and Muazzez Cig (the Turkish curators of the
Tablet Archives of the Istanbul Museum of the Ancient
Orient) and I—copied close to 300 additional tablets and
fragments.

In recent years, finally, a new stock of Sumerian literary
pieces became available. In 1948, the Oriental Institute of
the University of Chicago and the University Museum in
Philadelphia pooled their financial resources and sent out
a joint expedition to renew excavations at Nippur after a
lapse of some fifty years. Not unexpectedly, this new expedition uncovered hundreds of new tablets and fragments,
and these are being carefully studied by Thorkild Jacobsen
of the Oriental Institute, one of the world's outstanding cuneiformists, and the present writer. It is already apparent
that the newly discovered material will fill in many lacunae
in Sumerian belles-lettres. There is good reason to hope that
not a few Sumerian literary works will be made available
in the next decade, and that these, too, will reveal numerous "firsts" in man's recorded history.

HISTORY BEGINS AT SUMER

1 *Education*

THE FIRST SCHOOLS

The Sumerian school was the direct outgrowth of the invention and development of the cuneiform system of writing, Sumer's most significant contribution to civilization. The first written documents were found in a Sumerian city named Erech. They consist of more than a thousand small pictographic clay tablets inscribed primarily with bits of economic and administrative memoranda. But among them are several which contain word lists intended for study and practice. That is, as early as 3000 B.C., some scribes were already thinking in terms of teaching and learning. Progress was slow in the centuries that followed. But by the middle of the third millennium, there must have been a number of schools throughout Sumer where writing was taught formally. In ancient Shuruppak, the home city of the Sumerian "Noah," there were excavated, in 1902–3, a considerable number of school "textbooks" dating from about 2500 B.C.

However, it was in the last half of the third millennium that the Sumerian school system matured and flourished. From this period there have already been excavated tens of thousands of clay tablets, and there is little doubt that hundreds of thousands more lie buried in the ground, awaiting the future excavator. The vast majority are administrative in character; they cover every phase of Sumerian economic life. From them we learn that the number of scribes who practiced their craft throughout those years ran into the thousands. There were junior and "high" scribes, royal and temple scribes, scribes who were highly specialized for particular categories of administrative activities, and scribes who became leading officials in government. There is every reason to assume, therefore, that numerous scribal schools of considerable size and importance flourished throughout the land.

But none of these earlier tablets deal directly with the Sumerian school system, its organization, and its method of operation. For this type of information we must go to the first half of the second millennium B.C. From this later period there have been excavated hundreds of practice tablets filled with all sorts of exercises actually prepared by the pupils themselves as part of their daily school work. Their script ranges from the sorry scratches of the first-grader to the elegantly written signs of the far-advanced student about to become a "graduate." By inference, these ancient "copybooks" tell us not a little about the method of teaching current in the Sumerian school and about the nature of its curriculum. Fortunately, the ancient Sumerian teachers themselves liked to write about school life, and several of their essays on this subject have been recovered at least in part. From all these sources we get a picture of the Sumerian school—its aims and goals, its students and faculty, its curriculum and teaching techniques. This is unique for so early a period in the history of man.

The original goal of the Sumerian school was what we would term "professional"—that is, it was first established for the purpose of training the scribes required to satisfy the economic and administrative demands of the land, primarily those of the temple and palace. This continued to be the major aim of the Sumerian school throughout its existence. However, in the course of its growth and development, and particularly as a result of the ever widening curriculum, the school came to be the center of culture and learning in Sumer. Within its walls flourished the scholar-scientist, the man who studied whatever theological, botanical, zoological, mineralogical, geographical, mathematical, grammatical, and linguistic knowledge was current in his day, and who in some cases added to this knowledge.

Moreover, rather unlike present-day institutions of learning, the Sumerian school was also the center of what might be termed creative writing. It was here that the literary creations of the past were studied and copied; here, too, new ones were composed. While it is true that the majority of graduates from the Sumerian schools became scribes in the service of the temple and palace, and among the rich and powerful of the land, there were some who devoted their lives to teaching and learning. Like the university professor of today, many of these ancient scholars depended on their teaching salaries for their livelihood, and devoted themselves to research and writing in their spare time. The Sumerian school, which probably began as a temple appendage, became in time a secular institution; its curriculum, too, became largely secular in character. The teachers were paid, apparently, out of tuition fees collected from the students.

Education was neither universal nor compulsory. Most of the students came from wealthy families; the poor could hardly afford the cost and time which a prolonged education demanded. Until recently this was assumed *a priori* to be the state of affairs, but in 1946 a German cuneiformist, Nikolaus Schneider, ingeniously proved it from actual contemporary sources. In the thousands of published economic and administrative documents from about 2000 B.C., some five hundred individuals listed themselves as scribes, and for further identification many of them added the name of their father and his occupation. Schneider compiled a list of these data, and found that fathers of the scribes—that is, of the school graduates—were governors, "city fathers," ambassadors, temple administrators, military officers, sea captains, high tax officials, priests of various sorts, managers, supervisors, foremen, scribes, archivists, and accountants. In short, the fathers were the wealthier citizens of urban communities. Not a single woman is listed as a scribe in these documents, and it is therefore likely that the student body of the Sumerian school consisted of males only.

Head of the Sumerian school was the *ummia*, "expert," "professor," who was also called "school father," while the pupil was called "school son." The assistant professor was

known as "big brother," and some of his duties were to write
the new tablets for the pupils to copy, to examine the copies
made by the pupils, and to hear them recite their studies
from memory. Other members of the faculty were "the man
in charge of drawing" and "the man in charge of Sumerian."
There were also monitors in charge of attendance and "a
man in charge of the whip," who was presumably responsible for discipline. We know nothing of the relative rank
of the school personnel, except that the headmaster was the
"school father." Nor do we know anything about their
sources of income. Probably they were paid by the "school
father" from the tuition fees he received.

In regard to the curriculum of the Sumerian school, there
is at our disposal a wealth of data from the schools themselves, which is indeed unique in the history of early man.
In this case there is no need to depend on the statements
made by the ancients or on inference from scattered bits
of information. We actually have the written products of
the schoolboys themselves, from the beginner's first attempts to the copies of the advanced student, whose work
was so well prepared that it could hardly be distinguished
from that of the professor himself. It is from these school
products that we realize that the Sumerian school's curriculum consisted of two primary groups: the first may be described as semiscientific and scholarly; the second as literary
and creative.

In considering the first, or semiscientific group, it is important to stress that the subjects did not stem out of what
may be called the scientific urge—the search for truth for
truth's sake. Rather, they grew and developed out of the
main school aim: to teach the scribe how to write the Sumerian language. In order to satisfy this pedagogical need,
the Sumerian scribal teachers devised a system of instruction which consisted primarily in linguistic classification—
that is, they classified the Sumerian language into groups
of related words and phrases and had the students mem-
orize and copy them until they could reproduce them with
ease. In the third millennium B.C., these "textbooks" became increasingly more complete, and gradually grew to be
more or less stereotyped and standard for all the schools

of Sumer. Among them we find long lists of names of trees and reeds; of all sorts of animals, including insects and birds; of countries, cities, and villages; of stones and minerals. These compilations reveal a considerable acquaintance with what might be termed botanical, zoological, geographical, and mineralogical lore—a fact that is only now beginning to be realized by historians of science.

Sumerian schoolmen also prepared various mathematical tables and many detailed mathematical problems together with their solutions. In the field of linguistics the study of Sumerian grammar was well represented among the school tablets. A number are inscribed with long lists of substantive complexes and verbal forms, indicating a highly sophisticated grammatical approach. Moreover, as a result of the gradual conquest of the Sumerians by the Semitic Akkadians in the last quarter of the third millennium B.C., the Sumerian professors prepared the oldest "dictionaries" known to man. The Semitic conquerors not only borrowed the Sumerian script but also treasured highly the Sumerian literary works, which they studied and imitated long after Sumerian had become extinct as a spoken language. Hence, there arose the pedagogical need for "dictionaries" in which Sumerian words and phrases were translated into the Akkadian language.

As for the literary and creative aspects of the Sumerian curriculum, it consisted primarily in studying, copying, and imitating the large and diversified group of literary compositions which must have originated and developed mainly in the latter half of the third millennium B.C. These ancient works, running into the hundreds, were almost all poetic in form, ranging in length from less than fifty lines to close to a thousand. Those recovered to date are chiefly of the following genres: myths and epic tales in the form of narrative poems celebrating the deeds and exploits of the Sumerian gods and heroes; hymns to gods and kings; lamentations bewailing the destruction of Sumerian cities; wisdom compositions including proverbs, fables, and essays. Of the several thousand literary tablets and fragments recovered from the ruins of Sumer, not a few are in the immature hand of the ancient Sumerian pupils themselves.

Little is known as yet of the teaching methods and techniques practiced in the Sumerian school. In the morning, upon his arrival in school, the student evidently studied the tablet which he had prepared the day before. Then the "big brother"—that is, the assistant professor—prepared a new tablet, which the student proceeded to copy and study. Both the "big brother" and the "school father" probably examined his copies to see if they were correct. No doubt memorizing played a very large role in the students' work. The teachers and assistants must have supplemented, with considerable oral and explanatory material, the bare lists, tables, and literary texts which the student copied and studied. But these "lectures," which would have proved invaluable to our understanding of Sumerian scientific, religious, and literary thought, were in all probability never written down and hence are lost to us forever.

One fact stands out: the Sumerian school had none of the character of what we would call progressive education. In the matter of discipline, there was no sparing of the rod. While teachers probably encouraged their students, by means of praise and commendation, to do good work, they depended primarily on the cane for correcting the students' faults and inadequacies. The student did not have an easy time of it. He attended school daily from sunrise to sunset. He must have had some vacation in the school year, but on this we have no information. He devoted many years to his studies, staying in school from his early youth to the day when he became a young man. It would be interesting to know if, when, and to what extent the students were expected to specialize in one study or another. But on this point, as indeed on many other points concerned with school activities, our sources fail us.

What was the ancient Sumerian schoolhouse like? In several Mesopotamian excavations, buildings have turned up which for one reason or another were identified as possible schoolhouses—one in Nippur, another in Sippar, and a third in Ur. But, except for the fact that a large number of tablets were found in the rooms, there seems little to distinguish them from ordinary house rooms, and the identification may be erroneous. However, in the winter of 1934–35, the

French, who excavated ancient Mari far to the west of Nippur, uncovered two rooms which definitely seem to show physical features that might be characteristic of a schoolroom, especially since they contained several rows of benches made of baked brick, capable of seating one, two, or four people.

Just how did the students themselves feel about this system of education? For at least a partial answer, we turn, in Chapter 2, to a Sumerian essay on school life written almost four thousand years ago but only recently pieced together and translated. It is particularly informative on pupil-teacher relations and provides a unique "first" in the history of education.

2 *Schooldays*

THE FIRST CASE OF
''APPLE-POLISHING''

One of the most human documents ever excavated in the
Near East is a Sumerian essay dealing with the day-
to-day activities of a schoolboy. Composed by an anonymous schoolteacher who lived about 2000 B.C., its simple,
straightforward words reveal how little human nature has
really changed throughout the millenniums. In this ancient
essay, a Sumerian schoolboy, not unlike his modern counterpart, dreads being late to school "lest his teacher cane him."
On waking up, he urges his mother to prepare his lunch
hurriedly. In school, whenever he misbehaves, he is caned
by the teacher and his assistants; of this we are quite sure,
since the Sumerian sign for flogging consists of "stick" and
"flesh." As for the teacher, his pay seems to have been as
meager then as a teacher's pay is now; at least he was only
too happy to make a little extra from the parents to eke
out his earnings.

The composition, which was no doubt the creation of one
of the "professors" in the "tablet-house," begins with a direct question to the pupil: "Schoolboy, where did you go
from earliest days?" The boy answers: "I went to school."
The author then asks: "What did you do in school?" There
follows the pupil's reply, which takes up more than half
the document and reads in part: "I recited my tablet, ate
my lunch, prepared my (new) tablet, wrote it, finished it;

then they assigned me my oral work, and in the afternoon they assigned me my written work. When school was dismissed, I went home, entered the house, and found my father sitting there. I told my father of my written work, then recited my tablet to him, and my father was delighted. . . . When I awoke early in the morning, I faced my mother and said to her: 'Give me my lunch, I want to go to school.' My mother gave me two 'rolls' and I set out; my mother gave me two 'rolls' and I went to school. In school the monitor in charge said to me, 'Why are you late?' Afraid and with pounding heart, I entered before my teacher and made a respectful curtsy."

But curtsy or not, it seems to have been a bad day for this pupil. He had to take canings from the various members of the school staff for such indiscretions as talking, standing up, and walking out of the gate. Worst of all, the teacher said to him, "Your hand (copy) is not satisfactory," and caned him. This seems to have been too much for the lad, and he suggests to his father that it might be a good idea to invite the teacher home and mollify him with some presents—by all odds the first recorded case of "apple-polishing" in the history of man. The composition continues: "To that which the schoolboy said his father gave heed. The teacher was brought from school, and after entering the house he was seated in the seat of honor. The schoolboy attended and served him, and whatever he had learned of the art of tablet-writing he unfolded to his father."

The father then wined and dined the teacher, "dressed him in a new garment, gave him a gift, put a ring on his hand." Warmed by this generosity, the teacher reassures the aspiring scribe in poetic words, which read in part: "Young man, because you did not neglect my word, did not forsake it, may you reach the pinnacle of the scribal art, may you achieve it completely. . . . Of your brothers may you be their leader, of your friends may you be their chief, may you rank the highest of the schoolboys. . . . You have carried out well the school's activities, you have become a man of learning."

With these enthusiastic and optimistic words of the pro-

fessor, the "school days" essay comes to an end. Little did
he dream that his literary vignette on school life as he knew
it would be resurrected and restored some four thousand
years later by a twentieth-century professor in an American
university. Fortunately it was a popular essay in ancient
days, as can be seen from the fact that twenty-one copies,
in various states of preservation, have come to light: thirteen are in the University Museum in Philadelphia; seven
are in the Museum of the Ancient Orient in Istanbul, and
one is in the Louvre in Paris.

The story of the gradual piecing together of the text is
as follows: As early as 1909 the first bit of text from the
"school days" document was copied and published by a
young cuneiformist, Hugo Radau. It was an extract from
the middle of the composition, and Radau had no way of
knowing what it was all about. In the next twenty-five
years, additional bits were published by the late famed
Orientalists, Stephen Langdon, Edward Chiera, and Henri
de Genouillac. But still there was not enough material on
hand to gather the real significance of the text. In 1938,
during a prolonged stay in Istanbul, I succeeded in identifying five more pieces belonging to our document. One of
these was a fairly well-preserved four-column tablet which
had originally contained the entire text of our composition.
It enabled me to place the other pieces in their proper position. Since then, additional pieces in the University Museum have been identified, ranging in length from a well-
preserved four-column tablet to small fragments containing
no more than a few broken lines. As a result, except for
a few broken signs, practically the entire text of the document was pieced together and restored.

But this was only the first hurdle in the scholarly process
of making the contents of our ancient document available
to the world at large. A trustworthy translation is every bit
as important and far more difficult. Several portions of the
document have been successfully translated by the Sumerologists Thorkild Jacobsen, of the Oriental Institute of the
University of Chicago, and Adam Falkenstein, of the University of Heidelberg. These translations, together with a
number of suggestions by Benno Landsberger, formerly of

Leipzig and Ankara and now of the Oriental Institute of the University of Chicago, were utilized in the preparation of the first translation of the entire document. This was published in 1949 in the highly specialized *Journal of the American Oriental Society*. Needless to say, not a few of the Sumerian words and phrases in the ancient essay are still uncertain and obscure. No doubt some future professor will succeed in arriving at an exact rendering.

The Sumerian school was rather dreary and uninviting: the curriculum was "stiff," the teaching methods drab, the discipline harsh. No wonder then that at least some of the pupils played truant whenever possible, and became "problem" children. Which brings us to the first recorded example of "juvenile delinquency." Interestingly enough, it is also one of the earliest documents in which we find the Sumerian word for "humanity," *namlulu*, used, like its English counterpart, in the sense of conduct and behavior fit for humans.

3 *Father and Son*

THE FIRST CASE OF
JUVENILE DELINQUENCY

If juvenile delinquency is a serious problem in our day, it
might be consoling to know that things were not too different in ancient days. Wayward, disobedient, and ungrateful
children were the bane of their parents thousands of years
ago as well as today. They roamed the streets and boulevards and loitered in the public squares, perhaps even in
gangs, in spite of the fact that they were supervised by a
monitor. They hated school and education and made their
fathers sick to death with their everlasting gripes and complaints. All this we learn from the text of a Sumerian essay,
which was only very recently pieced together. The seven-
teen clay tablets and fragments on which the essay has been
found inscribed actually date back some 3,700 years; its
original composition may go back several centuries earlier.

The composition which concerns a scribe and his perverse son, begins with an introduction consisting of a more
or less friendly dialogue between father and son, in which
the latter is admonished to go to school, work diligently,
and report back without loitering in the streets. To make
sure that the lad has paid close attention, the father has
him repeat his words verbatim.

From here on the essay is a monologue on the part of
the father. It starts with a series of practical instructions
to help make a man of his son; not to gad about in the

streets and boulevards; to be humble before his monitor; to go to school and learn from the experience of man's early past. There follows a bitter rebuke to the wayward son, who, his father claims, has made him sick to death with his perennial fears and inhuman behavior. He, the father, is deeply disappointed at the son's ingratitude; he never made him work behind plow or ox, nor did he ever ask him to bring firewood, or support him as other fathers make their sons do. And yet his son turned out to be less of a man than the others.

Like many a disappointed parent of today, the father seems to be especially hurt that his son refuses to follow his professional footsteps and become a scribe. He admonishes him to emulate his companions, friends, and brothers; to follow his own profession, the scribal art, in spite of the fact that it is the most difficult of all professions which the god of arts and crafts thought up and brought into being. It is most useful, the father argues, for the poetic transmission of man's experience. But in any case, he continues, it is decreed by Enlil, the king of all the gods, that a son should follow his father's profession.

After a final upbraiding for the son's pursuit of materialistic success rather than humanistic endeavor, the text becomes rather obscure; it seems to consist of brief, pithy sayings, intended perhaps to guide the son in true wisdom. In any case the essay closes on a happy note, with the father blessing his son and praying that he find favor in the eyes of his personal god, the moon-god Nanna and his wife, the goddess Ningal.

Here now is a quite literal, if tentative, translation of the more intelligible portions of the essay only omitting here and there an obscure phrase or broken line.

The father begins by asking his son:

"Where did you go?"
"I did not go anywhere."
"If you did not go anywhere, why do you idle about? Go to school, stand before your 'school-father,' recite your assignment, open your schoolbag, write your tablet, let your 'big brother' write your new tablet for you. After you

have finished your assignment and reported to your moni-
tor, come to me, and do not wander about in the street.
Come now, do you know what I said?"

"I know, I'll tell it to you."

"Come, now, repeat it to me."

"I'll repeat it to you."

"Tell it to me."

"Come on, tell it to me."

"You told me to go to school, recite my assignment, open
my schoolbag, write my tablet, while my 'big brother' is
to write my new tablet. After finishing my assignment, I
am to proceed to my work and to come to you after I have
reported to my monitor. That's what you told me."

The father now continues with a long monologue:

"Come now, be a man. Don't stand about in the public
square, or wander about the boulevard. When walking in
the street, don't look all around. Be humble and show fear
before your monitor. When you show terror, the monitor
will like you."

. . . . [About fifteen lines destroyed.]

"You who wander about in the public square, would you
achieve success? Then seek out the first generations. Go to
school, it will be of benefit to you. My son, seek out the
first generations, inquire of them.

"Perverse one over whom I stand watch—I would not be
a man did I not stand watch over my son—I spoke to my kin,
compared its men, but found none like you among them.

"What I am about to relate to you turns the fool into
a wise man, holds the snake as if by charms, and will not
let you accept false phrases. Because my heart had been
sated with weariness of you, I kept away from you and
heeded not your fears and grumblings—no, I heeded not
your fears and grumblings. Because of your clamorings,
yes, because of your clamorings—I was angry with you—
yes, I was angry with you. Because you do not look to your
humanity, my heart was carried off as if by an evil wind.
Your grumblings have put an end to me, you have brought
me to the point of death.

"I, never in all my life did I make you carry reeds to the canebrake. The reed rushes which the young and the little carry, you, never in your life did you carry them. I never said to you 'Follow my caravans.' I never sent you to work, to plow my field. I never sent you to work to dig up my field. I never sent you to work as a laborer. 'Go, work and support me,' I never in my life said to you.

"Others like you support their parents by working. If you spoke to your kin, and appreciated them, you would emulate them. They provide 10 gur (72 bushels) barley each —even the young ones provided their fathers with 10 gur each. They multiplied barley for their father, maintained him in barley, oil, and wool. But you, you're a man when it comes to perverseness, but compared to them you are not a man at all. You certainly don't labor like them—they are the sons of fathers who make their sons labor, but me— I didn't make you work like them.

"Perverse one with whom I am furious—who is the man who can really be furious with his son—I spoke to my kin and found something hitherto unnoticed. The words which I shall relate to you, fear them and be on your guard because of them. Your partner, your yokemate—you failed to appreciate him; why do you not emulate him? Your friend, your companion—you failed to appreciate him; why do you not emulate him? Emulate your older brother. Emulate your younger brother. Among all mankind's craftsmen who dwell in the land, as many as Enki (the god of arts and crafts) called by name (brought into existence), no work as difficult as the scribal art did he call by name. For if not for song (poetry)—like the banks of the sea, the banks of the distant canals, is the heart of song distant—you wouldn't be listening to my counsel, and I wouldn't be repeating to you the wisdom of my father. It is in accordance with the fate decreed by Enlil for man that a son follows the work of his father.

"I, night and day am I tortured because of you. Night and day you waste in pleasures. You have accumulated much wealth, have expanded far and wide, have become fat, big, broad, powerful, and puffed. But your kin waits

*expectantly for your misfortune, and will rejoice at it be-
cause you looked not to your humanity."*

(Here follows an obscure passage of 41 lines which
seems to consist of proverbs and old saws; the essay then
concludes with the father's poetic blessing.)

*"From him who quarrels with you may Nanna, your god,
        save you,
From him who attacks you may Nanna, your god, save you,
May you find favor before your god,
May your humanity exalt you, neck and breast,
May you be the head of your city's sages,
May your city utter your name in favored places,
May your god call you by a good name,
May you find favor before your god Nanna,
May you be regarded with favor by the goddess Ningal."*

But though they may prefer not to admit it, it is not the
professors, poets, and humanists who run the world, but
the statesmen, politicians, and soldiers. And so our next
"first," in Chapter 4, is about "power politics," and a Sumerian ruler of five thousand years ago who could manage
"political incidents" successfully.

THE FIRST
"WAR OF NERVES"

Where the Sea of Marmara branches out into the gulf-like
Golden Horn and the river-like Bosphorus, is situated a part
of Istanbul known as Saray-burnu or "Palace-nose." Here,
in the shelter of high and impenetrable walls, Mehmed II,
the conqueror of Istanbul, built his palace and residence
almost five hundred years ago. In the centuries that followed, sultan after sultan added afresh to this palace complex, building new kiosks and mosques, installing new foun-
tains, laying out new gardens. In the well-paved courts and
terraced gardens wandered the ladies of the harem and
their attendants, the princes and their pages. Few were
privileged to enter the palace grounds, and fewer still were
permitted to witness its inner life.

But gone are the days of the sultans, and "Palace-nose"
has taken on a different aspect. The high towered walls are
largely broken down. The private gardens have been turned
into public parks for the people of Istanbul to find shade
and rest on hot summer days. As for the buildings themselves—the forbidden palaces and the secretive kiosks—most
of them have become museums. Gone forever is the sultan's
heavy hand. Turkey is a republic.

In a many-windowed room in one of these museums, the
Museum of the Ancient Orient, I sit at a large rectangular
table. On the wall facing me hangs a large photograph of

the broad-faced, sad-eyed Ataturk, the beloved founder and hero of the new Turkish Republic. Much is still to be said and written about this remarkable man, in some ways one of the most significant political figures of our century. But it is not with modern "heroes" that I am concerned, no matter how epoch-making their achievements. I am a Sumerologist, and my business is with the long-forgotten "heroes" of the far-distant past.

On the table before me is a clay tablet written by a scribe who lived almost four thousand years ago. The script is cuneiform, or wedge-shaped; the language is Sumerian. The tablet is square in shape, nine by nine inches; it is therefore smaller in area than a standard sheet of typewriter paper. But the scribe who wrote this tablet divided it into twelve columns. By using a minute script, he succeeded in inscribing in this limited space more than six hundred lines of a Sumerian heroic poem. We may call it "Enmerkar and the Lord of Aratta." Though its characters and events go back almost five thousand years, they have a strangely familiar ring to our modern ears, for the poem records a political incident suggestive of the power-politics techniques of our own day and age.

Once upon a time, this poem tells us, many centuries before the scribe who wrote it was born, there lived a far-famed Sumerian hero named Enmerkar. He ruled over Erech, a city-state in southern Mesopotamia, between the Tigris and Euphrates Rivers. Far to the north of Erech, in Iran, lay Aratta, another city-state. It was separated from Erech by seven mountain ranges, and was perched so high on a mountain top that it was difficult to approach. Aratta was a prosperous town, rich in metal and stone—the very materials that were entirely lacking in the flat lowlands of Mesopotamia, where Enmerkar's city, Erech, was situated. No wonder, then, that Enmerkar cast longing and covetous eyes upon Aratta and its riches. Determined to make its people and ruler his subjects, he proceeded to unloose a "war of nerves" against the lord of Aratta and its inhabitants. He succeeded in breaking down their morale to the point where they gave up their independence and became the vassals of Erech.

All this is told in the leisurely, roundabout style characteristic of epic poetry the world over. Our poem begins with
a preamble that sings the greatness of Erech and Kullab
(a district within Erech or in its immediate neighborhood)
from the very beginning of time, and stresses its superiority
over Aratta as a result of the goddess Inanna's preference.
The real action then begins with the words "once upon a
time."

The poet relates how Enmerkar, son of the sun-god Utu,
having determined to make a vassal state of Aratta, im-
plores his sister, Inanna, the powerful Sumerian goddess of
love and war, to see to it that the people of Aratta bring
gold, silver, lapis lazuli, and precious stones, and build for
him various shrines and temples, particularly the *Abzu*-
temple—that is, the "sea" temple of Enki, the Sumerian
water-god's main seat of worship in Eridu, a city near the
Persian Gulf.

Inanna, heeding Enmerkar's plea, advises him to seek out
a suitable herald to cross the imposing mountains of Anshan
(they separated Erech from Aratta) and assures him that
the people of Aratta will submit to him and carry out the
building operations he desires. Enmerkar selects his herald
and sends him to the lord of Aratta with a message threatening to destroy and make desolate his city unless he and
his people bring down silver and gold and build and decorate Enki's temple. To further impress the lord of Aratta,
Enmerkar instructs his herald to repeat to him the "spell
of Enki," which relates how the god Enki had put an end to
man's "golden age" under Enlil's universal sway over the
earth and its inhabitants.

The herald, after traversing seven mountains, arrives at
Aratta, duly repeats his master's words to its lord, and asks
for his answer. The latter, however, refuses to yield to Enmerkar, claiming that he is Inanna's protégé and that she
had brought him to Aratta as its ruler. Thereupon the herald informs him that Inanna, who is now "Queen of Eanna"
in Erech, has promised Enmerkar that Aratta would submit to him.

The lord of Aratta is stunned by this news. He composes
an answer for the herald to take back to his king, in which

he admonishes Enmerkar for resorting to arms and says that he prefers the "contest" (a fight between two selected champions). He goes on to say that, since Inanna has become his enemy, he is ready to submit to Enmerkar only if he will send him large quantities of grain. The herald returns to Erech posthaste and delivers the message to Enmerkar in the courtyard of the assembly hall.

Before making his next move, Enmerkar performs several acts, apparently ritualistic in character. First he takes counsel with Nidaba, the Sumerian goddess of wisdom. Then he has his beasts of burden loaded with grain. They are led to Aratta by the herald, who is to deliver to its lord a message eulogizing Enmerkar's scepter and commanding the lord to bring Enmerkar carnelian and lapis lazuli. On arrival, the herald piles up the grain in the courtyard and delivers his message. The people, delighted with the grain, are ready to present Enmerkar with the desired carnelian (nothing seems to be said of the lapis lazuli) and to have the "elders" build his "pure house" for him. But the hysterical lord of Aratta, after eulogizing his own scepter, insists, in words identical with those of Enmerkar, that the latter bring *him* carnelian and lapis lazuli.

On the herald's return to Erech, Enmerkar seems to consult the omens, in particular one involving a reed *sushima*, which he brings forth from "light to shade" and from "shade to light," until he finally cuts it down "after five years, after ten years had passed." He sends the herald forth once again to Aratta, this time merely placing the scepter in his hand without any accompanying message. The sight of the scepter seems to arouse terror in the lord of Aratta. He turns to his *shatammu,* and, after speaking bitterly of the plight of his city as a result of Inanna's displeasure, seems ready to yield to Enmerkar. Nevertheless, he once again issues a challenge to Enmerkar. This time he demands that Enmerkar select, as his representative, one of his "fighting men" to engage in single combat one of the lord of Aratta's "fighting men." Thus "the stronger will become known." The challenge, in riddlelike terms, asks that the selected retainer be neither black nor white, neither brown, yellow, nor dappled—all of which seems to make little sense when speaking of a man.

On the herald's arrival at Erech with this new challenge, Enmerkar bids him return to Aratta with a threefold message: (1) He (Enmerkar) accepts the lord of Aratta's challenge and is prepared to send one of his retainers to fight the lord of Aratta's representative to a decision. (2) He demands that the lord of Aratta heap up gold, silver, and precious stones for the goddess Inanna in Erech. (3) He once again threatens Aratta with total destruction unless its lord and people bring "stones of the mountain" to build and decorate for him the Eridu shrine.

In the first part of the message Enmerkar's words seem to clear up the lord of Aratta's riddlelike terms about the color of the retainer to be selected. Enmerkar substitutes the word "garment" for "fighting man." Presumably the color referred to garments worn by the combatants rather than to their bodies.

There follows a remarkable passage, which, if correctly interpreted, informs us that Enmerkar, the lord of Kullab, was, in the opinion of the poet, the first to write on clay tablets, and did so because his herald seemed "heavy of mouth" and unable to repeat the message (perhaps because of its length). The herald delivers the inscribed tablet to the lord of Aratta and awaits his answer. But help now seems to come to the lord of Aratta from an unexpected source. The Sumerian god of rain and storm, Ishkur, brings to Aratta wild-grown wheat and beans and heaps them up before the lord of Aratta. At the sight of the wheat the latter takes courage. His confidence regained, he informs Enmerkar's herald that Inanna had by no means abandoned Aratta and her house and bed in Aratta.

From here on the text becomes fragmentary and the context is difficult to follow, except for the statement that the people of Aratta did bring gold, silver, and lapis lazuli to Erech and heaped them up in the courtyard of Eanna for Inanna.

So ends the longest Sumerian epic tale as yet uncovered, the first of its kind in world literature. The text was restored from twenty tablets and fragments, of which the most important by far is the twelve-column tablet in the Istanbul Museum of the Ancient Orient, copied by me in 1946, and described in the foregoing paragraphs. The scientific edition of the poem for the specialist, consisting of the Sumerian text with translation and commentary, was published as a University Museum monograph in 1952. But even the nonspecialist will find this early example of heroic poetry of interest and merit. Following, therefore, is a literal translation of several of the better preserved passages in the first half of the poem which will serve to illustrate its particular mood, temper, and flavor. The passages include Enmerkar's plea to his patron deity Inanna; Inanna's advice; Enmerkar's instructions to his herald; the execution of these instructions by the herald; the lord of Aratta's indignant refusal; the herald's further argument that Inanna is now on Enmerkar's side and its distressing effect on the lord of Aratta. (Note that two, three, and four dots indicate the omission, for one reason or another, of one, two, and more than two words, respectively.)

Once upon a time the lord chosen by Inanna in her holy heart,
Chosen from the land Shuba by Inanna in her holy heart,
Enmerkar, the son of Utu,
To his sister, the queen of good . . . . . ,
To the holy Inanna makes a plea:
"O my sister, Inanna; for Erech
Let the people of Aratta fashion artfully gold and silver,
Let them bring down pure lapis lazuli from the slab,
Let them bring down precious stone and pure lapis lazuli;
Of Erech, the holy land . . . . ,
Of the house of Anshan where you stand,
Let them build its . . . . . ;
Of the holy gipar where you have established your dwelling,
May the people of Aratta fashion artfully its interior,
I, I would offer prayers . . . . in its midst;
Let Aratta submit to Erech,
Let the people of Aratta,

*Having brought down the stones of the mountains from
    their highland,*
*Build for me the great chapel, set up for me the great
    shrine,*
*Cause to appear for me the great shrine, the shrine of the
    gods,*
Carry out for me my divine laws in Kullab,
Fashion for me the Abzu like a holy highland,
Purify for me Eridu like a mountain,
*Cause to appear for me the holy chapel of the Abzu like
    a cavern;*
I, when I utter the hymns from the Abzu,
When I bring the divine laws from Eridu,
When I make blossom the pure en-ship like a . . . ,
When I place the crown on my head in Erech, in Kullab,
May the . . of the great chapel be brought into the gipar,
May the . . of the gipar be brought into the great chapel,
May the people admire approvingly,
May Utu look on with joyful eye."

*She who is . . . the delight of holy An, the queen who
    eyes the highland,*
The mistress whose kohl is Amaushumgalanna,
Inanna, the queen of all the lands,
Says to Enmerkar, the son of Utu:
*"Come, Enmerkar, instruction I would offer you, take my
    instruction,*
A word I would speak to you, give ear to it!
Choose a word-wise herald from . . . ,
*Let the great words of the word-wise Inanna be brought
    to him in . . ,*
Let him ascend the . . mountains,
Let him descend the . . mountains,
Before the . . of Anshan,
Let him prostrate himself like a young singer,
Awed by the dread of the great mountains,
Let him wander about in the dust—
Aratta will submit to Erech;
The people of Aratta,

Having brought down the stones of the mountains from
   their land,
Will build for you the great chapel, set up for you the great
   shrine,
Cause to appear for you the great shrine, the shrine of the
   gods,
Carry out for you your divine laws in Kullab,
Fashion for you the Abzu like a holy highland,
Purify for you Eridu like a mountain,
Cause to appear for you the holy chapel of the Abzu like
   a cavern;
You, when you utter the hymns from the Abzu,
When you bring the divine laws from Eridu,
When you make blossom the pure en-ship like a . . . ,
When you place the crown on your head in Erech, in
   Kullab,
The . . of the great chapel will be brought into the gipar,
The . . of the gipar will be brought into the great chapel.
The people will admire approvingly,
Utu will look on with joyful eye;
The people of Aratta,
. . . . [Four lines omitted.]
Will bend the knee before you like highland sheep;
O holy 'breast' of the house, whose coming out is like the
   sun,
You are its beloved provider,
O . . . . Enmerkar, son of Utu, praise!"

The lord gave heed to the word of the holy Inanna,
Chose a word-wise herald from . . . ,
Brought to him the great words of the word-wise Inanna
   in . . :
"Ascend the . . mountains,
Descend the . . mountains,
Before the . . of Anshan,
Prostrate yourself like a young singer,
Awed by the dread of the great mountains,
Wander about in the dust—
O herald, speak unto the lord of Aratta and say unto him:

'I will make the people of that city flee like the . . bird
    from its tree,
I will make them flee like a bird into its neighboring nest,
I will make it (Aratta) desolate like a place of . . . ,
I will make it hold dust like an utterly destroyed city,
Aratta, that habitation which Enki has cursed—
I will surely destroy the place, like a place which has been
    destroyed,
Inanna has risen up in arms behind it,
Has brought down the word, has turned it back,
Like the heaped-up dust, I will surely heap dust upon it;
Having made . . . gold in its ore,
Pressed . . silver in its dust,
Fashioned silver . . . ,
Fastened the crates on the mountain asses—
The . . . house of Sumer's junior Enlil,
Chosen by the lord Nudimmud in his holy heart,
Let the people of the highland of pure divine laws build
    for me,
Make it flower for me like the boxwood tree,
Light it up for me like Utu coming out of the ganun,
Adorn for me its thresholds.'"
. . . . [Twenty-seven lines omitted.]

The herald gave heed to the word of his king.
During the night he journeyed by the stars,
During the day he journeyed with Utu of heaven,
The great words of Inanna . . . . were brought unto him
    in . . ,
He ascends the . . mountains,
He descends the . . mountains,
Before the . . of Anshan,
He prostrated himself like a young singer,
Awed by the dread of the great mountains,
He wandered about in the dust;
Five mountains, six mountains, seven mountains he crossed,
Lifted his eyes, approached Aratta,
In the courtyard of Aratta he set a joyous foot,
Made known the exaltedness of his king,
Spoke reverently the word of his heart.

The herald says to the lord of Aratta:
"Your father, my king, has sent me to you,
The lord of Erech, the lord of Kullab, has sent me to you."
"Your king, what has he spoken, what has he said?"

"*My king, this is what he has spoken, this is what he has said—*
My king fit for the crown from his very birth,
The lord of Erech, the leading serpent of Sumer, who . . .
     like a . . ,
The ram full of princely might in the walled highland,
The shepherd who . . . . ,
Born of the faithful cow in the heart of the highland—
Enmerkar, the son of Utu, has sent me to you,
My king, this is what he says:
'*I will make the people of his city flee like the . . bird from*
     its tree,
I will make them flee like a bird into its neighboring nest,
I will make it desolate like a place of . . . ,
I will make it hold dust like an utterly destroyed city,
Aratta, that habitation which Enki has cursed—
I will surely destroy the place like a place which has been
     destroyed.
Inanna has risen up in arms behind it,
Has brought down the word, has turned it back,
Like the heaped-up dust, I will surely heap dust upon it;
Having made . . . gold in its ore,
Pressed . . silver in its dust,
Fashioned silver . . . ,
Fastened the crates on the mountain asses—
The . . . house of Sumer's junior Enlil,
Chosen by the lord Enki in his holy heart,
Let the people of the highland of the holy divine laws build
     for me,
Make it flower for me like the boxwood tree,
Light it up for me like Utu coming out of the ganun,
Adorn for me its thresholds.'
. . . . [Two lines omitted.]

"*Command what I shall say concerning this matter,*

And to the dedicated one who wears a long beard of lapis
    lazuli,
To him whose mighty cow . . s the land of pure divine laws.
To him whose seed came forth in the dust of Aratta,
To him who was fed milk in the fold of the faithful cow,
To him who was fit for lordship over Kullab, the land of
    all the great divine laws,
To Enmerkar, the son of Utu,
I will speak that word as a good word in the temple of
    Eanna;
In the gipar which bears fruit like a fresh . . plant,
I will deliver it to my king, the lord of Kullab."

After he had thus spoken to him,
"O herald, speak unto your king, the lord of Kullab, and
    say unto him:
'Me, the lord fit for the pure hand,
She who is the royal . . of heaven, the queen of heaven
    and earth,
The mistress of all the divine laws, the holy Inanna,
Has brought me to Aratta, the land of the holy divine laws,
Has made me close "the face of the highland" like a large
    door;
How then shall Aratta submit to Erech!
Aratta will not submit to Erech'—say unto him."

After he had thus spoken to him,
The herald answers the lord of Aratta:
"The great queen of heaven, who rides the fearful divine
    laws,
Who dwells in the mountains of the highland Shuba,
Who adorns the daises of the highland Shuba—
Because the lord, my king, who is her servant,
Made her the 'Queen of Eanna.'
'The lord of Aratta will submit'—
Thus said to him in the brickwork of Kullab."

Then was the lord depressed, deeply pained,
He had no answer, he kept seeking an answer,
At his own feet he cast a troubled eye, he finds an
    answer. . . .

The early rulers of Sumer, no matter how great their success as conquerors, were not unbridled tyrants and absolute monarchs. On all the more important questions of state, particularly those involving war and peace, they consulted their more important fellow citizens gathered in solemn assembly. One such crucial "congress" took place at the very dawn of Sumerian history, some five thousand years ago, although it is recorded in a heroic poem composed in a much later day. This "first" in political history is recorded in Chapter 5.

THE FIRST
BICAMERAL CONGRESS

Man's social and spiritual development is often slow, devious, and hard to trace. The full-grown tree may well be separated from its original seed by thousands of miles and years. Take, for example, the way of life known as democracy and its fundamental institution, the political assembly. On the surface it seems to be practically a monopoly of our Western civilization and an outgrowth of recent centuries. Who could imagine that there were political congresses thousands and thousands of years ago, and in parts of the world rarely associated with democratic institutions? But the patient archaeologist digs deep and wide, and he never knows what he will come up with. As a result of the efforts of the "pick and spade" brigade, we can now read the record of a political assembly that took place some five thousand years ago in—of all places—the Near East.

The first political "congress" in man's recorded history met in solemn session about 2800 B.C. It consisted, not unlike our own congress, of two "houses": a "senate," or an assembly of elders; and a "lower house," or an assembly of arms-bearing male citizens. It was a "war congress," called together to take a stand on the momentous question of war and peace; it had to choose between what we would describe as "peace at any price" or war and independence. The "senate," with its conservative elders, declared for peace at all cost, but its decision was "vetoed" by the king, who then brought the matter before the "lower house." This body declared for war and freedom, and the king approved.

In what part of the world did the first "congress" known to man meet? Not, as you might surmise, somewhere in the West, on the continent of Europe (the political assemblies in "democratic" Greece and republican Rome came much later). Our hoary congress met, surprising as it may seem, in that part of Asia now generally designated as the Near East, the traditional home of tyrants and despots, a part of the world where political assemblies were thought to be practically unknown. It was in the land known in ancient days as Sumer, situated north of the Persian Gulf between the Tigris and Euphrates Rivers, that the oldest known political assembly was convened. And when did this "congress" meet? In the third millennium B.C. In those days, this Near Eastern land Sumer (it corresponds roughly to the lower half of modern Iraq) was inhabited by a people who developed what was probably the highest civilization in the then known world.

Sumer, some four to five thousand years ago, boasted of many large cities centering about monumental and world-renowned public buildings. Its busy traders carried on an extensive commerce by land and sea with neighboring countries. Its more serious thinkers and intellectuals developed a system of religious thought which was accepted as gospel not only in Sumer but throughout much of the ancient Near East. Its gifted poets sang lovingly and fervently of their gods, heroes, and kings. To crown it all, the Sumerians gradually developed a system of writing by means of reed stylus on clay, which enabled man for the first time to make a detailed and permanent record of his deeds and thoughts, his hopes and desires, his judgments and beliefs. And so it is not surprising to find that in the field of politics, too, the Sumerians made important progress. Particularly, they took the first steps toward democratic government by curbing the power of the kings and recognizing the right of political assembly.

The political situation that brought about the convening of the oldest "congress" recorded in history may be described as follows: Like Greece of a much later day, Sumer, in the third millennium B.C., consisted of a number of city-states vying for supremacy over the land as a whole. One of the most important of these was Kish, which, according to Sumerian legendary lore, had received the "kingship" from heaven immediately after the "flood." But in time another city-state, Erech, which lay far to the south of Kish, kept gaining in power and influence until it seriously threatened Kish's supremacy in Sumer. The king of Kish at last realized the danger and threatened the Erechites with war unless they recognized him as their overlord. It was at this crucial moment that Erech's two assemblies were convened —the elders and the arms-bearing males—in order to decide which course to follow, whether to submit to Kish and enjoy peace or to take to arms and fight for independence.

The story of the struggle between Erech and Kish is told in the form of a Sumerian epic poem whose chief characters are Agga, the last ruler of the first dynasty of Kish, and Gilgamesh, the king of Erech and "lord of Kullab." The poem begins with the arrival in Erech of Agga's envoys bearing an ultimatum to its king Gilgamesh. Before giving them his answer, Gilgamesh goes before "the convened assembly of the elders of his city" with an urgent plea not to submit to Kish but to take up arms and fight for victory. The "senators," however, are of a different mind; they would rather submit to Kish and enjoy peace. Their decision displeases Gilgamesh, who then goes before "the convened assembly of the men of his city" and repeats his plea. The men of this assembly decide to fight rather than submit to Kish. Gilgamesh is delighted, and seems confident of the results of the expected struggle. In a very short time—in the words of our poet, "It was not five days, it was not ten days"—Agga besieges Erech, and the Erechites are dumfounded. The meaning of the remainder of the poem is not too clear, but it seems that Gilgamesh in some way succeeds in gaining the friendship of Agga and in having the siege lifted without a fight.

Here, now, are the ancient Sumerian poet's actual words dealing with the Erech "congress"; the translation is quite literal, but omits a number of lines whose contents are still unintelligible.

The envoys of Agga, the son of Enmebaraggesi,
Proceeded from Kish to Gilgamesh in Erech.
The lord Gilgamesh before the elders of his city
Put the matter, seeks out the word:
"Let us not submit to the house of Kish, let us smite it with
*   weapons."*

The convened assembly of the elders of his city
Answers Gilgamesh:
"Let us submit to the house of Kish, let us not smite it with
*   weapons."*

Gilgamesh, the lord of Kullab,
Who performs heroic deeds for the goddess Inanna,
Took not the words of the elders of his city to heart.

A second time Gilgamesh, the lord of Kullab,
Before the fighting men of his city put the matter, seeks
*   out the word:*
"Do not submit to the house of Kish, let us smite it with
*   weapons."*

The convened assembly of the fighting men of his city
Answers Gilgamesh:
"Do not submit to the house of Kish, let us smite it with
*   weapons."*

Then Gilgamesh, the lord of Kullab,
At the word of the fighting men of his city his heart re-
*   joiced, his spirit brightened.*

Our poet is all too brief; he merely mentions the Erech "congress" and its two assemblies, without giving any further details. What we would like to know, for example, is the size of the membership of each body, and just how the "congressmen" and "senators" were selected. Could each individual voice his opinion and be sure of a hearing? How was the final consensus of the body as a whole obtained? Did they have a device corresponding to the voting technique of our own day? Certainly there must have been a "speaker" in charge of the discussion who "spoke" for the assembly to the king. Then again, in spite of the poet's lofty language, we may rest assured that there was considerable "politicking" and "wire-pulling" among the old political "boys." The city-state of Erech was evidently split wide open into two opposing camps, a war party and a peace party. There was probably more than one behind-the-scenes conference of our own "smoke-filled room" type, before the leaders of each "house" announced the final and seemingly unanimous decisions.

But of all these ancient political bickerings and compromises we will probably never recover a trace. There is little likelihood that we will ever find any detailed historical records from the days of Agga and Gilgamesh, since, in their time, writing was not yet sufficiently developed for historiographic purposes. As for our epic poem, it must be borne in mind that it is inscribed on tablets written many centuries after the incidents it describes took place—probably about a thousand years after the Erech "congress" had met and adjourned.

There are known, at present, eleven tablets and fragments inscribed with our political-assembly poem. Four of the eleven pieces were copied and published in the past four decades. But the significance of their contents for the history of political thought and practice was not realized until 1943, when Thorkild Jacobsen, of the Oriental Institute of the University of Chicago, published a study on *Primitive Democracy*. Since then it was my good fortune to identify and copy the remaining seven pieces in Istanbul and Philadelphia. As a result, the poem, consisting of 115 lines, is now complete. A scientific edition of its text, together with a newly revised translation, appeared in 1949 in the *American Journal of Archaeology*.

The two political events described here and in Chapter 4 took place about 2800 B.C. They are known to us not from contemporary historical documents but from epic poems written down at a much later date, and these poems contain only a kernel of historic truth. It is not until some six centuries later that we come upon a number of inscrip-

tions recording and interpreting social and political events
in a style which stamps them as man's first attempt at
history-writing. One of these documents is described and
analyzed in Chapter 6, after an introductory comment on
the intellectual and psychological limitations of our first
"historians." It is primarily concerned with a bitter and
tragic civil war between two Sumerian city-states that
ended in a temporary and uneasy stalemate, the only vic-
tors being death and destruction.

6 Civil War in Sumer

THE FIRST HISTORIAN

The Sumerians, it is safe to say, produced no historiography in the generally accepted sense of the word. Certainly no Sumerian man of letters wrote history as the modern historian conceives it, in terms of unfolding processes and underlying principles. Bound by his particular world view, the Sumerian thinker saw historical events as coming ready-made and "full-grown, full-blown" on the world scene, and not as the slow product of man's interaction with his environment. He believed, for example, that his own country, which he knew as a land of thriving cities and towns, villages and farms, and in which flourished a well-developed assortment of political, religious, and economic institutions and techniques, had always been more or less the same from the very beginning of days—that is, from the moment the gods had planned and decreed it to be so, following the creation of the universe. It probably never occurred even to the most learned of the Sumerian sages that Sumer had once been desolate marshland with but few scattered settlements, and had only gradually come to be what it was after many generations of struggle and toil marked by human will and determination, manlaid plans and experiments, and diverse discoveries and inventions.

The psychological techniques of definition and generalization, which the modern historian takes more or less for granted, seem to have been unknown to the Sumerian teacher and thinker, at least on the level of explicit formulation. Thus, in the linguistic field, we have quite a number of Sumerian grammatical lists that imply an awareness of numerous grammatical classifications, but nowhere do we find a single explicit grammatical definition or rule. In mathematics we find many tables, problems, and solutions, but no statement of general principles, axioms, and theorems. In what might be termed the "natural sciences," the Sumerian teachers compiled long lists of trees, plants, animals, and stones. The reason for the particular ordering of the objects listed is still obscure, but certainly it does not stem from a fundamental understanding of, or approach to, botanical, zoological, or mineralogical principles and laws. The Sumerians compiled numerous law codes, which no doubt contained, in their original complete state, hundreds of individual laws, but nowhere is there a statement of legal theory. In the field of history, the Sumerian temple and palace archivists noted and wrote down a varied assortment of significant events of a political, military, and religious character. But this did not lead to the writing of connected and meaningful history. Lacking the relatively recent discovery that history is a constantly changing process, and seemingly ignorant of the methodological tool of comprehensive generalization, the Sumerian man of letters could not possibly have done his history-writing in the modern sense of the word.

While it is not surprising that the Sumerian writers failed to produce the "modern" type of historiography, it does seem strange that even historical works of the kind current among the Hebrews and Greeks were unknown in Sumer. No Sumerian writer or scribe, as far as we know, ever made a conscious effort to write a cultural or political history of Sumer or any of its component states, let alone of the then known world. To be sure, Sumerian men of letters originated and developed a number of written literary genres—myths and epic tales, hymns and lamentations, proverbs and essays—and several of these, the epics and lamentations in particular, do utilize, at least to a very limited extent, what might be termed historical data. But the thought of preparing a connected history, prompted either by the love of learning or even by what we would term purposes of propaganda, never seemed to occur to the Sumerian teachers and writers. The documents that come closest to what might be termed history are the votive inscriptions on statues, steles, cones, cylinders, vases, and tablets. But the events recorded on them are merely a by-product of the urge to find favor with the gods. Moreover, these inscriptions usually record single contemporaneous events, in very brief form. Nevertheless, there are several among them which do refer back to earlier circumstances and events, and these reveal a sense of historical detail which—for that early date, about 2400 B.C.—is without parallel in world literature.

All our earliest "historians," as far as extant material goes, lived in Lagash, a city in southern Sumer that played a dominant political and military role for over a century, beginning about 2500 B.C. It was the seat of an active dynasty of rulers founded by Ur-Nanshe. The dynasty included Ur-Nanshe's conquering grandson, Eannatum, who succeeded for a brief period in making himself ruler of practically all Sumer; Eannatum's brother, Enannatum; and the latter's son, Entemena. It was not until the reign of Urukagina, the eighth ruler following Ur-Nanshe, that Lagash's star finally set. Urukagina was defeated by Lugalzaggisi of Umma, who was conquered in turn by the great Sargon of Agade. It is the political history of this period, from the days of Ur-Nanshe to those of Urukagina, that is known to us from a varied group of contemporary records prepared by anonymous "historians" who, presumably as palace and temple archivists, had access to firsthand information on the events they described.

One of these documents is outstanding for its fullness of detail and clarity of meaning. It was prepared by one of the archivists of Entemena, the fifth in the line of Lagash rulers, starting with Ur-Nanshe. Its primary purpose was to record the restoration of the boundary ditch between Lagash and Umma, which had been destroyed in a struggle between the two cities. In order to set the event in its proper historical perspective, the archivist deemed it advisable to describe its political background. He recounted, ever so briefly to be sure, some of the important details in the struggle for power between Lagash and Umma from as far back

as his written records reached—that is, from the days of
Mesilim, the suzerain of Sumer about 2600 B.C. In do-
ing so, however, he did not use the straight factual
form of narrative writing expected of the historian. Instead
he strove to fit the historical events into the accepted framework of his theocratic world view, thus developing a rather
unique literary style, which constantly interweaves the
deeds of men and gods and often fails to distinguish
between them. As a consequence, the actual historical incidents are not readily apparent from the text of the document, but must be painstakingly extracted and discrimi-
nately filled in with the help of relevant data obtained from
other Sumerological sources. Cleared of its theological cloak
and polytheistic phraseology, the document records the
following series of political events in the history of Sumer
(they can be verified in large part from other extant
sources):

In the days when Mesilim was king of Kish, and at least
the nominal suzerain of Sumer, there arose a border dispute between Lagash and Umma, two Sumerian city-states
which evidently acknowledged Mesilim as their overlord.
He proceeded to arbitrate the controversy by measuring off
a boundary line between the two cities in accordance with
what was given out to be an oracle of Sataran, a deity in
charge of settling complaints, and he erected an inscribed
stele to mark the spot and prevent future disputes.

However, the decision, which was presumably accepted
by both parties, seemed to favor Lagash rather than Umma.
Not long afterward Ush, an *ishakku* of Umma, violated the
terms of the decision (the time is not stated, but there are
indications that this violation took place not long before Ur-
Nanshe founded his dynasty at Lagash). Ush ripped out
Mesilim's stele to indicate that he was not bound by its
terms, and then crossed the border and seized the north-
ernmost territory belonging to Lagash, known as the Guedinna.

This land remained in the hands of the Ummaites until
the days of Eannatum, the grandson of Ur-Nanshe, a military leader whose conquests had made him so powerful
that he dared assume, at least for a brief period, the title

"King of Kish," and thus claim the overlordship of all Sumer. It was this Eannatum, according to our document, who attacked and defeated the Ummaites; made a new border treaty with Enakalli, then the *ishakku* of Umma; dug a ditch in line with the new boundary which would help insure the fertility of the Guedinna; erected there for purposes of future record the old Mesilim stele, as well as several steles of his own; and constructed a number of buildings and shrines to several of the important Sumerian deities. To help minimize the possible source of future conflict between Umma and Lagash, he set aside a strip of fallow land on the Umma side of the boundary ditch, as a kind of "no-man's land." Finally, Eannatum, probably in an effort to alleviate the feelings of the Ummaites to some extent, since he was eager to expand his conquests in other directions, agreed to let them farm the fields lying in the Guedinna and even further south. But he granted this only under the condition that the Ummaites pay the Lagash rulers a share of the crops for the use of the land, thus assuring himself and his successors of a considerable revenue.

Thus far, Entemena's archivist dealt only with past events in the conflict between Umma and Lagash. He next turned to the most recent struggle between the cities, of which he was in all probability a contemporary witness—the battle between Ur-Lumma, the son of the unfortunate Enakalli, who had been compelled to agree to Eannatum's "shameful" terms, and Entemena, the son of Enannatum and nephew of Eannatum.

Despite Eannatum's mighty victory, it took the Ummaites less than a generation to recover their confidence, if not their former strength. Ur-Lumma repudiated the bitterly rankling agreement with Lagash, and refused to pay Enannatum the revenue imposed upon Umma. Moreover, he proceeded to "dry up" the boundary ditches; ripped out and put to fire both Mesilim's and Eannatum's steles with their irritating inscriptions; and destroyed the buildings and shrines which Eannatum had constructed along the boundary ditch to warn the Ummaites that they must not trespass on Lagash territory. He was now set to cross the border and enter the Guedinna. To assure himself of victory, he sought and obtained the military aid of the foreign ruler to the north of Sumer.

The two forces met in the Gana-ugigga of the Guedinna, not far south of the border. The Ummaites and their allies were under the command of Ur-Lumma himself, while the Lagashites were led by Entemena, since his father, Enannatum, must have been an old man at the time. The Lagashites were victorious. Ur-Lumma fled, hotly pursued by Entemena, and many of his troops were waylaid and killed.

But Entemena's victory proved to be ephemeral. Upon Ur-Lumma's defeat and probable death, a new enemy appeared on the scene. This new enemy, whose name was Il, was the temple-head of a city named Zabalam, situated not far from Umma to the north. Il had evidently been shrewd enough to "wait it out" while Entemena and Ur-Lumma were struggling for a decision. But as soon as the battle was over, he attacked the victorious Entemena, met with initial success, and penetrated deep into Lagash territory. Although he was unable to hold on to his gains south of the Umma-Lagash border, he did succeed in making himself *ishakku* of Umma.

Il proceeded to show his contempt for the Lagash claims in almost the same manner as his predecessor. He deprived the boundary ditches of the water so essential to the irrigation of the nearby fields and farms, and refused to pay all but a fraction of the revenue imposed upon Umma by the old Eannatum treaty. And when Entemena sent envoys demanding an explanation for his unfriendly acts, Il answered by arrogantly claiming the entire Guedinna as his territory and domain.

The issue between Il and Entemena, however, was not decided by war. Instead, a compromise seems to have been forced upon them by a third party, probably the northern non-Sumerian ruler who claimed overlordship over Sumer as a whole. By and large, the decision seemed to favor Lagash, since the old Mesilim-Eannatum line was retained as the fixed boundary between Umma and Lagash. On the other hand, nothing is said of compensation by the Ummaites for the revenue which they had withheld. Nor do they seem to have been held responsible any longer for

ensuring the water supply of the Guedinna. It was now up
to the Lagashites themselves to see to the water supply.

The historical events marking the struggle for power between Lagash and Umma are by no means self-evident
from a first study of the text of our document. Much of
the history is derived from reading between the lines. The
following literal translation of the inscription as a whole will
help to show how this was done, and at the same time
give the reader some idea of the unusual historiographic
style developed by the Sumerian men of letters:

> *Enlil (leading deity of the Sumerian pantheon), the king
> of all the lands, the father of all the gods, marked off the
> boundary for Ningirsu (the patron deity of Lagash), and
> Shara (the patron deity of Umma) by his steadfast word,
> (and) Mesilim, the king of Kish, measured it off in accord-
> ance with the word of Sataran, (and) erected a stele there.
> (But) Ush, the ishakku of Umma, violated (both) the de-
> cree (of the gods) and the word (given by man to man),
> ripped out its (the boundary's) stele, and entered the plain
> of Lagash.*
>
> *(Then) did Ningirsu, Enlil's foremost warrior, do battle
> with (the men of) Umma in accordance with his (Enlil's)
> straightforward word; by the word of Enlil he hurled the
> great net upon them, and heaped up their skeleton (?) piles
> in the plain in their (various) places. (As a result) Ean-
> natum, the ishakku of Lagash, the uncle of Entemena, the
> ishakku of Lagash, marked off the boundary with Enakalli,
> the ishakku of Umma; led out its (the boundary's) ditch
> from the Idnun (canal) to the Guedinna; inscribed (sev-
> eral) steles along that ditch; restored Mesilim's stele to its
> (former) place; (but) did not enter the plain of Umma.
> He (then) built there the Imdubba of Ningirsu, the Nam-
> nunda-kigarra, (as well as) the shrine of Enlil, the shrine
> of Ninhursag (the Sumerian "mother" goddess), the shrine
> of Ningirsu, (and) the shrine of Utu (the sun-god).*
>
> *(Moreover, following the boundary settlement) the Um-
> maites could eat the barley of (the goddess) Nanshe (an-
> other patron deity of Lagash) (and) the barley of Ningirsu
> to the amount of one karu (for each Ummaite, and only)*

*for interest; (also) he (Eannatum) levied a tax on them,
(and thus) brought in for himself (as revenue) 144,000
"large" karu.*

*Because this barley remained unpaid—(besides,) Ur-
Lumma, the ishakku of Umma, deprived the boundary ditch
of Ningirsu (and) the boundary ditch of Nanshe of water;
ripped out its (the boundary ditch's) steles (and) put them
to fire; destroyed the dedicated (?) shrines of the gods
which had been built in the Namnunda-kigarra; obtained
(the help of) the foreign lands; and (finally) crossed the
boundary ditch of Ningirsu—Enannatum fought with him
in the Gana-ugigga (where are) the fields and farms of
Ningirsu, (and) Entemena, Enannatum's beloved son, defeated him. Ur-Lumma (then) fled, (while) he (Entemena) slew (the Ummaite forces) up into Umma (itself);
(moreover) his (Ur-Lumma's) elite force (consisting of)
60 soldiers he wiped out (?) on the bank of the Lumma-
girnunta canal. (As for) its (Umma's fighting) men, he
(Entemena) left their bodies in the plain (for the birds and
beasts to devour) and (then) heaped up their skeleton (?)
piles in five (separate) places.*

*At that time (however) Il, the temple-head of Zabalam,
ravaged (?) (the land) from Girsu to Umma. Il took to
himself the ishakku-ship of Umma; deprived of water the
boundary ditch of Ningirsu, the boundary ditch of Nanshe,
the Imdubba of Ningirsu, that tract (of arable land) of
the Girsu tracts which lies toward the Tigris, (and) the
Namnunda-kigarra of Ninhursag; (and) paid (no more
than) 3600 karu of the barley (due) Lagash. (And) when
Entemena, the ishakku of Lagash, repeatedly sent (his)
men to Il because of that (boundary) ditch, Il, the ishakku
of Umma, the plunderer of fields and farms, the speaker
of evil, said: "The boundary ditch of Ningirsu, (and) the
boundary ditch of Nanshe are mine"; (indeed) he (even)
said: "I shall exercise control from the Antasurra to the
Dimgal-abzu temple." (However) Enlil and Ninhursag did
not grant this to him.*

*Entemena, the ishakku of Lagash, whose name was pro-
nounced by Ningirsu, made this (boundary) ditch from the
Tigris to the Idnun in accordance with the straightforward*

word of Enlil, in accordance with the straightforward word of Ningirsu, (and) in accordance with the straightforward word of Nanshe, (and) restored it for his beloved king Ningirsu and for his beloved queen Nanshe (after) he had constructed of bricks the foundation of the Namnunda-kigarra. May Shulutula, the (personal) god of Entemena, the ishakku of Lagash, whom Enlil gave the scepter, whom Enki (the Sumerian god of wisdom) gave wisdom, whom Nanshe fixed upon (in her) heart, the great ishakku of Ningirsu, the man who had received the words of the gods, step forward (in prayer) for the life of Entemena before Ningirsu and Nanshe unto distant days.

The Ummaite who (at any future time) will cross the boundary ditch of Ningirsu (and) the boundary ditch of Nanshe in order to take to himself fields and farms by force, whether he be (really) an Ummaite or a foreigner—may Enlil destroy him; may Ningirsu, after hurling his great net on him, bring down on him his lofty hand (and) his lofty foot; may the people of his city, having risen in rebellion, strike him down in the midst of his city.

The text of this unique historical inscription has been found inscribed in practically identical language on two clay cylinders. One of these cylinders was found near Lagash in 1895, and was copied and translated by the late François Thureau-Dangin, a towering figure in cuneiform studies for almost half a century. The second cylinder is in the Yale Babylonian Collection. It was obtained from an antique dealer. Its text was published in 1920 by Nies and Keiser in their *Historical, Religious, and Economic Texts.* In 1926 a brilliant paper on the document, with a detailed study of its style and contents, was published by the eminent Sumerologist Arno Poebel. It is primarily on this work that my translation and analysis are based.

Fortunately for us, the ancient Sumerian "historians" wrote, in their votive inscriptions, not only of battles and wars but also of significant social and economic events. Chapter 7 tells about one of the most precious documents in the history of political evolution—a contemporary account of a social reform, including a rather enviable tax-reduction program that took place about thirty years after the death of Entemena of Lagash. This document uses the word "freedom" (*amargi*) for the first time in all history.

7 Social Reform

THE FIRST CASE OF
TAX REDUCTION

The first recorded social reform took place in the Sumerian city-state of Lagash in the twenty-fourth century B.C. It was directed against the abuses of "former days" practiced by an obnoxious and ubiquitous bureaucracy, such as the levying of high and multifarious taxes and the appropriation of property belonging to the temple. In fact, the Lagashites felt so victimized and oppressed that they threw off the old Ur-Nanshe dynasty and selected a ruler from another family altogether. It was this new *ishakku*, Urukagina by name, who restored law and order in the city and "established the freedom" of its citizens. All this is told in a document composed and written by the Urukagina archivists to commemorate the dedication of a new canal. To better understand and appreciate the contents of this unique inscription, here is a background sketch of some of the more significant social, economic, and political practices in a Sumerian city-state.

The state of Lagash, in the early third millennium B.C., consisted of a small group of prosperous towns, each clustering about a temple. Nominally the city of Lagash, like the other Sumerian city-states, was under the overlordship of the king of the entire land of Sumer. Actually its secular ruler was the *ishakku*, who ruled the city as the representative of the tutelary deity to whom, in accordance with the

Sumerian world view, the city had been allotted after the creation. Just how the earlier *ishakku*'s came to power is uncertain; it may well be that they were selected by the freemen of the city, among whom the temple administrators (*sanga*'s) played a leading political role. In any case, the office became hereditary in time. The more ambitious and successful of the *ishakku*'s naturally tended to augment their power and wealth at the expense of the temple, and this led at times to a struggle for power between temple and palace.

By and large, the inhabitants of Lagash were farmers and cattle breeders, boatmen and fishermen, merchants and craftsmen. Its economy was mixed—partly socialistic and state-controlled, and partly capitalistic and free. In theory, the soil belonged to the city god, and therefore, presumably, to his temple, which held it in trust for all the citizens. In actual practice, while the temple corporation owned a good deal of land, which it rented out to some of the people as sharecroppers, much of the soil was the private property of the individual citizen. Even the poor owned farms and gardens, houses and cattle. Moreover, because of Lagash's hot, rainless climate, the supervision of the irrigation projects and waterworks, which were essential to the life and welfare of the entire community, necessarily had to be communally administered. But in many other respects the economy was relatively free and unhampered. Riches and poverty, success and failure, were, at least to some extent, the result of private enterprise and individual drive. The more industrious of the artisans and craftsmen sold their handmade products in the free town market. Traveling merchants carried on a thriving trade with the surrounding states by land and sea, and it is not unlikely that some of these merchants were private individuals rather than temple representatives. The citizens of Lagash were conscious of their civil rights and wary of any government action tending to abridge their economic and personal freedom, which they cherished as a heritage essential to their way of life. It was this "freedom" that the Lagash citizens had lost, according to our ancient reform document, in the days before

Urukagina's reign. It was restored by Urukagina when he came to power.

Of the events that led to the lawless and oppressive state of affairs, there is not a hint in the document. But we may surmise that it was the direct result of the political and economic forces unloosed by the drive for power that characterized the ruling dynasty founded by Ur-Nanshe about 2500 B.C. Inflated with grandiose ambitions for themselves and their state, some of these rulers resorted to "imperialistic" wars and bloody conquests. In a few cases they met with considerable success, and for a brief period one of them actually extended the sway of Lagash over Sumer as a whole, and even over several of the neighboring states. The earlier victories proved ephemeral, however, and in less than a century Lagash was reduced to its earlier boundaries and former status. By the time Urukagina came to power, Lagash had been so weakened that it was a ready prey for its unrelenting enemy to the north, the city-state of Umma.

It was during these cruel wars and their tragic aftermath that the citizens of Lagash found themselves deprived of their political and economic freedom. In order to raise armies and supply them with arms and equipment, the rulers found it necessary to infringe on the personal rights of the individual citizen, to tax his wealth and property to the limit, and to appropriate property belonging to the temple. Under the impact of war, these rulers met with little opposition. Once domestic controls were in the hands of the palace coterie, its members were most unwilling to relinquish them, even in peacetime, for the controls proved highly profitable. Indeed, our ancient bureaucrats devised a variety of sources of revenue and income, taxes and imposts, that might well be the envy of their modern counterparts.

But let the historian who lived in Lagash almost 4,500 years ago, and was therefore a contemporary of the events he reports, tell it more or less in his own words: The inspector of the boatmen seized the boats. The cattle inspector seized the large cattle, seized the small cattle. The fisheries inspector seized the fisheries. When a citizen of Lagash brought a wool-bearing sheep to the palace for shearing, he had to pay five shekels if the wool was white. If a man divorced his wife, the *ishakku* got five shekels, and his vizier got one shekel. If a perfumer made an oil preparation, the *ishakku* got five shekels, the vizier got one shekel, and the palace steward got another shekel. As for the temple and its property, the *ishakku* took it over as his own. To quote our ancient narrator literally: "The oxen of the gods plowed the *ishakku*'s onion patches; the onion and cucumber patches of the *ishakku* were located in the god's best fields." In addition, the more important temple officials, particularly the *sanga*'s, were deprived of many of their donkeys and oxen and of much of their grain.

Even death brought no relief from levies and taxes. When a dead man was brought to the cemetery for burial, a number of officials and parasites made it their business to be on hand to relieve the bereaved family of quantities of barley, bread, and beer, and various furnishings. From one end of the state to the other, our historian observes bitterly, "There were the tax collectors." No wonder the palace waxed fat and prosperous. Its lands and properties formed one vast, continuous, and unbroken estate. In the words of the Sumerian historian, "The houses of the *ishakku* and the fields of the *ishakku*, the houses of the palace harem and the fields of the palace harem, the houses of the palace nursery and the fields of the palace nursery crowded each other side to side."

At this low point in the political and social affairs of Lagash, our Sumerian historian tells us, a new and god-fearing ruler came to the fore, Urukagina by name, who restored justice and freedom to the long-suffering citizens. He removed the inspector of the boatmen from the boats. He removed the cattle inspector from the cattle, large and small. He removed the fisheries inspector from the fisheries. He removed the collector of the silver which had to be paid for the shearing of the white sheep. When a man divorced his wife, neither the *ishakku* nor his vizier got anything. When a perfumer made an oil preparation, neither the *ishakku*, nor the vizier, nor the palace steward got anything. When a dead man was brought to the cemetery for burial, the officials received considerably less of the dead man's goods than formerly, in some cases a good deal less than half. Temple property was now highly respected. From one end of the land to the other, our on-the-scene historian observes, "There was no tax collector." He, Urukagina, "established the freedom" of the citizens of Lagash.

But removing the ubiquitous revenue collectors and the parasitic officials was not Urukagina's only achievement. He also put a stop to the injustice and exploitation suffered by the poor at the hands of the rich. For example, "The house of a lowly man was next to the house of a 'big man,' and the 'big man' said to him, 'I want to buy it from you.' If, when he (the 'big man') was about to buy it from him, the lowly man said, 'pay me as much as I think fair,' and then he (the 'big man') did not buy it, that 'big man' must not 'take it out' on the lowly man."

Urukagina also cleared the city of usurers, thieves, and murderers. If, for instance, "a poor man's son laid out a fishing pond, no one would now steal its fish." No wealthy official dared trespass on the garden of a "poor man's mother," pluck the trees, and carry off their fruit, as had been their wont. Urukagina made a special covenant with Ningirsu, the god of Lagash, that he would not permit widows and orphans to be victimized by the "men of power."

How helpful and effective were these reforms in the struggle for power between Lagash and Umma? Unfortunately, they failed to bring about the expected strength and victory. Urukagina and his reforms were soon "gone with the wind." Like many another reformer, he seemed to have come "too late" with "too little." His reign lasted less than ten years, and he and his city were soon overthrown by Lugalzaggisi, the ambitious ruler of nearby Umma, who succeeded in making himself the king of Sumer and the surrounding lands, at least for a very brief period.

The Urukagina reforms and their social implications made a profound impression on our ancient "historians." The text of the documents has been found inscribed in four more or less varying versions on three clay cones and an oval-shaped plaque. All of them were excavated by the French at Lagash in 1878. They were copied and first translated by François Thureau-Dangin, the same painstaking

cuneiformist who treated the historical document described
in Chapter 6. However, the interpretation of the Urukagina
reforms in the present volume is based on a still unpublished
translation of the document prepared by Arno Poebel, the
leading Sumerologist of our time.

Freedom under law, it should now be evident, was a
way of life not unknown to the Sumerians of the third millennium B.C. Whether laws had already been written down
and promulgated in the form of codes in Urukagina's day
is still uncertain; at least no law codes from that period
have as yet been recovered. But that proves little. For a
long time the oldest law code known was one dating back
to about 1750 B.C., but only recently three earlier codes
have come to light. The oldest of these is the code of the
Sumerian ruler Ur-Nammu; it dates from the end of the
third millennium B.C. It was excavated in 1889–1900, but
it was not until 1952 that it was identified and translated,
and even then more or less by accident. For Ur-Nammu's
law code, see Chapter 8.

8 *Law Codes*

THE FIRST "MOSES"

The most ancient law code brought to light up till 1947
was that promulgated by Hammurabi, the far-famed Semitic king who began his rule about 1750 B.C. Written in
the cuneiform script and in the Semitic language known
as Babylonian, it contains close to three hundred laws sand-
wiched in between a boastful prologue and a curse-laden
epilogue. The diorite stele on which the code is inscribed
now stands solemn and impressive in the Louvre. From the
point of view of fullness of legal detail and state of preservation, it is the most imposing ancient law document as yet
uncovered—but not from the point of view of age and antiquity. In 1947 there came to light a law code promulgated
by King Lipit-Ishtar, who preceded Hammurabi by more
than one hundred and fifty years.

The Lipit-Ishtar code, as it is now generally called, is
inscribed not on a stele but on a sun-baked clay tablet. It
is written in the cuneiform script, but in the non-Semitic
Sumerian language. The tablet was excavated shortly before the turn of the century, but for various reasons had remained unidentified and unpublished. As reconstructed and
translated with my help by Francis Steele, formerly assistant curator in the University Museum, it is seen to contain
a prologue, epilogue, and an unknown number of laws, of
which thirty-seven are preserved wholly or in part.

But Lipit-Ishtar's claim to fame as the world's first law-

giver was short-lived. In 1948, Taha Baqir, the curator of
the Iraq Museum in Baghdad, was digging in an obscure
mound called Harmal, and he announced the discovery of
two tablets inscribed with an older law code. Like the Hammurabi code, these tablets were written in the Semitic
Babylonian language. They were studied and copied that
very year by the well-known Yale cuneiformist Albrecht
Goetze. In the brief prologue that precedes the laws (there
is no epilogue), a king by the name of Bilalama is mentioned. He may have lived some seventy years before Lipit-
Ishtar. It is this Semitic Bilalama code, therefore, which
seemed to be entitled to priority honors until 1952, when
I was privileged to copy and translate a tablet inscribed
with part of a law code promulgated by a Sumerian king
named Ur-Nammu. This ruler, who founded the now well-
known Third Dynasty of Ur, began his reign, even according to lowest chronological estimates, about 2050 B.C., some
three hundred years before the Babylonian King Hammurabi. The Ur-Nammu tablet is one of the hundreds of Sumerian literary tablets in the collection of the Museum
of the Ancient Orient in Istanbul, where I spent the year
1951–52 as Fulbright Research Professor.

In all probability I would have missed the Ur-Nammu
tablet altogether had it not been for an opportune letter
from F. R. Kraus, now Professor of Cuneiform Studies at
the University of Leiden in Holland. I had met Kraus a
number of years before, during my earlier Sumerological
researches in the Istanbul Museum of the Ancient Orient,
where he was curator. Hearing that I was once again in
Istanbul, he wrote me a letter of reminiscences and shop
talk. His letter said that some years ago, in the course of
his duties as curator in the Istanbul Museum, he had come
upon two fragments of a tablet inscribed with Sumerian
laws, had made a "join" of the two pieces, and had catalogued the resulting tablet as No. 3191 of the Nippur collection of the Museum. I might be interested in its contents,
he added, and perhaps would want to copy it.

Since Sumerian law tablets are extremely rare, I had No.
3191 brought to my working table at once. There it lay,
a sun-baked tablet, light brown in color, 20 by 10 centi-

meters in size. More than half of the writing was destroyed, and what was preserved seemed at first hopelessly unintelligible. But after several days of concentrated study, its contents began to become clear and take shape, and I realized with no little excitement that what I held in my hand was a copy of the oldest law code as yet known to man.

The tablet was divided by the ancient scribe into eight columns, four on the obverse and four on the reverse. Each of the columns contains about forty-five small ruled spaces, less than half of which are legible. The obverse contains a long prologue which is only partially intelligible, because of the numerous breaks in the text. Briefly, it runs as follows:

After the world had been created, and after the fate of the land Sumer and of the city Ur (the Biblical Ur of the Chaldees) had been decided, An and Enlil, the two leading deities of the Sumerian pantheon, appointed the moongod Nanna as the King of Ur. One day, Ur-Nammu was selected by the god to rule over Sumer and Ur as his earthly representative. The new king's first acts had to do with the political and military safety of Ur and Sumer. In particular he found it necessary to do battle with the bordering city-state of Lagash, which was expanding at Ur's expense. He defeated and put to death its ruler, Namhani, and then, "with the power of Nanna, the king of the city," he re-established Ur's former boundaries.

Now came the time to turn to internal affairs, and to institute social and moral reforms. He removed the "chiselers" and the grafters, or, as the code itself describes them, the "grabbers" of the citizens' oxen, sheep, and donkeys. He then established and regulated honest and unchangeable weights and measures. He saw to it that "the orphan did not fall a prey to the wealthy"; "the widow did not fall a prey to the powerful"; "the man of one shekel did not fall a prey to the man of one mina (sixty shekels)." Although the relevant passage is destroyed on the tablet, it was no doubt to ensure justice in the land and to promote the welfare of its citizens that he promulgated the laws which followed.

The laws themselves probably began on the reverse of the tablet. They are so badly damaged that the contents

of only five of them can be restored with some degree of
certainty. One of them seems to involve a trial by water
ordeal; another seems to treat of the return of a slave to
his master. But it is the other three laws, fragmentary and
difficult as their contents are, that are of very special importance for the history of man's social and spiritual growth.
For they show that, even before 2000 B.C., the law of "eye
for eye" and "tooth for tooth"—still prevalent to a large extent in the Biblical laws of a much later day—had already
given way to the far more humane approach in which a
money fine was substituted as a punishment. Because of
their historical significance, these three laws are here quoted
in the original Sumerian, as transcribed into our alphabet,
together with their literal translation:

tukum-bi	If
(*lu-lu-ra*	(a man to a man
gish- . . . -ta)	with a . . . -instrument)
. . . -a-ni	his . . .
gir in-kud	the foot has cut off,
10-gin-ku-babbar	10 silver shekels
i-la-e	he shall pay.
tukum-bi	If
lu-lu-ra	a man to a man
gish-tukul-ta	with a weapon
gir-pad-du	his bones
al-mu-ra-ni	of . . .
in-zi-ir	severed,
1-ma-na-ku-babbar	1 silver mina
i-la-e	he shall pay.
tukum-bi	If
lu-lu-ra	a man to a man
geshpu-ta	with a geshpu-instrument
ka- . . . in-kud	the nose (?) has cut off,
⅔-ma-na-ku-babbar	⅔ of a silver mina
i-la-e	he shall pay.

How long will Ur-Nammu retain his place as the world's
first lawgiver? Perhaps not for long. There are indications
that there were lawgivers in Sumer long before Ur-Nammu

was born. Sooner or later, a lucky "digger" will come up with a copy of a law code preceding that of Ur-Nammu by a century or more.

Law and justice were key concepts in ancient Sumer, in both theory and practice, and Sumerian social and economic life was permeated by them. In the past century, archaeologists have uncovered thousands of clay tablets inscribed with all sorts of Sumerian legal documents—contracts, deeds, wills, promissory notes, receipts, and court decisions. In ancient Sumer the advanced student devoted much of his schooltime to the field of law, and he constantly practiced the writing of the highly specialized legal terminology, as well as of law codes and those court decisions which had taken on the force of legal precedents. The full text of one such court decision became available in 1950. This document, which records what might be termed "the case of the silent wife," is discussed in Chapter 9.

9 Justice

THE FIRST LEGAL PRECEDENT

A murder was committed in the land of Sumer in 1850 B.C. or thereabouts. Three men—a barber, a gardener, and one whose occupation is not known—killed a temple official by the name of Lu-Inanna. The murderers, for some unstated reason, then informed the victim's wife, Nin-dada, that her husband had been killed. Strangely enough, she kept their secret and did not notify the authorities.

But the arm of the law was long and sure, even in those days, at least in the highly civilized state of Sumer. The crime was brought to the attention of King Ur-Ninurta, in his capital city Isin, and he turned the case over for trial to the Citizens Assembly at Nippur, which acted as a court of justice.

In this assembly, nine men arose to prosecute the accused. They argued that not only the three actual murderers, but the wife as well, should be executed, presumably because she had remained silent after learning of the crime and could thus be considered an accessory after the fact.

Two men in the assembly then spoke up in defense of the woman. They pleaded that the woman had taken no part in the murder of her husband, and that she should therefore go unpunished.

The members of the assembly agreed with the defense. They argued that the woman was not unjustified in remaining silent, since it seemed that her husband had failed to support her. Their verdict concluded with the statement that "the punishment of those who actually killed should suffice." Accordingly, only the three men were condemned, by the Nippur assembly, to be executed.

The record of this murder trial was found inscribed in the Sumerian language on a clay tablet that was dug up in 1950 by a joint expedition of the Oriental Institute of the University of Chicago and the University Museum of the University of Pennsylvania. Thorkild Jacobsen and I studied and translated it. The translation of some of the Sumerian words and phrases on the tablet is still in doubt, but the essential meaning is reasonably assured. One corner of the newly found tablet is destroyed, but it was possible to fill in the missing lines from a small fragment of another copy of the same record dug up at Nippur by the earlier expedition of the University Museum. The fact that two copies of the same record have been found shows that the decision of the Nippur Assembly in the case of the "silent wife" was celebrated throughout the legal circles of Sumer as a memorable precedent, not unlike a decision of our own Supreme Court.

Nanna-sig, the son of Lu-Sin, Ku-Enlil, the son of Ku-Nanna, the barber, and Enlil-ennam, the slave of Adda-kalla, the gardener, killed Lu-Inanna, the son of Lugal-apindu, the nishakku-official.

After Lu-Inanna, the son of Lugal-apindu, had been put to death, they told Nin-dada, the daughter of Lu-Ninurta, the wife of Lu-Inanna, that her husband Lu-Inanna had been killed.

Nin-dada, the daughter of Lu-Ninurta, opened not her mouth, (her) lips remained sealed.

Their case was (then) brought to (the city) Isin before the king, (and) the King Ur-Ninurta ordered their case to be taken up in the Assembly of Nippur.

(There) Ur-gula, son of Lugal- . . , Dudu, the bird-hunter, Ali-ellati, the dependent, Buzu, the son of Lu-Sin, Eluti, the son of . . -Ea, Shesh-Kalla, the porter (?), Lugal-Kan, the gardener, Lugal-azida, the son of Sin-andul, (and)

*Shesh-kalla, the son of Shara- . . , faced (the Assembly)
and said:*

> "They who have killed a man are not (worthy) of life.
> Those three males and that woman should be killed in
> front of the chair of Lu-Inanna, the son of Lugal-apindu,
> the nishakku-official."

*(Then) Shu . . -lilum, the . . -official of Ninurta, (and)
Ubar-Sin, the gardener, faced (the Assembly) and said:*

> "Granted that the husband of Nin-dada, the daughter
> of Lu-Ninurta, had been killed, (but) what had (?) the
> woman done (?) that she should be killed?"

*(Then) the (members of the) Assembly of Nippur faced
(them) and said:*

> "A woman whose husband did not support (?) her—
> granted that she knew her husband's enemies, and that
> (after) her husband had been killed she heard that her
> husband had been killed—why should she not remain si-
> lent (?) about (?) him? Is it she (?) who killed her
> husband? The punishment of those (?) who (actually)
> killed should suffice."

*In accordance with the decision (?) of the Assembly of
Nippur, Nanna-sig, the son of Lu-Sin, Ku-Enlil, the son of
Ku-Nanna, the barber, and Enlil-ennam, the slave of Adda-
kalla, the gardener, were handed over (to the executioner)
to be killed.*

(This is) a case taken up by the Assembly of Nippur.

After the translation had been made, it seemed relevant to compare the verdict with what the modern decision
might have been in a similar situation. We therefore sent
the translation to the late Owen J. Roberts, then dean of
the Law School, University of Pennsylvania (he had been
associate justice of the United States Supreme Court,
1930–45), and asked his opinion. His answer was of great
interest, for in this legal case modern judges would have
agreed with the Sumerian judges of long ago, and the ver-

dict would have been the same. To quote Justice Roberts, "The wife would not be guilty as an accessory after the fact under our law. An accessory after the fact must not only know that the felony was committed, but must also receive, relieve, comfort, or assist the felon."

But law is not the only field in which significant Sumerian documents have recently come to light. In 1954 a medical document, inscribed with man's first pharmacopoeia, was described in a preliminary report including a translation of the more intelligible part of the document. To be sure, the physician was known in Sumer throughout the third millennium B.C. A physician by the name of Lulu practiced his profession in Ur, the Biblical Ur of the Chaldees, as early as 2700 B.C. or thereabouts. But all other medical texts from Mesopotamia published before 1954 were from the first millennium B.C., and these are often full of spells and incantations rather than real medical treatment. The newly translated tablet, on the other hand, dates back to the last quarter of the third millennium B.C., and the prescriptions inscribed on it do not contain a trace of magic and sorcery. This tablet, the oldest medical document, is discussed in Chapter 10.

10 *Medicine*

THE FIRST PHARMACOPOEIA

An anonymous Sumerian physician, who lived toward the end of the third millennium B.C., decided to collect and record, for his colleagues and students, his more valuable medical prescriptions. He prepared a tablet of moist clay, 3¾ by 6¼ inches in size, sharpened a reed stylus to a wedge-shaped end, and wrote down, in the cuneiform script of his day, more than a dozen of his favorite remedies. This clay document, the oldest medical "handbook" known to man, lay buried in the Nippur ruins for more than four thousand years, until it was excavated by an American expedition and brought to the University Museum in Philadelphia.

I first learned of the existence of the tablet from a publication by my predecessor in the University Museum, Dr. Leon Legrain, curator emeritus of the Babylonian Section. In an article in the 1940 *Bulletin* of the University Museum, under the title "Nippur Old Drugstore," he made a valiant attempt to translate part of its contents. But it was obvious that this was not a task for the cuneiformist alone. The phraseology of the inscription was highly technical and specialized, and the cooperation of a historian of science was needed, particularly one trained in the field of chemistry. After I had become curator of the tablet collections in the University Museum, I often went longingly to the cupboard where this "medical" tablet was kept and brought it to my desk for study. More than once I was tempted to make another effort at translating its contents. Fortunately I did not succumb. Again and again I returned it to its place and awaited the opportune moment.

One Saturday morning in the spring of 1953, a young man came into my office and introduced himself as Martin Levey, a Philadelphia chemist. A doctorate in the history of science had just been conferred on him, and he asked if I knew of any tablets in the Museum's collection that he could help with from the point of view of the history of science and technology. Here was my opportunity! Once again I took the tablet from its cupboard, but this time it did not go back until it was at least tentatively translated. For several weeks Levey and I worked on its contents. I restricted myself primarily to the reading of the Sumerian signs and the analysis of the grammatical construction. It was Martin Levey, with his understanding and knowledge of the chemical and technological processes of the ancients, who brought to life again the intelligible portions of man's first pharmacopoeia.

The Sumerian physician, we learn from this ancient document, went, as does his modern counterpart, to botanical, zoological, and mineralogical sources for his materia medica. His favorite minerals were sodium chloride (salt) and potassium nitrate (saltpeter). From the animal kingdom he utilized milk, snake skin, and turtle shell. But most of his medicinals came from the botanical world, from plants such as cassia, myrtle, asafoetida, and thyme, and from trees such as the willow, pear, fir, fig, and date. These simples were prepared from the seed, root, branch, bark, or gum, and must have been stored, as today, in either solid or powdered form.

The remedies prescribed by our physician were both salves and filtrates to be applied externally, and liquids to be taken internally. The usual instructions for compounding salves were to pulverize one or more simples, to infuse the powder with "kushumma" wine, and to spread both common tree oil and cedar oil over the mixture. For one prescription in which pulverized river clay was one of the simples, the powder was to be kneaded in water and honey, and "sea" oil instead of tree oil was to be spread over the mixture.

The filtrate prescriptions were more complicated and were followed by directions for treatment. Three of the prescriptions (the Sumerian text is reasonably certain) made use of the process of decoction. In order to extract the sought-for principles, the ingredients were boiled in water, and alkali and salts were added, probably to obtain a greater yield of total extract. To separate the organic materials, the aqueous solution was no doubt subjected to filtration, although this is not stated explicitly in any of the prescriptions. The ailing organ was then treated with the filtrate, either by sprinkling or washing. Following this, oil was rubbed on it, and then one or more additional simples were added.

As for those remedies which were to be taken internally, beer was usually the vehicle chosen to make them palatable to the patient. The several simples were ground to a powder and dissolved in beer for the sick man to drink. In one case, however, where milk as well as beer seems to have been used for infusion, an unidentified "river" (?) oil was the vehicle.

Even from this lone tablet—the only medical text as yet recovered from the third millennium B.C.—it is clear that Sumerian pharmacology had made considerable progress. The tablet reveals, though indirectly, a broad acquaintance with quite a number of rather elaborate chemical operations and procedures. For example, in several of the prescriptions the instructions were to "purify" the simples before pulverization, a step which must have required several chemical operations. For another example, the pulverized alkali used as a simple in one of the prescriptions is probably the alkali ash produced by the pit-burning of one of a number of plants of the Chenopodiaceae (most likely the *Salicornia fruticosa*), which are rich in soda. Soda ash derived in this manner was used in the seventh century B.C., and in the Middle Ages it was used for glassmaking. Chemically speaking, it is of interest that the two prescriptions on our tablet that called for alkali used it together with substances which contain a great deal of natural fat, thus producing a soap for external application.

Another substance prescribed by our Sumerian doctor which could have been obtained only with some chemical knowledge is potassium nitrate, or saltpeter. To judge from much later Assyrian times, it is not unlikely that the Sumerians inspected the surface drains in which nitrogenous waste products, such as urine, flowed, and removed for purification whatever crystalline formation was to be found. The problem of separating the components, which no doubt included sodium chloride and other salts of sodium and potassium, as well as degradation products of nitrogenous matter, was probably solved by the method of fractional crystallization. In India and Egypt there is still current the ancient procedure of mixing lime or old mortar with decomposing nitrogenous organic matter to form calcium nitrate, which is then lixiviated and boiled with wood ash containing potassium carbonate to yield niter on evaporation of the filtrate.

In one respect our ancient text is most disappointing. It fails to name the diseases for which the remedies were intended, and we are unable to check their therapeutic value. The remedies were probably of little value, since the Sumerian physician seems to have made no use of experiment and verification. The selection of many of the drugs no doubt reflected the long-standing confidence of the ancients in the odoriferous properties of plants. Some of the prescriptions had their good points—for example, the making of a detergent was of value. And such substances as salt and saltpeter were effective, the former as an antiseptic and the latter as an astringent.

These Sumerian prescriptions suffer from at least one other obvious omission: they fail to specify the quantities to be used in compounding the simples, as well as the dosage and frequency of application of the medicine. This may have been the result of "professional jealousy," and the Sumerian physician may have purposely concealed the quantitative details in order to protect his secrets from nonmedical groups or perhaps even from his colleagues. More probably, the quantitative details just did not loom important to the Sumerian prescription-writer, since they could be figured out more or less empirically in the course of actual preparation and use of the remedies.

It is interesting to note that the Sumerian physician who wrote our tablet did not resort to magic spells and incantations. Not one god or demon is mentioned anywhere throughout the text. This does not mean that the use of charms and exorcisms to cure the sick was unknown in Sumer in the third millennium B.C. Quite the contrary is true, as is obvious from the contents of some three-score small tablets inscribed with incantations and so designated by the authors of the inscriptions. Like the Babylonians of later days, the Sumerians attributed numerous diseases to the unwelcome presence of harmful demons in the sick man's body. Half a dozen such demons are actually named in a Sumerian hymn dedicated to the patron deity of the art of medicine, a goddess variously known as Bau, Ninisinna, and Gula, and described as "the great physician of the blackheaded people (the Sumerians)." However, the startling fact remains that our clay document, the oldest "page" of medical text as yet uncovered, is completely free from mystical and irrational elements.

The discovery of a medical tablet written toward the end of the third millennium B.C. was a surprise even to the cuneiformist, since it is in the field of agriculture rather than medicine that our first "handbook" might have been expected. Agriculture was the mainstay of the Sumerian economy, the primary source of its wealth and well-being. Farming methods and techniques were already highly developed before the third millennium B.C. But the only farmers' "handbook" that has as yet come to light dates from the early second millennium B.C. It is discussed in Chapter 11.

11 *Agriculture*

THE FIRST
"FARMER'S ALMANAC"

A small clay tablet discovered by an American expedition in Iraq made possible the restoration of a document more than 3,500 years old that is of prime importance in the history of agriculture and its techniques. The 1949–50 expedition, sponsored jointly by the Oriental Institute of the University of Chicago and the University Museum of the University of Pennsylvania, excavated the 3- by 4½-inch inscription in the ancient Sumerian site Nippur. The tablet was in poor condition on its arrival. But after it had been baked, cleaned, and mended in the laboratory of the University Museum, practically its entire text became legible. Before the discovery at Nippur, eight other clay tablets and fragments inscribed with different parts of this agricultural "primer" were already known, but it was impossible to make a trustworthy restoration of the text as a whole until the new Nippur piece, with thirty-five lines from the middle of the composition, came to light.

The restored document, 109 lines in length, consists of a series of instructions addressed by a farmer to his son for the purpose of guiding him throughout his yearly agricultural activities, beginning with the inundation of the fields in May–June and ending with the cleaning and winnowing of the freshly harvested crops in the following April–May. Before the Nippur discovery, two similar farmer's "handbooks" were known from ancient days: Virgil's far-famed and highly poetic *Georgics* and Hesiod's *Work and Days*. The latter, which is by far the earlier of the two, was probably written in the eighth century B.C. On the other hand, the newly restored Sumerian clay document was actually inscribed about 1700 B.C., and thus antedates Hesiod's work by approximately a millennium.

The Sumerian farm "handbook" begins with the line, "In days of yore a farmer gave (these) instructions to his son." The directions that follow concern the more important chores and labors that a farmer must perform to ensure a successful crop. Since irrigation was essential for Sumer's parched soil, the instructions began with advice concerning irrigation works: Care must be taken that their water does not rise too high over the field; when the water subsides, the wet ground must be carefully guarded against trampling oxen and other prowlers; the field must then be cleared of weeds and stubble and fenced about.

The farmer was next counseled to have his household and hired help prepare in advance all the necessary tools, implements, baskets, and containers. He must see to it that he has an extra ox for the plow. Before beginning to plow, he should have the ground broken up twice by the mattock and once by the hoe. Where necessary the hammer must be used to pulverize the clods. He was counseled to stand over his laborers and see to it that they did not shirk their work.

The work of plowing and sowing was carried on simultaneously by means of a seeder—that is, a plow with an attachment that carried the seed from a container through a narrow funnel down to the furrow. The farmer was instructed to plow eight furrows to each strip of approximately twenty feet. He was told to see to it that the seed was placed at an even depth. In the words of the "handbook": "Keep an eye on the man who puts in the barley seed that he make the seed fall two fingers uniformly." If the seed failed to penetrate the earth properly, he must change the share, "the tongue of the plow." There were several kinds of furrows, according to the writer of the "handbook," who advised in particular: "Where you have plowed straight furrows, plow (now) diagonal furrows; where you have plowed diagonal furrows, plow (now) straight furrows." Following the sowing, the furrows had to be cleared of clods, so that the sprouting of the barley would not be impeded.

"On the day when the seed breaks through the ground," the Sumerian "handbook" continues, the farmer should say a prayer to Ninkilim, the goddess of field mice and vermin, lest these harm the growing grain; he should also scare away the birds. When the barley had grown sufficiently to fill the narrow bottoms of the furrows, he was to water it; and when it was dense enough to cover the field like the "mat in the middle of a boat," he was to water it a second time. A third time he was to water the "royal" grain. Should he then notice a reddening of the wet grain, it was the dread *samana*-disease that was endangering the crops. If the crop showed improvement, he was to water it a fourth time, and thus get an extra yield of 10 per cent.

When the time came for harvesting, the farmer was not to wait until the barley bent under its own weight, but was to cut it "in the day of its strength"; that is, just at the right moment. Three men worked as a team on the standing grain—a reaper, a binder, and a third whose duties are not clear.

The threshing which followed immediately upon the harvesting was done by means of a sledge drawn back and forth over the heaped-up grain stalks for a period of five days. The barley was then "opened" with an "opener," which was drawn by oxen. By this time, however, the grain had become unclean through contact with the ground. Therefore, following an appropriate prayer, the grain was winnowed with pitchforks, laid on sticks, and thus freed of dirt and dust.

The document closes with the statement that the agricultural rules laid down were not the farmer's own but those of the god Ninurta, the son and "true farmer" of the leading Sumerian deity, Enlil.

In order that the reader might taste the real flavor of the first farmer's handbook in man's recorded history, here is a literal translation of its first eighteen lines. The reader

*Fig. 2.   Plowing Scene. Reconstruction of plowing
scene from a cylinder-seal impression on Nippur tablet in University Museum. Note seeder-plow.*

is asked to bear in mind that the renderings are in some
cases tentative, since the text is full of obscure and per-
plexing technical terminology. The translation that follows
(it will no doubt be considerably improved over the years
as our knowledge of Sumerian language and culture grows)
has been worked out *provisionally* by Benno Landsberger
and Thorkild Jacobsen—cuneiformists of the Oriental Institute of the University of Chicago—and the present writer.

*In days of yore a farmer gave (these) instructions to his
son: When you are about to cultivate your field, take care
to open the irrigation works (so that) their water does not
rise too high in it (the field). When you have emptied it
of water, watch the field's wet ground that it stays even;
let no wandering ox trample it. Chase the prowlers and have
it treated as settled land. Clear it with ten narrow axes
(weighing no more than) ⅔ of a pound each. Its stubble
(?) should be torn up by hand and tied in bundles; its
narrow holes shall be gone over with a drag; and the four
sides of the field shall be fenced about. While the field is
burning (in the summer sun) let it be divided up into equal
parts. Let your tools hum with activity (?). The yoke-bar
should be made fast, your new whip should be fastened
with nails, and the handle to which your old whip was
fastened should be mended by the workers' children.*

Not only cereal farms but also vegetable gardens and fruit groves were sources of Sumer's economic wealth. One of the more significant horticultural techniques practiced in Sumer from earliest days was shade-tree gardening—that is, the planting of broad shade trees to protect the garden plants from sun and wind. This we learn from a Sumerian poem that is presented in Chapter 12.

THE FIRST EXPERIMENT IN
SHADE-TREE GARDENING

As annual professor of the American Schools of Oriental Research and representative of the University Museum, I traveled to Istanbul and Baghdad in 1946. In Istanbul I stayed some four months and copied more than a hundred tablets and fragments inscribed with Sumerian epics and myths. The majority of the copied pieces consisted of small and middle-sized fragments. But among them were a number of considerably longer tablets—for example, the twelve-column tablet inscribed with the "war of nerves" (see Chapter 4); the eight-column tablet inscribed with the disputation between summer and winter (see Chapter 18); and a six-column piece inscribed with a hitherto unknown myth which I have titled "Inanna and Shukallituda: The Gardener's Mortal Sin."

This last-mentioned document originally must have measured 6 by 7¼ inches, but now measures only 4¼ by 7 inches. The first and last columns are almost entirely destroyed, but the remaining four columns permit the restoration of some two hundred lines of text, of which more than half are complete. As the contents of the myth gradually became intelligible, it was obvious that not only was its plot unusual, but the poem was highly significant in two other respects. In the first place, it features an incident in which a deity, angered by the impious deed of a mortal, turns the water of an entire land into blood. The only parallel to this "blood-plague" motif in the entire range of ancient literature is the Biblical exodus story in which Jahweh turns the water of all Egypt into blood when Pharaoh refuses to send forth the enslaved Israelites to serve him. Secondly, the author of our ancient myth seems to explain the origin of shade-tree gardening, and thus reveals that the horticultural technique of planting shade trees in a garden or grove to protect the plants from wind and sun was known and practiced thousands of years ago. The plot of this myth runs as follows:

Once upon a time there lived a gardener by the name of Shukallituda, whose diligent efforts at gardening had met with nothing but failure. Although he had carefully watered his furrows and garden patches, the plants had withered away. The raging winds smote his face with the "dust of the mountains." All that he had carefully tended turned desolate. He thereupon lifted his eyes east and west to the starry heavens, studied the omens, observed and learned the divine laws. Having acquired new wisdom, he planted the (as yet unidentified) *sarbatu* tree in the garden, a tree whose broad shade lasts from sunrise to sunset. As a consequence of this horticultural experiment, Shukallituda's garden blossomed forth with all kinds of greens.

One day the goddess Inanna (the Sumerian counterpart of the Greek Aphrodite and the Roman Venus), after having traversed heaven and earth, lay down to rest her tired body not far from the garden of Shukallituda. He spied on her from the edge of his garden. Then he took advantage of her extreme weariness and cohabited with her. When morning came and the sun rose, Inanna looked about her in consternation and determined to ferret out, at all costs, the mortal who had so shamefully abused her. She therefore sent three plagues against Sumer: (1) She filled all the wells of the land with blood, so that all the palm groves and vineyards became saturated with blood. (2) She sent destructive winds and storms against the land. (3) The nature of the third plague is uncertain, since the relevant lines are too fragmentary.

Despite the three plagues, Inanna was unable to locate

her defiler. After each plague Shukallituda went to his father's house and informed him of his danger. The father
advised his son to direct his step to his brothers, the "blackheaded people" (the people of Sumer), and to stay close to
the urban centers. Shukallituda followed this advice, and
as a result Inanna did not find him. She realized bitterly
that she was unable to avenge the outrage committed
against her. She therefore decided to go to the city Eridu,
to the house of Enki, the Sumerian god of wisdom, to seek
his advice and help. Here the tablet breaks off, and the
end of the story remains unknown.

   The following is a tentative translation of one of the relevant and more intelligible portions of the poem:

Shukallituda, ... ,
When pouring water over the furrows,
When digging wells by the patches, ... ,
Stumbled over its roots, was cut up by them;
The raging winds with whatever they carried,
With the dust of the mountains, struck his face,
At his . . face and . . hands,
They blew it about, he knew not its . .

He (thereupon) lifted his eyes toward the lands below,
   Looked up at the stars in the east,
Lifted his eyes toward the lands above,
   Looked up at the stars in the west,
Gazed at the auspicious inscribed heaven,
From the inscribed heaven learned the omens,
Saw there how to carry out the divine laws,
Studied the decrees of the gods.
In the garden, in five to ten unapproachable places,
In those places he planted one tree as a protecting cover,
The tree's protecting cover—the sarbatu-*tree of wide shade—*
Its shade below, dawn,
Noon, and dusk, did not turn away.

One day my queen, after crossing heaven, crossing earth,
Inanna, after crossing heaven, crossing earth,
After crossing Elam and Shubur,
After crossing . . . . ,

*The hierodule (Inanna) in her weariness approached (the
        garden), fell fast asleep,*
Shukallituda saw her from the edge of his garden, ...
Copulated with her, kissed her,
Returned to the edge of his garden.

Dawn broke, the sun rose,
The woman looked about her in dread.
Inanna looked about her in dread.
*Then, the woman, because of her pudendum, what harm
        she did!*
Inanna, because of her pudendum, what did she do!
All the wells of the land she filled with blood,
All the groves and gardens of the land she sated with blood,
*The (male) slaves coming to gather firewood, drink noth-
        ing but blood,*
*The (female) slaves coming to fill up with water, fill up
        with nothing but blood,*
*"I must find him who copulated with me among all the
        lands," she said.*

But him who copulated with her she found not,
For the young man entered his father's house,
Shukallituda says to his father:
"Father, when pouring water over the furrows,
When digging wells by the patches, ... ,
I stumbled over its roots, was cut up by them;
The raging winds, with whatever they carried,
With the dust of the mountains, struck my face,
At my . . face and . . hands,
They blew it about, I knew not its . .

"I (thereupon) lifted my eyes toward the lands below,
*   Looked up at the stars in the east,*
Lifted my eyes toward the lands above,
*   Looked up at the stars in the west,*
Gazed at the auspicious inscribed heaven,
From the inscribed heaven learned the omens,
Saw there how to carry out the divine laws,
Studied the decrees of the gods.
In the garden, in five to ten unapproachable places,

In those places I planted one tree as a protecting cover.
The tree's protecting cover—the sarbatu-*tree of wide shade—*
Its shade below, dawn,
Noon, and dusk, did not turn away.

"One day my queen, after crossing heaven, crossing earth,
Inanna, after crossing heaven, crossing earth,
After crossing Elam and Shubur,
After crossing . . . . ,
The hierodule in her weariness approached (the garden),
    fell fast asleep;
I saw her from the edge of my garden,
Copulated with her, kissed her,
Returned to the edge of my garden.

"Dawn broke, the sun rose,
The woman looked about her in dread,
Inanna looked about her in dread.
Then, the woman, because of her pudendum, what harm
    she did!
Inanna, because of her pudendum, what did she do!
All the wells of the land she filled with blood,
All the groves and gardens of the land she sated with blood,
The (male) slaves coming to gather firewood, drink noth-
    ing but blood,
The (female) slaves coming to fill up with water, fill up
    with nothing but blood,
'I must find him who copulated with me,' she said."

But him who copulated with her she found not,
For his father answers the young man,
His father answers Shukallituda:
"Son, stay close to your brothers' cities,
Direct your step and go to your brothers, the blackheaded
    people,
The woman (Inanna) will not find you in the midst of the
    lands."
He (Shukallituda) stayed close to his brothers' cities,
Directed his step to his brothers, the blackheaded people,
The woman found him not in the midst of all the lands.

*Then, the woman, because of her pudendum, what harm
     she did!*
Inanna, because of her pudendum, what did she do! . . . .
     (The poem continues with the second plague.)

We turn now from the material to the spiritual, from
technology to philosophy. The Sumerians of the third millennium B.C., there is good reason to believe, evolved a
number of metaphysical and theological concepts which,
though never explicitly formulated, became more or less
paradigmatic for the entire Near East, and even left their
imprint on the Hebrew and Christian dogmas of later days.
The more significant of their concepts are presented in
Chapter 13, together with an analysis of the largely un-
formulated and unarticulated rational and logical inferences
behind them. The chapter also shows how the Sumerian
intellectual speculations and philosophical conclusions were
isolated and adduced primarily from the Sumerian myths
and epic tales, in spite of the fact that these resort to fantasy and imagination rather than reason and logic for their
literary effect.

MAN'S FIRST COSMOGONY

AND COSMOLOGY

The Sumerians failed to develop a systematic philosophy in the accepted sense of the word. It never occurred to them to raise any questions concerning the fundamental nature of reality and knowledge, and they therefore evolved practically nothing corresponding to the philosophical subdivision which is commonly known today as epistemology. They did, however, speculate on the nature and, more particularly, the origin of the universe, and on its method of operation. There is good reason to infer that in the third millennium B.C. there emerged a group of Sumerian thinkers and teachers who, in their quest for satisfactory answers to some of the problems raised by their cosmic speculations, evolved a cosmology and theology carrying such high intellectual conviction that their doctrines became the basic creed and dogma of much of the ancient Near East.

These cosmological ideas and theological speculations are nowhere explicitly formulated in philosophical terms and systematic statements. Sumerian philosophers had failed to discover that all-important intellectual tool which we take for granted: the scientific method of definition and generalization, without which our present-day science would never have reached its prominence. To take even so relatively simple a principle as cause and effect, the Sumerian thinker, while fully aware of the innumerable concrete examples of its operation, never came upon the idea of formulating it as a general, all-pervading law. Almost all our information concerning Sumerian philosophy, theology, cosmology, and cosmogony, has to be ferreted out and pieced together from Sumerian literary works, particularly myths, epic tales, and hymns.

What were some of the "scientific" data at their disposal, which underpinned their assumptions and led to the narrowing down of their philosophical speculations to theological certainties? In the eyes of the Sumerian teachers and sages, the major components of the universe were heaven and earth; indeed, their term for universe was *an-ki*, a compound word meaning "heaven-earth." The earth, they thought, was a flat disk; heaven, a hollow space enclosed at top and bottom by a solid surface in the shape of a vault. Just what this heavenly solid was thought to be is still uncertain. To judge from the fact that the Sumerian term for tin is "metal of heaven," it may have been tin. Between heaven and earth they recognized a substance which they called *lil*, a word whose approximate meaning is "wind" (air, breath, spirit); its most significant characteristics seem to be movement and expansion, and it therefore corresponds roughly to our "atmosphere." The sun, moon, planets, and stars were taken to be made of the same stuff as the atmosphere, but endowed, in addition, with the quality of luminosity. Surrounding the "heaven-earth" on all sides and at top and bottom was the boundless sea, in which the universe somehow remained fixed and immovable.

From these basic assumptions concerning the structure of the universe, which seemed to the Sumerian thinkers obvious and indisputable facts, they evolved a cosmogony to fit. First, they concluded, was the primeval sea; the indications are that they looked upon the sea as a kind of "first cause" and "prime mover," and that they never asked themselves just what was prior to the sea in time and space. In this primeval sea was somehow engendered the universe, the "heaven-earth," consisting of a vaulted heaven superimposed over a flat earth and united with it. In between, separating heaven from earth, was the moving and expanding "atmosphere." Out of this atmosphere were fashioned the luminous bodies—the moon, sun, planets, and stars. Following the separation of heaven and earth—and the creation of the light-giving astral bodies—plant, animal, and human life came into existence.

Who created this universe and kept it operating, day in day out, year in year out, throughout the ages? From as far back as our written records go, the Sumerian theologian assumed as axiomatic the existence of a pantheon consisting of a group of living beings, manlike in form but superhuman and immortal, who, though invisible to mortal eye, guide and control the cosmos in accordance with well-laid plans and duly prescribed laws. Each of these anthropomorphic but superhuman beings was deemed to be in charge of a particular component of the universe and to guide its activities in accordance with established rules and regulations. One or another of these beings had charge of the great realms of heaven and earth, sea and air; the major astral bodies, sun, moon, and planet; atmospheric forces such as wind, storm, and tempest; and, in the realm of the earth, natural entities such as river, mountain, and plain; cultural entities such as city and state, dike and ditch, field and farm; even implements such as the pickax, brickmold, and plow.

Behind this axiomatic assumption of the Sumerian theologians, no doubt, lay a logical inference, since they could hardly have seen any of these humanlike beings with their own eyes. They took their cue from human society as they knew it, and reasoned of course from the known to the unknown. They noted that lands and cities, palaces and temples, fields and farms—in short, all imaginable institutions and enterprises—are tended and supervised, guided and controlled, by living human beings, without whom lands and cities become desolate, temples and palaces crumble, fields and farms turn to desert and wilderness. Surely, therefore, the cosmos and all its manifold phenomena must also be tended and supervised, guided and controlled, by living beings in human form. But the cosmos being far larger than the sum total of human habitations, and its organization being far more complex, these living beings must obviously be far stronger and much more effective than ordinary humans. Above all, they must be immortal. Otherwise the cosmos would turn to chaos upon their death and the world would come to an end—alternatives which, for obvious reasons, did not recommend themselves to the Sumerian metaphysician. It was each of these invisible, anthropomorphic yet superhuman and immortal beings that the Sumerian designated by his word *dingir*, which we translate by the word "god."

How did this divine pantheon function? In the first place, it seemed reasonable to the Sumerians to assume that the gods constituting the pantheon were not all of the same importance or rank. The god in charge of the pickax or brickmold could hardly be expected to compare with the god in charge of the sun. Nor could the god in charge of dikes and ditches be expected to equal in rank the god in charge of the earth as a whole. And, on analogy with the political organization of the human state, it was natural to assume that at the head of the pantheon was a god recognized by all the others as king and ruler. The Sumerian pantheon was therefore conceived as functioning as an assembly with a king at its head, its most important groups consisting of seven gods who "decree the fates" and fifty known as "the great gods." But a more significant division set up by the Sumerian theologians within their pantheon was that between creative and noncreative gods, a notion arrived at as a result of their cosmological views. According to these views, the basic components of the cosmos were heaven and earth, sea and atmosphere; every other cosmic phenomenon could exist only within one or another of these realms. Hence it seemed reasonable to infer that the four gods in control of heaven, earth, sea, and air were the creating gods, and that one or another of these four created every other cosmic entity in accordance with plans originating with them.

As for the creating technique attributed to these deities, Sumerian philosophers developed a doctrine which became dogma throughout the Near East—the doctrine of the creative power of the divine word. All that the creating deity had to do, according to this doctrine, was to lay his plans, utter the word, and pronounce the name. Probably this notion of the creative power of the divine word was the result of an analogical inference based on observation of human society. If a human king could achieve almost all he wanted by command—by no more than the words of his mouth—the immortal and superhuman deities in charge of the four realms of the universe could achieve much more. But perhaps this "easy" solution of the cosmological problems, in which thought and word alone are so important, is a reflection of the drive to escape into wish fulfillment characteristic of practically all humans in times of stress and misfortune.

Similarly, the Sumerian theologians arrived at what was for them a satisfying metaphysical inference to explain what keeps the cosmic entities and cultural phenomena, once created, operating continuously and harmoniously, without conflict and confusion. This is the concept designated by the Sumerian word *me*, whose exact meaning is still uncertain. In general it would seem to denote a set of rules and regulations assigned to each cosmic entity and cultural phenomenon for the purpose of keeping it operating forever in accordance with the plans laid down by the deities creating it. Here was another superficial, but evidently not altogether ineffective, answer to an insoluble cosmological problem, which merely hid the fundamental difficulties from view with a layer of largely meaningless words.

The Sumerian men of letters developed no literary genre comparable in any way to a systematic treatise of their philosophical, cosmological, and theological concepts. The modern scholar is compelled to "dig" out these concepts from the numerous myths recovered to date, wholly or in part. And this is no simple task, since the myth-makers and myth-writers must not be confused with the metaphysician and theologian. Psychologically and temperamentally they are poles apart, although often, no doubt, they were combined in one and the same person.

The mythographers were scribes and poets whose main concern was the glorification and exaltation of the gods and their deeds. Unlike the philosophers, they were not interested in discovering cosmological and theological truths. They accepted the current theological notions and practices without worrying about their origin and development. The aim of the myth-makers was to compose a narrative poem that would explain one or another of these notions and practices in a manner that would be appealing, inspiring, and entertaining. They were not concerned with proofs and arguments directed to the intellect. Their first interest was in telling a story that would appeal to the emotions. Their main literary tools, therefore, were not logic and reason, but imagination and fantasy. In telling their story, these poets did not hesitate to invent motives and incidents patterned on human action which could not possibly have any basis in reasonable and speculative thought. Nor did they hesitate to adopt legendary and folkloristic motifs that had nothing to do with rational cosmological inquiry and inference.

The failure to distinguish between the Sumerian mythographer and philosopher has confused some of the modern students of ancient Oriental thought, particularly those strongly affected by the current demands for "salvation" rather than "truth," and has led them into both underestimating and overestimating the minds of the ancients. On the one hand, they argued, the ancients were mentally incapable of thinking logically and intelligently on cosmic problems. On the other hand, they argued, the ancients were blessed with an intellectually "unspoiled" mythopoeic mind, which was naturally profound and intuitive and could therefore penetrate cosmic truths far more perceptively than the modern mind with its analytic and intellectual approach. For the most part, this is just stuff and nonsense. The more mature and reflective Sumerian thinker had the mental capacity of thinking logically and coherently on any problems, including those concerned with the origin and operation of the universe. His stumbling block was the lack of scientific data at his disposal. Furthermore, he lacked such fundamental intellectual tools as definition and generalization, and had practically no insight into the processes of growth and development, since the principle of evolution, which seems so obvious now, was entirely unknown to him.

No doubt, in some future day, with the continued ac-

cumulation of new data and the discovery of hitherto
undreamed-of intellectual tools and perspectives, the limitations and shortcomings of the philosophers and scientists
of our own day will become apparent. There is, however,
this significant difference: modern thinking man is usually
prepared to admit the relative character of his conclusions
and is skeptical of all absolute answers. Not so the Sumerian
thinker; he was convinced that his thoughts on the matter
were absolutely correct and that he knew exactly how the
universe was created and operated.

What evidence do we have of the Sumerian conception
of the creation of the universe? Our major source is the
introductory passage to a poem I have titled "Gilgamesh,
Enkidu, and the Nether World." The plot of this poem is
described in Chapter 23. What is of interest here is not the
poem as a whole but its introduction, for the Sumerian
poets usually began their myths or epic poems with a cosmological statement that had no direct bearing on the composition as a whole. Part of this introduction to "Gilgamesh,
Enkidu, and the Nether World" consists of the following
five lines:

> *After heaven had been moved away from earth,*
> *After earth had been separated from heaven,*
> *After the name of man had been fixed,*
> *After (the heaven-god) An carried off the heaven,*
> *After (the air-god) Enlil carried off the earth . . . .*

Upon having prepared the translation of these lines, I
analyzed them and deduced that they contained the following cosmogonic concepts:

1. At one time heaven and earth were united.
2. Some of the gods existed before the separation of
   heaven and earth.
3. Upon the separation of heaven and earth, it was the
   heaven-god An who carried off heaven, but it was the
   air-god Enlil who carried off the earth.

Among the crucial points *not stated or implied* in this
passage are the following:

1. Were heaven and earth conceived as created, and if so by whom?
2. What was the shape of heaven and earth as conceived by the Sumerians?
3. Who separated heaven from earth?

I hunted around among the available Sumerian texts and found the following answers to these three questions:

1. In a tablet, which gives a list of the Sumerian gods, the goddess Nammu, written with the pictograph for primeval "sea," is described as "the mother, who gave birth to heaven and earth." Heaven and earth were therefore conceived by the Sumerians as the created product of the primeval sea.
2. The myth "Cattle and Grain," which describes the birth in heaven of the gods of cattle and grain, who were sent down to earth to bring prosperity to mankind (see Chapter 14), begins with the following two lines:

> On the mountain of heaven and earth
> An begot the Anunnaki.

3. A poem which describes the fashioning and dedication of the pickax, the valuable agricultural implement, is introduced with the following passage:

The lord, in order to bring forth what was useful,
The lord whose decisions are unalterable,
Enlil, who brings up the seed of the "land" from the earth,
Planned to move away heaven from earth,
Planned to move away earth from heaven.

From the first line of "Cattle and Grain," it is not unreasonable to assume that heaven and earth united were conceived as a mountain whose base was the bottom of the earth and whose peak was the top of the heaven. And the poem about the pickax answers the question, Who separated heaven from earth? It was the air-god Enlil.

After my hunt among available Sumerian texts had led to these conclusions, it was possible to sum up the cosmogonic or creation concepts evolved by the Sumerians. Their concepts explained the origin of the universe as follows:

1. First was the primeval sea. Nothing is said of its origin or birth, and it is not unlikely that the Sumerians conceived it as having existed eternally.
2. The primeval sea engendered the cosmic mountain consisting of heaven and earth united.
3. Conceived as gods in human form, An (i.e., heaven) was the male and Ki (i.e., earth) was the female. From their union was begotten the air-god Enlil.
4. Enlil, the air-god, separated heaven from earth, and while his father An carried off heaven, Enlil himself carried off the earth, his mother. The union of Enlil and his mother earth set the stage for the organization of the universe—the creation of man, animals, and plants, and the establishment of civilization.

For the origin and nature of the luminous bodies—moon, sun, planets, and stars—practically no direct explanation is given. But from the fact that, as far back as our written sources go, the Sumerians considered the moon-god, known by the two names Sin and Nanna, to be the son of the air-god Enlil, it is not unreasonable to infer that they thought of the moon as a bright, airlike body that was fashioned in some way from the atmosphere. And since the sun-god Utu and the Venus-goddess Inanna are always referred to in the texts as children of the moon-god, the probability is that these two luminous bodies were conceived as having been created from the moon after the latter had been fashioned from the atmosphere. This is also true of the remaining planets and the stars, which are described poetically as "the big ones who walk about (the moon) like wild oxen," and "the little ones who are scattered about (the moon) like grain."

Concerning the birth of the moon-god Sin, we have a charming and very human myth which seems to have been evolved to explain the begetting of the moon-god and of three deities who were doomed to spend their lives in the nether world instead of in the eastern sky where the more fortunate deities dwelt. My first attempt to piece together and translate this myth was published in *Sumerian Mythology* in 1944. However, the interpretation of the plot contained several serious errors of omission and commission. These were clarified and corrected by Thorkild Jacobsen in a careful and constructive review published in 1946 in Volume V of the *Journal of Near Eastern Studies*. Moreover, in 1952 the expedition to Nippur sponsored jointly by the Oriental Institute and the University Museum dug up a well-preserved tablet that fills in some of the gaps in the first part of the poem and clarifies it considerably. The plot of the myth, as revised in accordance with most of Jacobsen's suggestions and the contents of the newly discovered piece from Nippur, follows:

When man had not yet been created and the city of Nippur was inhabited by gods alone, "its young man" was the god Enlil; "its young maid" was the goddess Ninlil; and "its old woman" was Ninlil's mother Nunbarshegunu. One day the latter, having evidently set her mind and heart on Ninlil's marriage to Enlil, instructs her daughter thus:

"In the pure stream, woman, bathe in the pure stream,
Ninlil, walk along the bank of the stream Nunbirdu,
The bright-eyed, the lord, the bright-eyed,
The 'great mountain,' Father Enlil, the bright-eyed, will see
*   you,*
The shepherd . . . who decrees the fates, the bright-eyed,
*   will see you,*
Will forthwith embrace (?) you, kiss you."

Ninlil joyfully follows her mother's instructions:

In the pure stream, the woman bathes, in the pure stream,
Ninlil walks along the bank of the stream Nunbirdu,
The bright-eyed, the lord, the bright-eyed,
The "great mountain," father Enlil, the bright-eyed, saw
*   her,*
The shepherd . . . who decrees the fates, the bright-eyed,
*   saw her.*

The lord speaks to her of intercourse (?), she is unwilling,
Enlil speaks to her of intercourse (?), she is unwilling;

"My vagina is too little, it knows not to copulate,
My lips are too small, they know not to kiss". . . . .

Whereupon Enlil calls his vizier Nusku and tells him of
his desire for the lovely Ninlil. Nusku brings up a boat,
and Enlil rapes Ninlil while sailing on the stream, and impregnates her with the moon-god Sin. The gods are dis-
mayed by this immoral deed, and, though Enlil is their
king, they seize him and banish him from the city to the
nether world.

The relevant passage, one of the few to shed some light
on the organization of the pantheon and its method of operation, reads:

Enlil walks about in the Kiur (Ninlil's private shrine),
As Enlil walks about in the Kiur,
The great gods, the fifty of them,
The fate-decreeing gods, the seven of them,
Seize Enlil in the Kiur (saying):
"Enlil, immoral one, get you out of the city,
Nunamnir (an epithet of Enlil), immoral one, get you out
    of the city."

And so Enlil, in accordance with the fate decreed by the
gods, departs in the direction of the Sumerian Hades. Ninlil,
however, now big with child, refuses to remain behind and
follows Enlil on his forced journey to the nether world. This
disturbs Enlil, for it would mean that his son Sin, originally
destined to be in charge of the largest luminous body, the
moon, would have to dwell in the dark, gloomy nether
world instead of in the sky. To circumvent this, he devises
a rather complicated scheme. On the way to Hades from
Nippur, the traveler meets up with three individuals, probably minor deities: the gatekeeper in charge of the gates,
the "man of the nether-world river," and the ferryman
(the Sumerian "Charon" who ferries the dead across to
Hades). What does Enlil do? He takes the form of each
of these in turn (the first known example of divine meta-
morphosis) and impregnates Ninlil with three nether-world
deities as substitutes for their older brother Sin, who is thus
free to ascend to heaven.

Here, now, are several of the relevant passages (it should be stressed that the real meaning of a number of the lines is still far from clear, and that the significance of this part of the myth may ultimately be modified):

Enlil, in accordance with what was decreed for him,
Nunamnir, in accordance with what was decreed for him,
Enlil came, Ninlil followed,
Nunamnir came, Ninlil enters,
Enlil says to the man of the gate:

"Man of the gate, man of the lock,
Man of the bolt, man of the silver lock,
Your queen has come;
If she asks you about me,
Tell her not my whereabouts."

Ninlil says to the man of the gate:
"Man of the gate, man of the lock,
Man of the bolt, man of the silver lock,
Enlil, your lord, whence . . . ."

Enlil speaks up for the man of the gate:
"My lord did not . . the fairest, the fair,
Enlil did not . . the fairest, the fair,
He . . d in my anus, he . . d in my mouth;
My true distant heart . . . . ,
Thus has Enlil, the lord of all the lands, commanded me."

"Enlil is indeed your lord, but I am your lady."
"If you are my lady, let my hand touch your cheek (?)."
"The seed of your lord, the all-bright seed, is in my womb,
The seed of Sin, the all-bright seed, is in my womb."
"Let then my lord's seed go to the heaven above,
*   Let my seed go to the earth below,*
Let my seed in my lord's seed's stead go to the earth below."
Enlil, as [that is, impersonating] the man of the gate, lay
*   with her in the bedchamber,*
Copulated with her, kissed her,
Having copulated with her, kissed her,
He plants in her womb the seed of Meslamtaea . . .

Enlil then proceeds to the "nether-world river" (the

Sumerian Styx), followed by Ninlil, and there exactly the
same conversations take place between Enlil, the "man of
the nether-world river," and Ninlil. Here Enlil, impersonating the "man of the river," impregnates Ninlil with the
seed of the nether-world deity known as Ninazu. From
there Enlil, followed by Ninlil, proceeds to where the Sumerian "Charon" is stationed. The scene is repeated a third
time, and Enlil, impersonating the ferryman, impregnates
Ninlil with the seed of a third deity (his name is destroyed,
but he too is no doubt a god doomed to dwell in Hades).
The myth then closes with a brief paean to Enlil as the
lord of plenty and prosperity, whose word is unalterable.

   This myth illustrates vividly the anthropomorphic character of the Sumerian gods. Even the most powerful and
most knowing among them were regarded as human in
form, thought, and deed. Like man, they planned and
acted, ate and drank, married and raised families, supported large households, and were addicted to human pas-
sions and weaknesses. By and large, they preferred truth
and justice to falsehood and oppression, but their motives
are by no means clear, and man is often at a loss to understand them. They were thought to live on the "mountain
of heaven and earth, the place where the sun rose," at least
when their presence was not necessary in the particular
cosmic entities over which they had charge. Just how they
traveled from place to place is by no means certain. From
available data we can infer that the moon-god traveled in
a boat; the sun-god in a chariot or, according to another
version, by foot; the storm-god on the clouds. But the Sumerian thinkers seem not to have troubled themselves too
much with such realistic problems, and so we are not informed just how the gods were supposed to arrive at their
various temples and shrines in Sumer, nor how they performed such human activities as eating and drinking. The
priests presumably saw only the statues of the gods, which
no doubt were tended and handled with great care. But
just how the stone, wooden, and metal objects were to be
regarded as having bone, muscle, and the breath of life
was a question that never occurred to the Sumerian thinkers. Nor did they seem to be troubled by the inherent con-

tradiction between immortality and anthropomorphism. Although the gods were believed to be immortal, they nevertheless had to have their sustenance; could become sick to the point of death; fought, wounded, and killed; and could themselves be wounded and killed.

No doubt Sumerian sages developed numerous theological notions in a futile attempt to resolve the inconsistencies and contradictions inherent in a polytheistic system of religion. But to judge from available material, they never wrote them down in systematic form, and we may therefore never learn much about them. In any case, it is hardly likely that they resolved many of the inconsistencies. What saved them from spiritual and intellectual frustration was no doubt the fact that many a question which according to our way of thinking should have troubled them, never came to their mind.

The Sumerians of the third millennium B.C. had hundreds of deities, at least by name. We know the names of many of them, not merely from lists compiled in the schools but also from lists of sacrifices on tablets which have been unearthed over the past century. We know others from such proper names as "X is a shepherd," "X has a great heart," "who is like X," "the servant of X," "the man of X," "the beloved X," "X has given me," and so on, X representing the name of a deity in each case. Many of these deities are secondary—that is, they are the wives and children and servants of the major deities thought up for them on the human pattern. Others are perhaps names and epithets of well-known deities who cannot at present be identified. But a large number of deities were actually worshiped throughout the year with sacrifices, adoration, and prayer. Of all these hundreds of deities, the four most important were the heaven-god, An; the air-god, Enlil; the water-god, Enki; and the great mother-goddess, Ninhursag. These four usually head the god-lists and are often listed as a group performing significant acts together. At divine meetings and banquets they took the seats of honor.

There is good reason to believe that An, the heaven-god, was at one time regarded by the Sumerians as the supreme ruler of the pantheon, although in our available sources, reaching to about 2500 B.C., it is the air-god, Enlil, who seems to have been the leader of the pantheon. The city-state in which An had his main seat of worship was called Uruk, or, as it is vocalized in the Bible, Erech, a city which played a pre-eminent political role in the history of Sumer. (At the site of Uruk, not long before the Second World War, a German expedition uncovered hundreds of small clay tablets, inscribed with semipictographic signs, which date from about 3000 B.C., not long after writing was first invented.) An continued to be worshiped in Sumer throughout the millenniums, but he lost much of his prominence. He became a rather shadowy figure in the pantheon and is rarely mentioned in the hymns and myths of later days, by which time most of his powers had been conferred upon the god Enlil.

By far the most important deity in the Sumerian pantheon, one who played a dominant role throughout in rite, myth, and prayer, was the air-god, Enlil. The events leading up to his general acceptance as a leading deity of the Sumerian pantheon are unknown, but from the earliest intelligible records Enlil is known as "the father of the gods," "the king of heaven and earth," "the king of all the lands." Kings and rulers boasted that it was Enlil who gave them the kingship of the land, who made the land prosperous for them, who gave them all the lands to conquer by their strength. It was Enlil who pronounced the king's name, gave him his scepter, and looked upon him with favorable eye.

From later myths and hymns we learn that Enlil was regarded as a beneficent deity who was responsible for the planning and creating of most productive features of the cosmos. He was the god who made the day come forth, who took pity on humans, who laid the plans that brought forth all seeds, plants, and trees from the earth. It was he who established plenty, abundance, and prosperity in the land. It was he who fashioned the pickax and the plow as the prototypes of the agricultural implements to be used by man.

I stress the beneficent features of Enlil's character in order to correct a misconception which has found its way into practically all handbooks and encyclopedias treating Sumerian religion and culture—namely, that Enlil was a violent and destructive storm deity whose word and deed nearly always brought nothing but evil. As not infrequently happens, this misunderstanding is due largely to an archaeological accident. Among the earliest Sumerian compositions published there was an unusually large number, proportionately, of the "lamentation" type in which Enlil had the unhappy duty of carrying out the destruction and misfortunes decreed by the gods for one reason or another. As a result he was stigmatized as a fierce and destructive deity by earlier scholars and even by later ones. Actually, when we analyze the hymns and myths, especially those which have been published since 1930, we find Enlil glorified as a friendly, fatherly deity who watches over the safety and well-being of all humans, particularly the inhabitants of Sumer.

One of the most important hymns to Enlil was pieced together in 1953 from a number of tablets and fragments. In 1951–52, while working in the Istanbul Museum of the Ancient Orient, I was fortunate enough to uncover the lower half of a four-column tablet whose upper half is in the University Museum in Philadelphia and had been published as early as 1919 by the late cuneiformist Stephen Langdon. And in 1952 the expedition to Nippur under the joint auspices of the Oriental Institute of the University of Chicago and the University Museum uncovered another large fragment of the hymn. The text is still incomplete, and its translation is no simple matter. It begins with a paean to Enlil himself, particularly as a god who punishes evildoers; continues with a glorification of his great temple in Nippur known as the Ekur; and closes with a poetic summary of civilization's debt to him. The following are some of the more intelligible passages of the 170-line hymn:

Enlil, whose command is far-reaching, whose word is holy,
The lord whose pronouncement is unchangeable, who forever decrees destinies,
Whose lifted eye scans the lands,
Whose lifted light searches the heart of all the lands,

Enlil who sits broadly on the white dais, on the lofty dais,
Who perfects the decrees of power, lordship, and prince-
ship,
The earth-gods bow down in fear before him,
The heaven-gods humble themselves before him . . . . .

The city (Nippur), its appearance is fearsome and awe-
some, ... ,
The unrighteous, the evil, the oppressor,
The . . . , the informer,
The arrogant, the agreement-violator,
He does not tolerate their evil in the city,
The great net . . . . ,
He does not let the wicked and evildoer escape its meshes.

Nippur—the shrine where dwells the father, the "great
mountain,"
The dais of plenty, the Ekur which rises . . . ,
The high mountain, the pure place . . . ,
Its prince, the "great mountain," Father Enlil,
Has established his seat on the dais of the Ekur, lofty
shrine;
The temple—its divine laws like heaven cannot be over-
turned,
Its pure rites, like the earth cannot be shattered,
Its divine laws are like the divine laws of the abyss, none
can look upon them,
Its "heart" like a distant shrine, unknown like heaven's
zenith . . . . ,
Its words are prayers,
Its utterances are supplication . . . . ,
Its ritual is precious,
Its feasts flow with fat and milk, are rich with abundance,
Its storehouses bring happiness and rejoicing, ... ,
Enlil's house, it is a mountain of plenty . . . . .
The Ekur, the lapis-lazuli house, the lofty dwelling place,
awe-inspiring,
Its awe and dread are next to heaven,
Its shadow is spread over all the lands
Its loftiness reaches heaven's heart,

1. Nippur scribal quarter—old excavations.

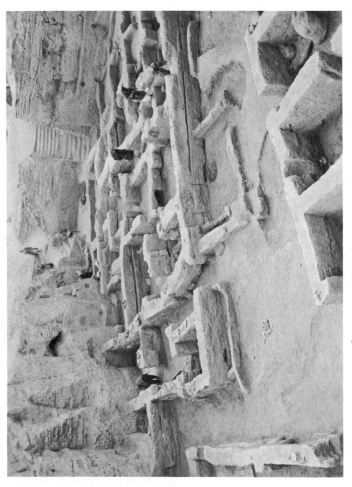

2. Nippur scribal quarter—new excavations.

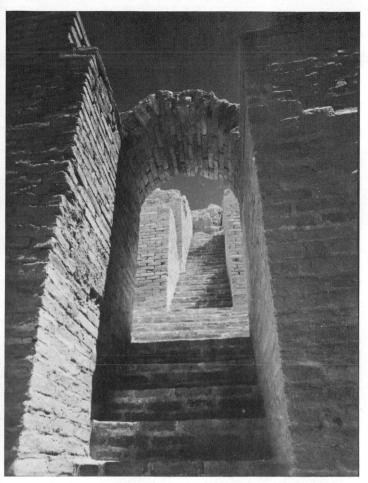

3. Stairs of the Ziggurat of Tchoga-Zanbil, in Western Persia.

4. Tell Harmal: temple, palace, and school (?)

5. War and Peace: The "standard" from Ur.

6. "Netting" the enemy.

7. Gudea, the "architect."

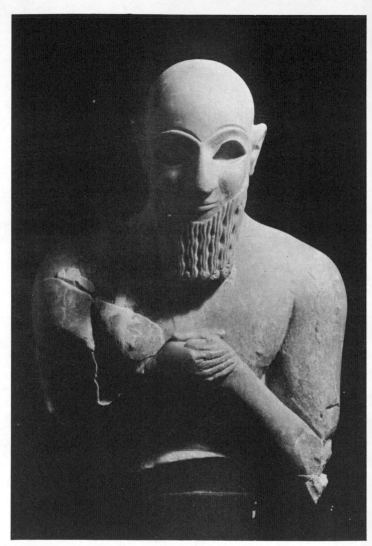

8. Idi-Narum, an official of Mari.

All the lords and princes conduct thither their holy gifts,
    offerings,
Utter there prayer, supplication, and petition.

Enlil, the shepherd upon whom you gaze (favorably),
Whom you have called and made high in the land, ... ,
Who prostrates the foreign lands wherever he steps forth,
Soothing libations from everywhere,
Sacrifices from heavy booty,
Has brought; in the storehouse,
In the lofty courtyards he has directed his offerings;
Enlil, the worthy shepherd, ever on the move,
Of the leading herdsman of all who have breath (the king),
Brought into being his princeship,
Placed the holy crown on his head . . . . .

Heaven—he is its princely one; earth—he is its great one,
The Anunnaki—he is their exalted god;
When, in his awesomeness, he decrees the fates,
No god dare look on him.
Only to his exalted vizier, the chamberlain Nusku,
The command, the word of his heart,
Did he make known, did he inform,
Did he commission to execute his all-embracing orders,
Did he entrust all the holy rules, all the holy laws.

Without Enlil, the great mountain,
No cities would be built, no settlements founded,
No stalls would be built, no sheepfolds established,
No king would be raised, no high priest born,
No mah-priest, no high-priestess would be chosen by sheep-
    omen,
Workers would have neither controller nor super-
    visor, ... ,
The rivers—their floodwaters would not bring overflow,
The fish of the sea would lay no eggs in the canebrake,
The birds of heaven would not build nests on the wide
    earth,
In heaven the drifting clouds would not yield their moisture,
Plants and herbs, the glory of the plain, would fail to grow,
In field and meadow the rich grain would fail to flower,

*The trees planted in the mountain-forest would not yield
      their fruit . . . . .*

The third of the Sumerian leading deities was Enki, the
god in charge of the abyss, or, as the Sumerian word for
it reads, the *abzu*. Enki was the god of wisdom, and it was
primarily he who organized the earth, in accordance with
the decisions of Enlil, who made only general plans. The
actual details and execution were left to Enki, the resource-
ful, skillful, hardy, and wise. For example, in a myth that
may be titled "Enki and the World Order: The Organization of the Earth and Its Cultural Processes," an account
is given of Enki's creative activities in instituting the natural
and cultural phenomena essential to civilization. This myth,
the contents of which I sketched for the first time in *Sumerian Mythology* (pages 59–62), also serves as a vivid
illustration of the Sumerians' relatively superficial notions
about nature and its mysteries. Nowhere is there an attempt to get at the fundamental origins, either of the natural or cultural processes. Instead they are ascribed to
Enki's creative efforts, in words approximating the statement "Enki did it." Where the creative technique is mentioned at all, it consists of the god's word and command,
nothing more.

The contents of the poem "Enki and the World Order"
(which is altogether about 450 lines in length) can now
be sketched as follows: After a hymnal passage addressed
to Enki, perhaps by the author of the poem, glorifying him
as the god who provides for the needs of both gods and
men, Enki utters a paean of praise for himself which reads:

"My father, the king of heaven and earth,
Brought about my epiphany on heaven and earth;
My ancestor (?), the king of all the lands,
*Gathered together all the divine laws, placed them in my
      hand;*
From the Ekur, the house of Enlil,
I brought craftsmanship to my Abzu in Eridu.
*I am the true seed engendered by the great wild ox, the
      eldest son of An,*

The great storm who comes forth in the "Great Below,"
    the great lord of the Land,
The first among the chieftains, the father of all the lands,
The "big brother" of the gods, who generates prosperity,
Who budgets the accounts of the universe,
The "ear" and "mind" of all the lands,
Who directs judgment with the king An in the shrine of
    heaven,
Who decrees the fates with Enlil in the land of wisdom—
He (Enlil) had placed in my hands the decreeing of the
    fates of the place where the sun rises—
I am truly cherished by the goddess Nintu,
I am he who was called a good name by Ninhursag,
The leader of the Anunnaki (the great gods) am I,
The first son born of holy An . . . ."

There follows a brief hymnal prayer by the Anunnaki,
and then for a second time Enki, "because of his great joy,"
utters a paean of self-praise which begins with the lines:

"I, the lord, firm is my command, I lead it forth,
At my command stalls are built, sheepfolds are enclosed;
I approach heaven, the rain pours down from above,
I approach the earth, there is a mighty inundation . . . ."

and ends with the lines:

"The lands of . . . Magan and Dilmun looked up at me
    (Enki),
The ships of Dilmun brought (?) wood,
The ships of Magan are loaded sky-high,
The magilum-boats of Meluhha
Transport gold and silver,
Bring them to Nippur for Enlil, the king of all the lands."

Following another brief hymnal song uttered by the
Anunnaki, Enki is all set to "go forth in his land" in order to
perform his divine duties. After a broken and obscure
passage involving "lords," "chieftains," and the holy men
of Eridu and Sumer, we find Enki decreeing the fate of
Sumer:

"O Sumer, great land, of the lands of the universe,

*Filled with steadfast light, dispensing from sunrise to sun-
    set the divine laws to (all) the people,*
Your divine laws are exalted laws, unreachable,
Your heart is profound, unfathomable,
*The true learning which you bring . . . , like heaven is
    untouchable,*
*The king to whom you give birth is adorned with the ever-
    lasting diadem,*
The lord to whom you give birth sets ever crown on head,
*Your lord is an honored lord; with An, the king, he sits on
    the heavenly dais,*
Your king is the great mountain, the father Enlil, ... ,
The Anunnaki, the great gods,
In your midst have taken up their dwelling place,
In your large groves they consume (their) food.
*O house of Sumer, may your stables be many, may your
    cows multiply,*
*May your sheepfolds be many, may your sheep be myr-
    iad, ... ,*
May your steadfast temples lift hand to heaven,
May the Anunnaki decree the fates in your midst."

Enki then goes to Ur (probably the capital of Sumer at
the time this poem was composed) and blesses it.

To Ur, the shrine, he came,
Enki, king of the abyss, decrees the fate:
*"O City, well-supplied, washed by much water, firm-
    standing ox,*
*Dais of abundance of the land, knees opened, green like the
    mountain,*
Hashur-forest, wide of shade, heroic beyond . . ,
May your perfected divine laws be well directed,
*The great mountain, Enlil, in heaven and earth has uttered
    your exalted name;*
City whose fates have been decreed by Enki,
Shrine Ur, may you rise heaven high."

Enki then comes to Meluhha, the "black mountain"
(it can probably be identified with Ethiopia). Remarkably
enough, Enki is almost as favorably disposed to this land

as to Sumer itself. He blesses its trees and reeds, its oxen
and birds, its silver and gold, its bronze and copper, its human beings.

From Meluhha, Enki goes to the Tigris and Euphrates
Rivers. He fills them with sparkling water and places the
god Enbilulu in charge. Enki then fills the rivers with fishes
and makes a deity described as the "son of Kesh" responsible for them. He next turns to the sea (Persian Gulf),
sets up its rules, and appoints the goddess Sirara in charge.

Enki now calls to the winds and appoints over them the
god Ishkur, who rides the thundering storms. Next, Enki
directs the plow and yoke, fields and vegetation:

The plow and the yoke he directed,
The great prince Enki . . . . ,
Opened the holy furrows,
Made grain grow in the perennial field,
The lord, the jewel and ornament of the plain,
Fitted out on its strength, Enlil's farmer,
Enkimdu, the god of the canals and ditches,
Enki placed in their charge.
The lord called to the perennial field, caused it to produce
  gunu-grain,
Enki made it bring forth abundantly its small and large
  beans,
The . . . . grains he heaped up for the granary,
Enki added granary to granary,
With Enlil he multiplied abundance for the people; . . . . ,
The lady who . . , the source of strength of the land, the
  steadfast support of the blackheaded people,
Ashnan, strength of all things,
Enki placed in charge.

Enki now turns to the pickax and the brickmold, and appoints the brick-god Kabta in charge. He then directs the
building implement *gugun*, lays foundations, and builds
houses, and places them under the charge of Mushdamma,
the "great builder of Enlil." He then fills the plain with
plant and animal life, and places Sumugan, "King of the
Mountain," in control. Enki now builds stables and sheepfolds, fills them with milk and cream, and puts them in

the care of the shepherd-god Dumuzi. He then sets up boundaries according to agreement, and places the sun-god Utu, "the judge and arbiter of the gods," in charge of them "in the entire universe." Finally Enki "wove a thread," perfected "that which goes with womanhood," and placed Uttu, the goddess of weaving, in charge of it.

The myth then takes a rather unexpected turn, in that it introduces the ambitious and belligerent Inanna, goddess of love and war. What seems to irk Inanna is that, in the course of the distribution of powers and rights to the various female deities, she was left aside entirely. She therefore "entered Enki's house" and brings her complaint, though "humbly" according to the author, beginning with the following four lines:

> *"The fates of the Anunnaki, the great gods,*
> *Enlil has confirmed as your right.*
> *Me, the woman, why did you treat differently?*
> *Me, the holy Inanna, where are my powers?"*

She then proceeds to name the other more important female deities and to list their powers. There was the goddess Aruru (alias Nintu), who has taken for herself "the lapis-lazuli pot," whose right it is to fashion "king and lord" in the Land. Her sister Ninisinna, Inanna continues, has taken for herself "the precious jewels" and has become the special favorite of the heaven-god An. Her sister Ninmug has taken to herself "the golden spindle (?)" (the line listing her powers is largely broken). Finally her sister Nidaba has taken for herself the measuring-rod, she draws up boundaries and treaties, and has charge of the "food and drink of the gods." But as for herself, she complains once again:

> *"Me, the woman, why did you treat differently?*
> *Me, the holy Inanna, where are my powers?"*

Enki's answer is quite long and detailed; he seems to have assigned to her many rights and powers. But unfortunately the last fifty lines of the poem are rather poorly preserved, and the meaning, even of the better preserved lines, is often obscure. He seems to endow Inanna, among other things, with "the crook of shepherdship," with various kinds of garments, with love of battle and destruction, and with the power to attract men.

Fourth among the creating deities was the mother-goddess Ninhursag, also known as Ninmah ("the exalted lady"). In an earlier day, this goddess was of even higher rank, and her name often preceded that of Enki in the god-lists of one type or another. There is reason to believe that her name had originally been Ki ("Earth"), and that she was taken to be the consort of An ("Heaven"), and that they were the parents of all the gods. She was also known as Nintu ("the lady who gave birth"). All the early Sumerian rulers liked to describe themselves as "nourished by the trustworthy milk of Ninhursag." She was regarded as the mother of all living things, the mother-goddess. In one myth involving this goddess, she plays an important role in the creation of man (see Chapter 14), and in another myth she starts a chain of divine births which lead up to a "forbidden fruit" motif (see Chapter 19).

Finally we come to the *me's*, the divine laws, rules, and regulations which, according to the Sumerian philosophers, governed the universe from the days of its creation and kept it operating. In this case we have considerable direct evidence, particularly in regard to the *me's* governing man and his culture. One of the ancient Sumerian poets, in composing or redacting one of his myths, found it desirable to list all these cultural *me's*. He therefore divided civilization as he knew it into over one hundred elements. Only sixty-odd of these elements are at present intelligible, and some are only bare words which, because of lack of context, give but a hint of their real significance. But enough remains to show the character and import of this first recorded attempt at culture analysis, resulting in a considerable list of what are now generally termed "culture traits and complexes." These consist of various institutions, priestly offices, ritualistic paraphernalia, mental and emotional attitudes, and sundry beliefs and dogmas.

Here are the more intelligible portions of the list in the exact order given by the ancient Sumerian writer himself: (1) lordship; (2) godship; (3) the exalted and enduring crown; (4) the throne of kingship; (5) the exalted scepter;

(6) the royal insignia; (7) the exalted shrine; (8) shepherdship; (9) kingship; (10) lasting ladyship; (11) "divine lady" (the priestly office); (12) *ishib* (the priestly office); (13) *lumah* (the priestly office); (14) *gutug* (the priestly office); (15) truth; (16) descent into the nether world; (17) ascent from the nether world; (18) *kurgarru* (the eunuch); (19) *girbadara* (the eunuch); (20) *sagursag* (the eunuch); (21) the (battle) standard; (22) the flood; (23) weapons (?); (24) sexual intercourse; (25) prostitution; (26) law (?); (27) libel (?); (28) art; (29) the cult chamber; (30) "hierodule of heaven"; (31) *gusilim* (the musical instrument); (32) music; (33) eldership; (34) heroship; (35) power; (36) enmity; (37) straightforwardness; (38) the destruction of cities; (39) lamentation; (40) rejoicing of the heart; (41) falsehood; (42) the rebel land; (43) goodness; (44) justice; (45) art of woodworking; (46) art of metal working; (47) scribeship; (48) craft of the smith; (49) craft of the leatherworker; (50) craft of the builder; (51) craft of the basket weaver; (52) wisdom; (53) attention; (54) holy purification; (55) fear; (56) terror; (57) strife; (58) peace; (59) weariness; (60) victory; (61) counsel; (62) the troubled heart; (63) judgment; (64) decision; (65) *lilis* (the musical instrument); (66) *ub* (the musical instrument); (67) *mesi* (the musical instrument); (68) *ala* (the musical instrument).

We owe the preservation of this bit of ancient anthropological lore to the fact that it was utilized in the plot of a Sumerian myth involving the popular Sumerian goddess Inanna. The list of more than one hundred cultural elements is repeated *four* times in the story, and hence, in spite of the numerous breaks in the text, can be reconstructed in large part. As early as 1911, a fragment belonging to this myth (it is in the University Museum) was published by David W. Myhrman. Three years later, Arno Poebel published another Philadelphia tablet inscribed with part of the composition—a large, well-preserved six-column tablet whose upper left corner was broken off. This broken corner piece I was fortunate enough to uncover in 1937, in the Museum of the Ancient Orient at Istanbul. Although a large part of the myth had been copied and published by 1914, no translation had been attempted, since the story seemed to make no connected sense and to lack intelligent motivation. The small piece that I located and copied in Istanbul supplied the missing clue, and as a result this charming tale of the all-too-human Sumerian gods was sketched and analyzed for the first time in *Sumerian Mythology* (pages 64–68).

Inanna, Queen of Heaven, the tutelary goddess of Erech, is anxious to increase the welfare and prosperity of her city, to make it the center of Sumerian civilization, and thus to exalt her name and fame. She therefore decides to go to Eridu, the ancient seat of Sumerian culture, where Enki, the Lord of Wisdom, "who knows the very heart of the gods," dwells in his watery abyss, the Abzu. Enki has under his charge all the divine laws that are fundamental to civilization, and if she can obtain them, by fair means or foul, and bring them to her city, Erech, its glory and her own will be unsurpassed. As she approaches the Abzu of Eridu, Enki, no doubt taken in by her charm, calls his messenger Isimud, whom he addresses as follows:

"Come, my messenger Isimud, give ear to my instructions,
A word I shall say to you, take my word.
The maid, all alone, has directed her step to the Abzu,
Inanna, all alone, has directed her step to the Abzu,
Have the maid enter the Abzu of Eridu,
Have Inanna enter the Abzu of Eridu,
Give her to eat barley cake with butter,
Pour for her cold water that freshens the heart,
Give her to drink beer in the 'face of the lion'
At the holy table, the Table of Heaven,
Speak to Inanna words of greeting."

Isimud does exactly as bidden by his master, and Inanna and Enki sit down to feast and banquet. After their hearts have become happy with drink, Enki exclaims:

"By the name of my power, by the name of my power,
To holy Inanna, my daughter, I shall present the divine
laws."

He thereupon presents, several at a time, the more than one hundred divine laws that are the basis of the culture pattern of civilization. Inanna is only too happy to accept the gifts offered her by the drunken Enki. She takes them and loads them on her Boat of Heaven, and makes off for Erech with her precious cargo. But after the effects of the banquet have worn off, Enki notices that the *me*'s are gone from their usual place. He turns to Isimud, who informs him that he, Enki himself, presented them to his daughter Inanna. Enki bitterly rues his munificence and decides to prevent the Boat of Heaven from reaching Erech at all costs. He therefore dispatches his messenger Isimud, together with a group of sea monsters, to follow Inanna and her boat to the first of the seven stopping stations that are situated between the Abzu of Eridu and Erech. Here the sea monsters are to seize the Boat of Heaven from Inanna, but Inanna herself must be permitted to continue her journey to Erech afoot.

The passage covering Enki's instructions to Isimud and Isimud's conversation with Inanna, who reproaches her father for expecting his gift to be returned, is, in its way, a poetic gem. It runs as follows:

The prince calls his messenger Isimud,
Enki gives the word to the Good Name of Heaven.
"O my messenger Isimud, my Good Name of Heaven."
"O my king, here I stand, forever is praise."
"The Boat of Heaven, where now has it arrived?"
"At the wharf Idal it has arrived."
"Go and let the sea monsters seize it from her."

Isimud does as bidden, overtakes the Boat of Heaven, and says to Inanna:

"O my queen, your father has sent me to you,
O Inanna, your father has sent me to you,
Your father, exalted is his speech,
Enki, exalted is his utterance,
His great words are not to go unheeded."

Holy Inanna answers him:

*"My father, what has he spoken to you, what has he said
    to you?*
*His great words that are not to go unheeded, what, pray,
    are they?"*

"My king has spoken to me,
Enki has said to me:
'Let Inanna go to Erech,
But you, bring me back the Boat of Heaven to Eridu.'"

Holy Inanna says to the messenger Isimud:
"My father, why, pray, has he changed his word to me?
Why has he broken his righteous word to me?
Why has he defiled his great words to me?
My father has spoken to me falsely, has spoken to me falsely,
*Falsely has he sworn by the name of his power, by the
    name of the Abzu."*

Barely had she uttered these words,
The sea monsters seized the Boat of Heaven.

Inanna says to her messenger Ninshubur:
"Come, my true messenger of Inanna,
My messenger of favorable words,
My carrier of true word,
Whose hand never falters, whose foot never falters,
*Save the Boat of Heaven and Inanna's presented divine
    laws."*

This Ninshubur does. But Enki is persistent. He sends
Isimud, accompanied by various sea monsters, to seize the
Boat of Heaven at each of the seven stopping points between Eridu and Erech. And each time Ninshubur comes
to Inanna's rescue. Finally Inanna and her boat arrive safe
and sound at Erech, where, amidst jubilation and feasting
on the part of the delighted inhabitants, she unloads the
divine laws one at a time.

The Sumerian thinkers did not formulate a system of
philosophy, nor did they evolve an explicit system of moral
laws and principles. They produced no formal treatises on
ethics. What we do know about Sumerian ethics and morals has to be searched out in various Sumerian literary
works. Chapter 14 analyzes some of the Sumerian ethical
ideas, together with relevant evidence.

THE FIRST MORAL IDEALS

Sumerian thinkers, in line with their world view, had no exaggerated confidence in man and his destiny. They were firmly convinced that man was fashioned of clay and created for one purpose only: to serve the gods by supplying them with food, drink, and shelter, so that they might have full leisure for their divine activities. Life, they believed, is beset with uncertainty and haunted by insecurity, since man does not know beforehand the destiny decreed for him by the unpredictable gods. When he dies, his emasculated spirit descends to the dark, dreary nether world, where life is but a dismal and wretched reflection of earthly life.

One fundamental moral problem, a favorite with Western philosophers, never troubled the Sumerian thinkers at all—namely, the delicate problem of free will. Convinced beyond all need for argument that man was created by the gods solely for their benefit and pleasure, the thinkers accepted man's dependent status just as they accepted the divine decision that death is man's lot and that only the gods are immortal. To the gods was attributed all credit for the high moral qualities and ethical virtues that the Sumerians had no doubt evolved gradually and painfully from their social and cultural experiences. It was the gods who planned; man only followed divine orders.

The Sumerians, according to their own records, cherished goodness and truth, law and order, justice and freedom, righteousness and straightforwardness, mercy and compassion. And they abhorred evil and falsehood, lawlessness and disorder, injustice and oppression, sinfulness and perversity, cruelty and pitilessness. Kings and rulers constantly boasted of the fact that they had established law and order in the land; protected the weak from the strong, the poor from the rich; and wiped out evil and violence. In the unique document analyzed in Chapter 7, the Lagashite ruler Urukagina, who lived in the twenty-fourth century B.C., proudly recorded that he restored justice and freedom to the long-suffering citizens, did away with ubiquitous and oppressive officials, put a stop to injustice and exploitation, and protected the widow and the orphan. Less than four centuries later, Ur-Nammu, founder of the Third Dynasty of Ur, promulgated his law code (see Chapter 8), which lists in its prologue some of his ethical achievements: he did away with a number of prevalent bureaucratic abuses, regulated weights and measures to ensure honesty in the market place, and saw to it that the widow, the orphan, and the poor were protected from ill-treatment and abuse. Some two centuries later, Lipit-Ishtar of Isin promulgated a new law code, in which he boasted that he was especially selected by the great gods An and Enlil for "the princeship of the land in order to establish justice in the lands, to banish complaints, to turn back enmity and rebellion by force of arms, and to bring well-being to the Sumerians and Akkadians." The hymns of a number of Sumerian rulers abound in similar claims of high ethical and moral conduct.

The gods, too, according to the Sumerian sages, preferred the ethical and moral to the unethical and immoral, and practically all the major deities of the Sumerian pantheon are extolled in Sumerian hymns as lovers of the good and the just, of truth and righteousness. Indeed, there were several deities who had the supervision of the moral order as their main function—the sun-god Utu, for example. Another deity, a Lagashite goddess by the name of Nanshe, is also sporadically mentioned in the texts as devoted to truth, justice, and mercy. But it is only now that we are beginning to get some idea of the significant role played by this goddess in the sphere of man's ethical and moral conduct. In

1951 a Sumerian hymn consisting of about 250 lines was pieced together from 19 tablets and fragments excavated in Nippur, and this hymn contains some of the most explicit ethical and moral statements yet found in Sumerian documents. It describes the goddess Nanshe as follows:

Who knows the orphan, who knows the widow,
Knows the oppression of man over man, is the orphan's
    mother,
Nanshe, who cares for the widow,
Who seeks out (?) justice (?) for the poorest (?).
The queen brings the refugee to her lap,
Finds shelter for the weak.

In a passage whose meaning is still largely obscure, Nanshe is pictured as judging mankind on New Year's day. By her side are Nidaba, the goddess of writing and accounts, and Nidaba's husband Haia, as well as numerous witnesses. The evil human types who suffer her displeasure are described as follows:

(People) who walking in transgression reached out with
    high hand, ... ,
Who transgress the established norms, violate contracts,
Who looked with favor on the places of evil, ... ,
Who substituted a small weight for a large weight,
Who substituted a small measure for a large meas-
    ure, ... ,
Who having eaten (something not belonging to him) did
    not say "I have eaten it."
Who having drunk, did not say "I have drunk it," . . . . ,
Who said "I would eat that which is forbidden."
Who said "I would drink that which is forbidden."

Nanshe's social conscience is further revealed in lines which read:

To comfort the orphan, to make disappear the widow,
To set up a place of destruction for the mighty,
To turn over the mighty to the weak, ... ,
Nanshe searches the heart of the people.

Although the leading gods were assumed to be moral in

their conduct, the fact remains that in the world view of the Sumerians these were the very gods who, in the process of establishing civilization, also planned evil and falsehood, violence and oppression—in short, all the immoral modes of human conduct. For example, the list of *me*'s—the rules and regulations devised by the gods to make the cosmos run smoothly and effectively—included not only rules concerning "truth," "peace," "goodness," "justice," but also rules concerning "falsehood," "strife," "lamentation," "fear." Why did the gods find it necessary to plan and create sin and evil, suffering and misfortune? (One Sumerian pessimist could say, "Never has a sinless child been born to his mother.") To judge from our available material, the Sumerian sages, if they asked the question at all, were prepared to admit their ignorance in this respect; the will of the gods and their motives were at times inscrutable. The proper course for a Sumerian "Job" to pursue was not to argue and complain in the face of seemingly unjustifiable misfortune, but to plead and wail, to lament, and to confess his inevitable sins and failings.

But would the gods give heed to him, a lone and not very effective mortal, even if he prostrated and humbled himself in heartfelt prayer? Probably not, it seemed to the Sumerian teachers. As they saw it, gods were like the mortal rulers the world over, and no doubt had more important things to attend to. And so, as in the case of kings, man must have an intermediary to intercede in his behalf, one whom the gods would be willing to hear and favor. The Sumerian thinkers therefore evolved the notion of a personal god, a kind of good angel to each particular individual and family head—his divine father who had begot him, as it were. It was to *him*, to his personal deity, that the individual sufferer bared his heart in prayer and supplication, and it was through him that he found his salvation.

The Sumerian ethical concepts and ideals were dominated by the dogma that man was fashioned of clay to serve the gods. The pertinent evidence comes primarily from two myths. One is devoted entirely to the creation of man. The other consists largely of a disputation between two minor deities, but contains an introduction which gives a detailed statement of the purpose for which man was created.

The composition narrating the creation of man has been found inscribed on two duplicating tablets: one is a Nippur tablet in the University Museum; the other is in the Louvre, which acquired it from an antique dealer. The Louvre tablet and the greater part of the University Museum tablet had been copied and published by 1934, yet the contents remained largely unintelligible, primarily owing to the fact that the University Museum tablet, which is better preserved than the Louvre fragment, arrived in Philadelphia, some four or five decades ago, broken into four parts. By 1919 two of the pieces had already been recognized and joined; these were copied and published by Stephen Langdon. In 1934 Edward Chiera published the third piece, but he failed to recognize that it joined the two pieces published by Langdon in 1919. I realized this fact a decade or so later while trying to piece together the text of the myth for my *Sumerian Mythology*. At that time I identified in the University Museum tablet collection the fourth —and still unpublished—fragment of the tablet, which actually joins the three published pieces. It was now possible for the first time to arrange the contents of the myth in their proper order and to prepare at least a tentative interpretation of the myth, although the text was still difficult, obscure, and far from complete (see *Sumerian Mythology*, pages 68–72).

The poem begins with what may be a description of the difficulties of the gods in procuring their bread, especially after the female deities had come into being. The gods complain, but Enki, the water-god—as the Sumerian god of wisdom he might have been expected to come to their aid— is lying asleep in the deep and fails to hear them. Thereupon his mother, the primeval sea, "the mother who gave birth to all the gods," brings the tears of the gods before Enki, saying:

"O my son, rise from your bed, from your . . . work what is wise,

Fashion servants of the gods, may they produce their doubles (?)."

Enki gives the matter thought, leads forth the host of "good and princely fashioners," and says to his mother, Nammu, the primeval sea:

"O my mother, the creature whose name you uttered, it exists,
  Bind upon it the image (?) of the gods;
Mix the heart of the clay that is over the abyss,
The good and princely fashioners will thicken the clay,
  You, do you bring the limbs into existence;
Ninmah (the earth-mother goddess) will work above you,
The goddesses (of birth) . . . . will stand by you at your fashioning;
O my mother, decree its (the newborn's) fate,
  Ninmah will bind upon it the image (?) of the gods,
It is man . . . . ."

Here the poem turns from the creation of man as a whole to the creation of certain imperfect human types in an attempt to explain the existence of these abnormal beings. It tells of a feast arranged by Enki for the gods, no doubt to commemorate man's creation. At this feast, Enki and Ninmah drink much wine and become somewhat exuberant. Thereupon Ninmah takes some of the clay that is over the abyss and fashions six different types of abnormal individuals, and Enki decrees their fate and gives them bread to eat. The character of only the last two imperfect types—the barren woman and the sexless creature—is intelligible. The lines read:

The . . . she (Ninmah) made into a woman who cannot give birth.
Enki, upon seeing the woman who cannot give birth,
Decreed her fate, destined her to be stationed in the "woman house."
The . . . she (Ninmah) made into one who has no male organ, who has no female organ.

Enki, upon seeing him who has no male organ, who has no
 female organ,
To stand before the king, decreed as his fate.

After Ninmah has created these six types of man, Enki
decides to do some creating of his own. The way in which
he goes about it is not clear, but, whatever it is that he
does, the resulting creature is a failure; it is weak and feeble
in body and spirit. Enki, anxious that Ninmah help this for-
lorn creature, addresses her as follows:

"Of him whom your hand has fashioned, I have decreed
 the fate,
 Have given him bread to eat;
Do you decree the fate of him whom my hand has fash-
 ioned,
 Do you give him bread to eat."

Ninmah tries to be good to the creature, but to no avail.
She talks to him, but he fails to answer. She gives him
bread to eat, but he does not reach out for it. He can neither sit nor stand, nor bend his knees. A long conversation
between Enki and Ninmah then follows. (The tablets are
so badly broken at this point that it is impossible to make
out the sense.) Finally Ninmah seems to utter a curse
against Enki because of the sick, lifeless creature he has
produced—a curse which Enki seems to accept as his due.

The second myth significant for the Sumerian conception
of the creation of man, which may be titled "Cattle and
Grain," represents a variation of the disputation genre of
compositions, which was very popular with Sumerian writers. The protagonists of the myth are the cattle-god Lahar
and his sister, the grain-goddess Ashnan. These two, according to the myth, were created in the creation chamber
of the gods in order that the Anunnaki, the children of the
heaven-god An, might have food to eat and clothes to
wear. But the Anunnaki were unable to make effective use
of cattle and grain until man was created. All this is told
in an introductory passage which reads:

After on the mountain of heaven and earth,

An (*the heaven-god*) *had caused the Anunnaki* (*his followers*) *to be born,*
Because the name Ashnan (*the grain-goddess*) *had not been born, had not been fashioned,*
Because Uttu (*the goddess of weaving*) *had not been fashioned,*
Because to Uttu no temenos had been set up,
There was no ewe, no lamb was dropped,
There was no goat, no kid was dropped,
The ewe did not give birth to its two lambs,
The goat did not give birth to its three kids.

Because the name of Ashnan, the wise, and Lahar (*the cattle-god*),
The Anunnaki, the great gods, did not know,
The shesh-grain of thirty days did not exist,
The shesh-grain of forty days did not exist,
The small grains, the grain of the mountain, the grain of the pure living creatures did not exist.

Because Uttu had not been born, because the crown (*of vegetation?*) had not been raised,
Because the lord . . . had not been born,
Because Sumugan, the god of the plain, had not come forth,
Like mankind when first created,
They (*the Anunnaki*) knew not the eating of bread,
Knew not the wearing of garments,
Ate plants with their mouth like sheep,
Drank water from the ditch.

In those days, in the creation chamber of the gods,
In their house Duku, Lahar and Ashnan were fashioned;
The produce of Lahar and Ashnan,
The Anunnaki of the Duku eat, but remain unsated;
In their pure sheepfolds shum-*milk*, the good,
The Anunnaki of the Duku drink, but remain unsated;
For the sake of their pure sheepfolds, the good,
Man was given breath.

The passage following the introduction describes the de-

scent of Lahar and Ashnan from heaven to earth, and the
cultural benefits which they bestow on mankind:

In those days Enki says to Enlil:
"Father Enlil, Lahar and Ashnan,
They who have been created in the Duku,
Let us cause them to descend from the Duku."

At the pure word of Enki and Enlil,
Lahar and Ashnan descended from the Duku.
For Lahar they (Enlil and Enki) set up the sheepfold,
Plants and herbs in abundance they present to him;
For Ashnan they establish a house,
Plow and yoke they present to her.

Lahar standing in his sheepfold,
A shepherd increasing the bounty of the sheepfold is he;
Ashnan standing among the crops,
A maid kindly and bountiful is she.

Abundance which comes from heaven,
Lahar and Ashnan caused to appear (on earth),
In the assembly they brought abundance,
In the land they brought the breath of life,
The laws of the gods they direct,
The contents of the warehouses they multiply,
The storehouses they fill full.

In the house of the poor, hugging the dust,
Entering they bring abundance;
The pair of them, wherever they stand,
Bring heavy increase into the house;
The place where they stand they sate, the place where
*   they sit they supply,*
They made good the heart of An and Enlil.

But then Lahar and Ashnan drink much wine, and so
they begin to quarrel in the farms and fields. In the arguments that ensue, each deity extolls his achievements and
belittles those of his opponent. Finally Enlil and Enki intervene and declare Ashnan the victor.

The Sumerian sages believed and taught the doctrine

that man's misfortunes are the result of his sins and misdeeds, and that no man is without guilt. They argued that there are no cases of unjust and undeserving human suffering; it is always man who is to blame, not the gods. In moments of adversity more than one sufferer must have been tempted to challenge the fairness and justice of the gods. It was, perhaps, in an effort to forestall such resentment against the gods and to ward off disillusionment with the divine order, that one of the Sumerian sages composed the edifying essay presented in Chapter 15, which contains the earliest known example of the "Job" motif.

15 *Suffering and Submission*

THE FIRST "JOB"

A paper I read before the Society of Biblical Literature on December 29, 1954, was titled "Man and His God: A Sumerian Version of the Job Motif." It was based on a Sumerian poetic essay consisting of about 139 lines. The text of the essay was pieced together from six clay tablets and fragments excavated by the first University of Pennsylvania expedition to Nippur, about a hundred miles south of modern Baghdad in Iraq. Four of the six pieces are now in the University Museum in Philadelphia, and two are in the Museum of the Ancient Orient in Istanbul.

Up to the date of my lecture, only two of the six pieces, both from the University Museum, had been published, and the text of the poem had therefore remained largely unknown and unintelligible. While in Istanbul in 1951–52 as Fulbright Research Professor, I recognized and copied the two pieces belonging to the poem in the Museum of the Ancient Orient. Upon my return to Philadelphia, I identified the two additional fragments in the University Museum with the help of Edmund Gordon, then a research assistant in the Mesopotamian Section of the museum. While we were going over my translation of the poem for final publication, it dawned upon us that the two Istanbul fragments join two of the four Philadelphia pieces—that is, they actually belong to the very same tablets but had become detached either in very ancient days or in the course of the excavations, and had been brought separately to the two far-flung museums on the Marmara and the Schuylkill. Fortunately I was able to verify these long-distance "joins" in 1954 on a visit to Istanbul as a Bollingen Fellow.

The new identifications and the "joins" across the ocean made it possible for me to piece together and translate the larger part of the text of the poem. It then became obvious that here was the first written essay on human suffering and submission, the theme made famous in world literature and religious thought by the Biblical Book of Job. The Sumerian poem in no way compares with the latter in breadth of scope, depth of understanding, and beauty of expression. Its major significance lies in the fact that it represents man's first recorded attempt to deal with the age-old yet very modern problem of human suffering. All the tablets and fragments on which our Sumerian essay is inscribed date back to more than a thousand years before the compilation of the Book of Job.

The main thesis of our poet is that in cases of suffering and adversity, no matter how seemingly unjustified, the victim has but one valid and effective recourse, and that is to glorify his god continually, and keep wailing and lamenting before him until he turns a favorable ear to his prayers. The god concerned is the sufferer's "personal" god; that is, the deity who, in accordance with the accepted Sumerian credo, acted as the man's representative and intercessor in the assembly of the gods. To prove his point, our poet does not resort to philosophical speculation and theological argumentation; instead, with characteristic Sumerian practicality, he cites a case. Here is a man, unnamed to be sure, who had been wealthy, wise and righteous, or at least seemingly so, and blessed with both friends and kin. One day sickness and suffering overwhelmed him. Did he defy the divine order and blaspheme? Not at all! He came humbly before his god, with tears and lamentation, and poured out his heart in prayer and supplication. As a result, his god was highly pleased and moved to compassion; he gave heed to his prayer, delivered him from his misfortunes, and turned his suffering to joy.

Structurally, the poem may be tentatively divided into four sections. First comes a brief introductory exhortation that man should praise and exalt his god and soothe him with lamentations. The poet then introduces the unnamed individual who, upon being smitten with sickness and misfortune, addresses his god with tears and prayers. There follows the sufferer's petition, which constitutes the major part of the poem. It begins with a description of the ill-treatment accorded him by his fellow men—friend and foe alike; continues with a lament against his bitter fate, including a rhetorical request to his kin and to the professional singers to do likewise; and concludes with a confession of guilt and a direct plea for relief and deliverance. Finally comes the "happy ending," in which the poet informs us that the man's prayer did not go unheeded, and that his god accepted the entreaties and delivered him from his afflictions. All of this leads to a further glorification of his god.

To illustrate the mood and temper of the poem, some of its more intelligible passages are quoted here. The reader must constantly bear in mind that Sumerian is still not fully understood, and that in time some of the translations will be modified and improved. Here is part of the sufferer's petition in his own words:

"I am a man, a discerning one, yet who respects me prospers
     not,
My righteous word has been turned into a lie,
The man of deceit has covered me with the Southwind, I
     am forced to serve him,
Who respects me not has shamed me before you.

"You have doled out to me suffering ever anew,
I entered the house, heavy is the spirit,
I, the man, went out to the streets, oppressed is the heart,
With me, the valiant, my righteous shepherd has become
     angry, has looked upon me inimically.

"My herdsman has sought out evil forces against me who
     am not his enemy,
My companion says not a true word to me,
My friend gives the lie to my righteous word,
The man of deceit has conspired against me,

And you, my god, do not thwart him. . . .

"I, the wise, why am I bound to the ignorant youths?
I, the discerning, why am I counted among the ignorant?
Food is all about, yet my food is hunger,
On the day shares were allotted to all, my allotted share
*   was suffering.*

"My god, (I would stand) before you,
Would speak to you, . . . , my word is a groan,
I would tell you about it, would bemoan the bitterness of
*   my path,*
(Would bewail) the confusion of . . . .

"Lo, let not my mother who bore me cease my lament be-
*   fore you.*
Let not my sister utter the happy song and chant.
Let her utter tearfully my misfortunes before you,
Let my wife voice mournfully my suffering,
Let the expert singer bemoan my bitter fate.

"My god, the day shines bright over the land, for me the
*   day is black.*
The bright day, the good day has . . like the . . .
Tears, lament, anguish, and depression are lodged within
*   me,*
Suffering overwhelms me like one chosen for nothing but
*   tears,*
Evil fate holds me in its hand, carries off my breath of life,
Malignant sickness bathes my body. . . .

"My god, you who are my father who begot me, lift up my
*   face.*
Like an innocent cow, in pity . . . the groan,
How long will you neglect me, leave me unprotected?
Like an ox, ... ,
How long will you leave me unguided?

"They say—valiant sages—a word righteous and straight-
*   forward:*
'Never has a sinless child been born to its mother,
. . . . a sinless youth has not existed from of old.'"

So much for the man's prayer and supplication. The "happy ending" reads as follows:

The man—his god harkened to his bitter tears and weeping,
The young man—his lamentation and wailing soothed the
*   heart of his god.*
The righteous words, the pure words uttered by him, his
*   god accepted.*
The words which the man prayerfully confessed,
Pleased the . . . . , the flesh of his god, and his god with-
*   drew his hand from the evil word,*
. . which oppresses the heart, ... he embraces,
The encompassing sickness-demon, which had spread wide
*   its wings, he swept away.*
The (disease) which had smitten him like a . . . , he
*   dissipated,*
The evil fate which had been decreed for him in accordance
*   with his sentence, he turned aside,*
He turned the man's suffering into joy,
Set by him the kindly genii as a watch and guardian,
Gave him . . angels with gracious mien.

We now turn from the sublime to the mundane, from Sunday's preaching to Monday's practice, from poetic prayers to prosaic proverbs. It is in its proverbs that a people gives itself away, as it were, for proverbs reveal the characteristic attitudes, the basic drives, and the inner motives behind man's day-to-day actions, which the more poetic literary works tend to cloak and disguise. Sumerian proverbs by the hundreds are now in the process of restoration and translation, primarily through the efforts of Edmund Gordon, and some are presented in Chapter 16.

THE FIRST PROVERBS AND SAYINGS

The Hebrew Book of Proverbs was long believed to be the oldest collection of maxims and sayings in man's recorded history. With the discovery and unraveling of the ancient Egyptian civilization, in the past century and a half, collections of Egyptian proverbs and precepts were uncovered which antedate the Biblical Book of Proverbs by many years. But these are by no means the oldest of man's recorded aphorisms and adages. The Sumerian proverb collections antedate most, if not all, of the known Egyptian compilations by several centuries.

Until about two decades ago, almost no Sumerian unilingual proverbs were known. A small number of bilingual sayings, written in Sumerian with Akkadian translations, had been published, and these were practically all inscribed on tablets dating from the first millennium B.C. In 1934, however, Edward Chiera published several proverb tablets and fragments from the University Museum's Nippur collection, which were inscribed in the eighteenth century B.C. They indicated that the Sumerian men of letters must have compiled quite a number of collections of proverbs and sayings. Since 1937 I have devoted much time to this literary genre, identifying a large number of proverb pieces in the Istanbul Museum of the Ancient Orient and the University Museum in Philadelphia, and actually copying a number of them in both museums. But it was not until 1951–52, during my stay in Turkey as a Fulbright Research Professor, that I succeeded in copying practically all the Istanbul material, consisting of more than eighty tablets and fragments.

On my return to Philadelphia and the University Museum, with its hundreds of proverb fragments, it became evident that, because there was so much to do on Sumerian literature in general, I would not have the time to concentrate on this huge collection of proverb material. I therefore turned over my Istanbul copies and other pertinent data to Edmund Gordon, now Research Associate in the University Museum. After months of devoted effort, Gordon found that more than a dozen Sumerian collections, each containing scores and even hundreds of proverbs, could be pieced together and restored from the available material. He has already prepared definitive editions of four such collections and pieced together over three hundred practically complete proverbs, many of which were unknown. Some of his material is utilized in this chapter. The reader should bear in mind, however, that proverbs are particularly difficult to translate because of their laconic language, and that future study may show that some of the sayings here quoted miss the meaning, wholly or in part.

One of the significant characteristics of proverbs in general is the universal relevance of their content. If you ever begin to doubt the brotherhood of man and the common humanity of all peoples and races, turn to their sayings and maxims, their precepts and adages. More than any other literary products, they pierce the crust of cultural contrasts and environmental differences, and lay bare the fundamental nature of all men, no matter where and when they live. The Sumerian proverbs were compiled and written down more than thirty-five hundred years ago, and many had no doubt been repeated by word of mouth for centuries before they were put in written form. They concern a people that differs from us in language and physical environment, in manners and customs, in politics, economics, and religion, and yet the basic character revealed by the Sumerian proverbs is remarkably like our own. We have little difficulty in recognizing in them reflections of our own drives and attitudes, foibles and weaknesses, confusions and dilemmas.

For example, we find there the whiner, who attributes all his failures to fate and keeps complaining, "I was born on an ill-fated day."

Then there are the perpetual explainers who parade their transparent excuses in spite of the clearest evidence to the contrary. Of them, the ancients said:

> *Can one conceive without intercourse,*
> *Can one get fat without eating!*

What the Sumerians thought of their misfits is shown in their saying:

> *You are put in water, the water becomes foul,*
> *You are put in a garden, the fruit begins to rot.*

As in our own times, confusion and hesitation in economic matters beset not a few. Our ancients put it this way:

> *We are doomed to die, let us spend;*
> *We will live long, let us save.*

And in another way:

> *The early barley will thrive—how do we know?*
> *The late barley will thrive—how do we know?*

Sumer had, of course, its perennial poor with their troubles, and these are rather nicely summed up in the contrasting lines:

> *The poor man is better dead than alive;*
> *If he has bread, he has no salt,*
> *If he has salt, he has no bread,*
> *If he has meat, he has no lamb,*
> *If he has a lamb, he has no meat.*

The poor man frequently had to dig into his savings. As the Sumerian proverb-writer puts it, "The poor man nibbles away at his silver." When his savings gave out, he had

to borrow from the ancient counterparts of our own loan
sharks. Hence the saying: "The poor man borrows and wor-
ries." This is the Sumerian equivalent of our own: "Money
borrowed is soon sorrowed."

No doubt the poor as a whole were submissive. There is
nothing to indicate that the Sumerian poor consciously re-
belled against the rich ruling classes. Nevertheless, their
proverb, "Not all the households of the poor are equally
submissive," if the translation is correct, does indicate a certain degree of class consciousness.

Suggestive of Ecclesiastes 5:12, "The sleep of a labouring
man is sweet," and particularly of the Talmudic "Who
multiplies possessions multiplies worry," is this Sumerian
proverb:

> *Who possesses much silver may be happy,*
> *Who possesses much barley may be happy,*
> *But who has nothing at all can sleep.*

Occasionally the poor man realized that he was a failure
not through a fault of his own but because he had tied up
with the wrong associates:

> *I am a thoroughbred steed,*
> *But I am hitched to a mule*
> *And must draw a cart,*
> *And carry reeds and stubble.*

Of the poor artisan who, ironically enough, could not
afford to have the very things he made, the Sumerian said:
"The valet always wears dirty clothes."

Clothes, incidentally, were highly appreciated by the Sumerians, for they said, "Everybody takes to the well-
dressed man."

In any case there were some valets who evidently succeeded in getting a formal education, to judge from the
saying, "He is a valet who has actually studied Sumerian."

Evidently not all ancient scribes, any more than all their
modern counterparts, the stenographers, were perfect at
taking dictation. Hence the Sumerian saying:

> *A scribe whose hand moves in accordance with the mouth*
> *(that is, the dictated word),*

He is indeed a scribe!

The Sumerians even had their quota of scribes who could not spell properly, as is implied in this rhetorical question:

> *A scribe who does not know Sumerian,*
> *What kind of scribe is he!*

The so-called weaker sex is well represented in Sumerian sayings, and not always to its advantage. To be sure, the "gold-digger" seems to have been unknown in Sumer, but Sumerians had their share of practical virgins. As one marriageable young lady who had grown weary of waiting for a wealthy match, and decided to stop picking and choosing, said:

> *Who is well-provided, who is rich?*
> *For whom shall I hold my love?*

Marriage among the Sumerians was no light burden. They put it in a negative way:

Who has not supported a wife or child,
His nose has not borne a leash (the allusion is to the nose leash of prisoners).

The Sumerian husband felt himself frequently neglected, as shown in the saying:

My wife is in "church" (literally "the outdoor shrine"),
My mother is down by the river (probably attending some religious rite),
And here am I starving of hunger.

As for the restless, discontented wife who just did not know what was wrong with her, even in those ancient days the doctor was her refuge. At least so we might gather, if the translation is correct, from the saying:

> *A restless woman in the house*
> *Adds ache to pain.*

No wonder, then, that the Sumerian male at times regretted his marriage, as is evident from the proverb:

> *For his pleasure: marriage.*
> *On his thinking it over: divorce.*

No wonder the bride and groom entered into marriage in quite different spirits, to judge from these terse words:

> *A joyful heart: the bride.*
> *A sorrowful heart: the groom.*

As for the mother-in-law, she seems to have been far less difficult than her modern counterpart; at least, no Sumerian mother-in-law stories have as yet come to light. In ancient Sumer it was the daughter-in-law who had an unenviable reputation. This seems evident from a Sumerian epigram on what is good and bad for a man, which reads:

> *The desert canteen is a man's life,*
> *The shoe is a man's eye,*
> *The wife is a man's future,*
> *The son is a man's refuge,*
> *The daughter is a man's salvation,*
> *The daughter-in-law is a man's devil.*

Friendship was highly valued by the Sumerians. But, as with ourselves, "blood was thicker than water." As they put it:

> *Friendship lasts a day,*
> *Kinship endures forever.*

Interestingly enough from the point of view of comparative culture, the dog was by no means considered a "man's best friend" by the Sumerians. Rather, he was thought of as essentially disloyal to man, to judge from such sayings as these:

> *The ox plows,*
> *The dog spoils the deep furrows.*

> *It is a dog that does not know its home.*

> *The smith's dog could not overturn the anvil;*
> *He (therefore) overturned the waterpot instead.*

If the Sumerian's attitude toward the dog seems a bit strange to us, here are several psychological insights which are practically identical with our own, though expressed in different words: "The boatman is a man of belligerence" compares with our "A sailor will fight at the drop of a hat."

The Sumerian saying,

> *He did not yet catch the fox,*
> *Yet he is making a neck-stock for it,*

is the equivalent of our "Don't count your chickens before they are hatched."

Finally,

> *Upon my escaping from the wild ox,*
> *The wild cow confronted me,*

is just another way of saying: "Out of the frying pan, into the fire."

The need for diligence has, no doubt, been preached in all places and at all times. But even "Poor Richard" could hardly have put it better than the Sumerian who said:

> *Hand and hand, a man's house is built;*
> *Stomach and stomach, a man's house is destroyed.*

At least some Sumerians tried hard to "keep up with the Joneses." For them, this rather drastic warning was coined:

> *Who builds like a lord, lives like a slave;*
> *Who builds like a slave, lives like a lord.*

With respect to war and peace, our ancients found themselves in the same dilemma that confronts us. On the one hand, preparedness seems to be necessary for self-preservation, or, as they put it:

> *The state weak in armaments—*
> *The enemy will not be driven from its gates.*

On the other hand, the futility of war and its tit-for-tat character are only too obvious:

> *You go and carry off the enemy's land;*
> *The enemy comes and carries off your land.*

But war or peace, the thing to do is to "keep your eye on the ball" and not be fooled by appearances. The Sumerian put it in words which are not untimely:

> *You can have a lord, you can have a king,*
> *But the man to fear is the "governor"!*

The Sumerian men of letters included in their numerous proverb collections not only sayings of all kinds, such as maxims, truisms, adages, bywords, and paradoxes, but fables as well. These approach quite closely the classical "Aesopic" fable in that they consist of a short introductory passage in narrative form, followed by a brief quoted speech serving as a punch line. Occasionally there is even a protracted dialogue between the characters. Chapter 17 will cite numerous examples of these early "Aesopica" from translations prepared by Dr. Edmund Gordon in the past year or two.

THE FIRST ANIMAL FABLES

Among the Greeks and Romans, the invention of the literary genre of animal fables was ascribed to Aesop, who lived in Asia Minor during the sixth century B.C. Today, however, it is well known that at least some of the fables attributed to Aesop were already in existence long before Aesop. In any case the animal fable of the "Aesopic" type is found in Sumer more than a millennium before Aesop was born.

Animals, as might well have been expected, played a large role in Sumerian wisdom literature. In the past several years Gordon has pieced together and translated a total of 295 proverbs and fables relating to some 64 different species of animal life: mammals, birds, and members of the so-called lower classes of animal life down to insects. The order of frequency of the various animals in these texts, if we may judge from the extant material, is in itself not uninstructive. The *dog* comes first, being referred to in some 83 proverbs and fables. Next come *domestic cattle*, and then the *donkey*. Then the *fox*, followed by the *pig*, and only then the *domestic sheep*. Next in prominence come the *lion* and *wild ox* (that is, the now extinct *Bos primigenius*), followed by the *domestic goat* and the *wolf*, and so on. Here now are Gordon's tentative translations of some of the better preserved and more intelligible Sumerian fables, starting with the dog and ending with the monkey.

The greediness of the dog is illustrated by these two brief fables:

1. The donkey was swimming in the river, and the dog held tightly onto him, saying: "When is he going to climb out, and be eaten."

2. The dog went to a banquet, but when he looked at the bones there, he went away, saying: "Where I am going now, I shall get more to eat than this."

On the other hand, one of the finest expressions of mother love is voiced in a dog fable which reads:

Thus speaks the bitch with pride: Whether I have fawn-colored (puppies) or whether I have brindled ones, I love my young.

In the case of the wolf, it was his predatory nature that was foremost in the minds of the Sumerians, to judge from the better-preserved fables in which he appears. In one fable, which unfortunately has two short breaks in the text, a pack of ten wolves have attacked some sheep, but one of the wolves manages to play a deceitful trick on the others with a shrewd bit of sophistry, thus:

Nine wolves and a tenth one slaughtered some sheep. The tenth one was greedy and did not (one or two words broken) . . . *When he had treacherously* (one or two words broken) . . . *he said: "I will divide them for you! There are nine of you, and so one sheep will be your joint share. Therefore I, being one, shall take nine. This shall be my share."*

The wild animal whose character seems to be *most* clearly delineated is the fox. In the Sumerian proverbs, the fox is an animal full of conceit, who constantly exhibits—in both his actions and speech—a tendency to exaggerate his own role in the world. But, being at the same time a coward, he is frequently not equal to the task of living up to his bravado. For example:

The fox trod upon the hoof of the wild ox, saying: "Didn't it hurt?"

Or:

*The fox could not build his own house, and so he went
to the house of his friend as a conqueror!*

Or:

*The fox had a stick with him (and said): "Whom shall
I hit?"*

*He carried a legal document with him (and said):
"What can I challenge?"*

Or:

The fox gnashes its teeth, but its head is trembling!

Here are two of the longest fables about the fox, which
further illustrate his cowardice and conceit. Both are rather
complex and seem to leave us hanging in mid-air at the
end, but by and large their meaning and implications are
clear:

The fox says to his wife:

*"Come! Let us crush the city of Uruk with our teeth,
as though it were a leek! Let us strap the city of Kullab
upon our feet as though it were a sandal!" But when they
had not even come within a distance of 600 gar (about
two miles) from the city, the dogs began to howl at them
from within the city: "Geme-Tummal, Geme-Tummal!
(presumably the name of the fox's wife) Go home! Get
along now!" they howled menacingly from within the city.*

And we can assume that the fox and his wife turned on
their heels, and did exactly that.

The other Sumerian fable uses a motif which later occurs in Aesop, not in connection with the fox, but in the
fable of "The Rats and the Weasels." It reads as follows:

*The fox requested the horns of a wild ox from the god
Enlil (and so) the horns of a wild ox were attached to him.
But then the wind and rain were stirred up, and he could
not enter his burrow. Toward the end of the night, when
the cold north wind and storm clouds and rain had show-
ered (?) down upon him, he said: "As soon as it gets light
. . . (unfortunately the text breaks off here, and we can
only guess that the fox begged that the horns be removed).*

Thus, the fox of the Sumerians seems to have little in common with the clever and sly beast that he is in much of the later European folklore, although in a number of ways he is very much akin to the fox in several of Aesop's fables, including the "Sour Grapes" fable. It should also be noted that two Sumerian fables exist—both of them unfortunately in a poor state of preservation—in which the fox appears with the raven or the crow, a combination which occurs also in the later fables of Aesop.

The bear is represented by only two Sumerian fables, in one of which there seems to be an allusion to his annual hibernation.

While very little can be said about the bear, there is a good bit of information to be gleaned from the proverbs about the mongoose. The mongoose was kept as a domestic animal in ancient Mesopotamia, as it is in modern Iraq, for the purpose of killing rats. To the Sumerians, the mongoose seems to have been noted for its directness in attacking its prey, in contrast to the cat's patient and apparently deliberate manner before pouncing upon its quarry. Thus they said:

> A cat—for its thoughts;
> A mongoose—for its actions!

On the other hand, the food-stealing and alcohol-filching habits of the mongoose seem to have been regarded with a sort of bitter tolerance:

> If there is any food around, the mongoose consumes it;
> If it leaves any food for me, a stranger comes and consumes
>   it!

In one proverb, however, a pet mongoose was regarded by its owner as a source of amusement, because of its "poor taste":

> My mongoose, which eats only spoiled food, will not climb up after beer and ghee!

The hyena may be alluded to in one proverb, but even in this case the meaning of the allusion is uncertain.

As for the cat, it occurs but rarely in Sumerian literature, and there are two references in the proverbs. One was just cited above in connection with the mongoose. In the other, a cow who follows a basket carrier around is compared to the cat.

The lion, according to the proverbs and fables, was at home in a type of terrain overgrown with trees and reeds, which can be referred to as "the bush," although at least two fables, which are either badly broken or obscure, locate him in the open steppe country. While the "bush" provided the lion with a protective cover, men had to protect themselves from him by learning his habits. Thus:

O lion, the dense "bush" is your ally!
And:
In the "bush," the lion does not eat up the man who knows him!

The latter proverb sounds at least superficially like the motif of "Androcles and the Lion."

Another fable, which is badly broken, tells of a lion who had fallen into a trap, and a fox. In a number of fables, the lion's natural role as predatory beast par excellence is played up, his prey there being sheep, goats, and the "bush"-pig; thus:

When the lion came to the sheepfold, the dog was wearing a leash of spun wool!
And:
The lion had caught a "bush"-pig and proceeded to bite him, saying: "Up until now, your flesh has not filled my mouth, but your squeals have created a din in my ears!"

But the lion is not always the victor, for he can even be outwitted by the flattery of the "helpless she-goat." Here we have one of the longer Sumerian fables, which most closely resembles those of Aesop:

The lion had caught a helpless she-goat. "Let me go, (and) I will give you a sheep, one of my companions!" (said the she-goat). "If I am to let you go, (first) tell me your name!" (said the lion). The she-goat (then) answered the lion: "Do you not know my name? My name is 'You-

*are-clever'!" (And so,) when the lion came to the sheepfold,
he roared out: "Now that I have arrived at the sheepfold,
I will release you!" She (then) answered him from the
other side (of the fence [?]), saying: "So you have re-
leased me! Were you (really so) clever? Instead of (giving
you) the sheep (which I promised you), even I shall not
stay here!"*

There is one Sumerian fable concerned with the elephant.
It presents the beast as a boaster, who must be "taken down
a peg" by one of the smallest of birds, the wren:

*The elephant boasted (?) about himself, saying: "There
is nothing like me in existence! Do not* (the text is broken
at the end of this line, but we might expect some such
phrase as *"Do not compare yourself to me!) . . . !" The
wren (then) answered him, saying: "But I, too, in my own
small way, was created just as you were!"*

The donkey, as is well known, served as the chief beast
of burden and draught animal in ancient Mesopotamia, and
the Sumerians good-humoredly represented him as the same
slow-moving, and frequently foolish, creature that he is in
European literature of a later date. His main objective in
life seems to be to act contrary to the wishes of his master;
for example:

*One must drive him (by force) into a plague-stricken
city like a pack ass!*

Or:

The donkey eats its own bedding!

Or:

*"Your helpless donkey has no more speed left! O Enlil,
your helpless man has no more strength left!"*

Or:

*My donkey was not destined to run quickly, he was des-
tined to bray!*

Or:

*The donkey lowered its face, and its owner patted it on
the nose, saying:*

*"We must get up and away from here! Quickly now!
Come on!"*

9. Lion attacking bull.

10. Man's oldest prescription.

11. Hymn to the "Great Physician of the Blackheaded People."

12. Sumerian "painted temple."

13. Ur-Nammu, the first "Moses."

14. Ebih-il, the "steward."

15. Ur-Nanshe, the "singer."

16. Woman with a "stole."

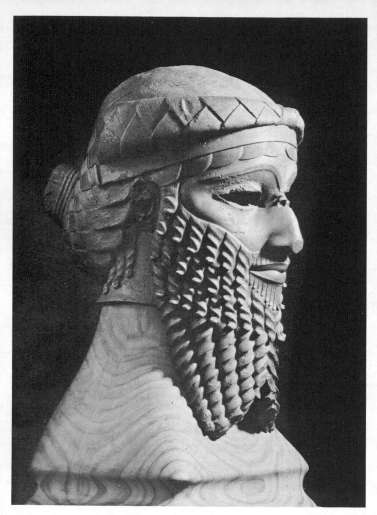

17. A Semitic king of Sumer.

At times the donkey even threw off his burden, and was berated for it:

The donkey, after he had thrown off his packs, said: "The woes of the past are still plentiful in my ears!"

And on occasion the donkey might run away, and not return to its master. The runaway donkey provides an interesting simile in two proverbs:

Like a runaway donkey, my tongue does not turn around and come back!

And:

My youthful vigor has quit my thighs like a runaway donkey.

There are also allusions to certain unpleasant physical traits of the donkey, as for example:

Were there a donkey without a stench, he would be a donkey without a groom!

Finally, there is a proverb which gives us an interesting bit of sociological information, since this proverb which reads:

I will not marry a wife who is only three years old as the donkey does!

apparently indicates disapproval of child marriage.

As for the horse, one Sumerian fable has now quite unexpectedly thrown some new light on the early history of the horse's domestication, for it provides us with what is clearly the earliest reference to horseback riding now known. To be sure, the tablets on which this proverb is inscribed date from about 1700 B.C. But since this fable is found both on a large tablet from the city of Nippur, as well as on a roughly contemporaneous school tablet from the city of Ur, one may deduce a considerably older date for the actual original composition of the fable to allow time, not only for its diffusion, but also for its inclusion within one of the standard proverb collections. It is not unlikely therefore that the horse was already being used for riding in Mesopotamia by about 2000 B.C., even though the next oldest allusion to horseback riding now known is some three centuries later. The fable reads:

The horse, after he had thrown off his rider, said: "If my burden is always to be this, I shall become weak!"

Another proverb seems to refer to the sweating of the horse:

You sweat like a horse; it is what you have been drinking!

which is essentially our colloquial English phrase "He sweats like a horse."

There is only one extant proverb about the hybrid mule, and that proverb, interestingly enough, actually alludes to the animal's parentage! It reads:

O mule, will your sire recognize you, or will your dam recognize you?

The pig, interestingly enough was for the Sumerians one of the most "kosher" of animals, since the animal most frequently mentioned in the proverbs as being slaughtered for food is actually the pig! For example:

The fatted pig is about to be slaughtered, and so he says: "It was the food which I ate!"

Or:

He was at the end of his means (?), and so he slaughtered his pig!

Or:

The pork butcher slaughters the pig, saying: "Must you squeal? This is the road which your sire and your grandsire traveled, and now you are going on it too! (And yet) you are squealing!"

As yet no Sumerian fables concerned with the monkey have come to light. But we have one proverb, and a related mock letter from a monkey to his mother, and these both indicate that the monkey was used for entertainment in the Sumerian music halls, and that he was treated rather shabbily. The proverb reads:

All of Eridu is prosperous, but the monkey of the Great Music Hall sits in the garbage heap!

The related letter goes as follows:

To Lusalusa, my "mother," speak!
Thus says Mr. Monkey:
"Ur is the delightful city of the god Nanna,
Eridu is the prosperous city of the god Enki;
But here am I, sitting behind the doors of the Great Music
     Hall,
I must eat garbage; may I not die from it!
I don't even get a taste of bread; I don't even get a taste
     of beer.
Send me a special courier—Urgent!"

It would seem, therefore, that a monkey belonging to the Great Music Hall at Eridu, the prosperous lake-port city of southeastern Sumer, went unfed and was forced to seek his own food in the garbage heaps of the city. For some reason, the poor animal's predicament became proverbial; and, as seems probable, eventually one of the scribes with a bent for satire expanded the proverb into a mock letter addressed to the monkey's "mother," whose name Lusalusa may possibly be intended to mean "Aping Man." The "letter," in view of the fact that at least four copies have come down to us, seems to have become a minor literary classic, while the original proverb itself found its way into one of the proverb collections.

Compilations of proverbs and fables constitute only one category of Sumerian wisdom literature. The Sumerian men of letters also developed the didactic essay, which may consist of a collection of precepts or instructions such as the "Farmer's Almanac" (Chapter 11) or may be devoted to a description of life in school (Chapter 2). But there was one type of wisdom composition that was a particular favorite with Sumerian writers: the disputation, a battle of words utilizing the rivalry motif. It consists primarily of a dispute between two rivals, each of whom may personify a season, animal, plant, metal, stone, or, as in the highly abbreviated Biblical Cain-Abel story, an occupation. The subject of the first literary debates in history is discussed in Chapter 18.

THE FIRST LITERARY
DEBATES

Sumerian teachers and men of letters were not—and indeed could not be—systematic philosophers and profound thinkers. But they were keen observers of nature and the immediate world about them. The long lists of plants, animals, metals, and stones which the professors compiled for pedagogic purposes (see Chapter 1) imply a careful study of at least the more obvious characteristics of natural substances and living organisms. Too, the Sumerian forerunners of our modern cultural anthropologists consciously set about analyzing civilization as they knew it, and divided it into more than one hundred institutions, occupations, crafts, attitudes, and modes of action.

One of the obvious features in the world about us is the natural clustering into pairs of certain seasons, animals, plants, metals, and implements; so much so that the mere mention of the one immediately brings the other to mind. In the agricultural milieu typified by Sumerian society, such pairs were, for example, summer and winter, cattle and grain, bird and fish, tree and reed, silver and bronze, pickax and plow, shepherd and farmer. To some degree and in certain respects, each of the pair was the opposite of the other; their common feature was the significant and useful role they played in man's life. The question that naturally comes to mind is, Which was *more useful* for man? This particular problem of evaluation struck a sympathetic chord among Sumerian schoolmen, and the more creative among them devised a literary genre devoted especially to it—the debate or disputation. Its major component is the argument between two protagonists, which goes back and forth several times, and in its course each of the rivals "talks up" his own importance and "talks down" that of his opponent. All this is written in poetic form, since the Sumerian men of letters were the direct heirs and descendants of the illiterate minstrels of much earlier days, and poetry came to them more naturally than prose. The composition was rounded out formally with an appropriate mythological introduction, which usually told of the creation of the protagonists, and with a suitable ending in which the dispute was settled by the decision of one or more of the leading deities of the Sumerian pantheon.

We now have the text, wholly or in part, of seven such literary debates, but only three of these have been more or less adequately studied to date. One is the debate between cattle and grain sketched in considerable detail in Chapter 14. The second may be titled "Summer and Winter: Enlil Chooses the Farmer-God." It is one of the longest of the group, and once the text has been pieced together from all available material, it will probably prove to be one of the most informing from the point of view of ancient agricultural practice. Its contents may be tentatively sketched as follows:

Enlil, the air-god, has set his mind on bringing forth all sorts of trees and grain, and on establishing abundance and prosperity in the land. For this purpose, two cultural beings, the brothers Emesh (Summer) and Enten (Winter) are created, and Enlil assigns to each his specific duties. The following lines tell how these duties were executed:

Enten made the ewe give birth to the lamb, the goat give birth to the kid,
Cow and calf to multiply, cream and milk to increase,
In the plain he made rejoice the heart of the wild goat, sheep, and donkey,

*The birds of heaven—in the wide earth he made them set
    up their nests,*
*The fish of the sea—in the canebrake he made them lay
    their eggs,*
*In the palm grove and vineyard he made honey and wine
    abound,*
The trees, wherever planted, he caused to bear fruit,
*The gardens he decked out in green, made their plants lux-
    uriant,*
Made grain increase in the furrows,
*Like Ashnan (the grain goddess), the kindly maid, he made
    it come forth sturdily.*

*Emesh brought into being the trees and fields, made wide
    the stalls and the sheepfolds,*
*In the farms he multiplied produce, bedecked the
    earth . . . . ,*
*Caused the abundant harvest to be brought into the houses,
    the granaries to be heaped high,*
*Cities and habitations to be founded, houses to be built in
    the land,*
Temples to rise mountain-high.

Their mission accomplished, the two brothers decide
to go to Nippur to the "house of life," and bring thank-
offerings to their father Enlil. Emesh brings sundry wild
and domestic animals, birds, and plants as his gift, while
Enten chooses precious metals and stones, trees, and fish
as his offering. But right at the door of the "house of life,"
the jealous Enten starts a quarrel with his brother. The arguments go back and forth between them, and finally
Emesh challenges Enten's claim to the position of "farmer
of the gods." And so they betake themselves to Enlil's great
temple, the *Ekur*, and each states his case. Enten complains
to Enlil:

*"Father Enlil, you have given me charge of the canals, I
    brought the water of abundance,*
Farm I made touch farm, heaped high the granaries,
I made grain increase in the furrows,
Like Ashnan, the kindly maid, I made it come forth sturdily,

Now Emesh, the . . . . , who has no understanding for
  fields,
Has jostled my . . . arm and . . shoulder,
At the king's palace. . . ."

Emesh's version of the quarrel, which begins with several flattering phrases cunningly directed to win Enlil's favor, is brief but (as yet) unintelligible. Then Enlil answers Emesh and Enten:

"The life-producing waters of all the lands—Enten is in
  charge of them,
Farmer of the gods—he produces everything,
Emesh, my son, how do you compare yourself with your
  brother Enten!"
The exalted word of Enlil, with meaning profound,
Whose verdict is unalterable—who dares transgress it!

Emesh bent the knee before Enten, offered him a prayer,
Into his house he brought nectar, wine, and beer,
They sate themselves with heart-cheering nectar, wine, and
  beer,
Emesh presents Enten with gold, silver, and lapis lazuli,
In brotherhood and companionship, they pour joyous
  libations . . . .

In the dispute between Emesh and Enten,
Enten, the faithful farmer of the gods, having proved him-
  self the victor over Emesh,
. . . . Father Enlil, praise!

The third of the disputation compositions may be titled, "The Wooing of Inanna." In formal structure it actually differs from the others of this genre. It is built up more like a playlet, with a number of characters, each having his say in his proper place, and there is therefore no mythological introduction. Moreover, the main body of the poem does not take the form of an argument, but rather consists of a long uninterrupted speech by one of the characters, who, feeling rejected and frustrated, is impelled to enumerate his superior qualities. To be sure, at a later moment this character actually goes looking for a quarrel with his rival, but the latter proves to be a peaceful, cautious type who would rather appease than fight.

There are four characters in this poem: the goddess Inanna; her brother, the sun-god Utu; the shepherd-god Dumuzi; and the farmer-god Enkimdu. Its contents may be summarized as follows: After a brief (but largely fragmentary) introduction, Utu addresses his sister and urges her to become the wife of the shepherd Dumuzi.

Her brother, the hero, the warrior, Utu
Says to the pure Inanna:
"O my sister, let the shepherd marry you,
O maid Inanna, why are you unwilling?
His cream is good, his milk is good,
The shepherd, everything his hand touches is bright,
O Inanna, let the shepherd Dumuzi marry you,
O you who are bedecked with jewels, why are you un-
        willing?
His good cream he will eat with you,
O protector of the king, why are you unwilling?"

Inanna's answer is a flat refusal; she is determined to marry the farmer Enkimdu.

"Me the shepherd shall not marry,
In his new garment he shall not drape me,
His fine wool shall not cover me,
Me, the maid, the farmer shall marry,
The farmer who makes plants grow abundantly,
The farmer who makes grain grow abundantly . . ."

After several fragmentary lines of uncertain meaning, the text continues with a long address by the shepherd, which is probably directed to Inanna. In it he details his superior qualities as compared with the farmer.

"The farmer more than I, the farmer more than I, the
        farmer what has he more than I?
Enkimdu, the man of dike, ditch, and plow,
More than I, the farmer, what has he more than I?
Should he give me his black garment,
I would give him, the farmer, my black ewe for it,
Should he give me his white garment,

I would give him, the farmer, my white ewe for it,
Should he pour me his prime beer,
I would pour him, the farmer, my yellow milk for it,
Should he pour me his good beer,
I would pour him, the farmer, my kisim-milk for it,
Should he pour me his seductive beer,
I would pour him, the farmer, my . . -milk for it,
Should he pour me his diluted beer,
I would pour him, the farmer, my plant-milk for it,
Should he give me his good portions,
I would give him, the farmer, my itirda-milk,
Should he give me his good bread,
I would give him, the farmer, my honey-cheese for it,
Should he give me his small beans,
I would give him, the farmer, my small cheeses for them;
After I shall have eaten, shall have drunk,
I would leave for him the extra cream,
I would leave for him the extra milk;
More than I, the farmer, what has he more than I?"

We then find the shepherd rejoicing on the riverbank, perhaps because his argument had convinced Inanna and induced her to change her mind. There he meets Enkimdu and starts a quarrel with him.

He rejoiced, he rejoiced on the riverbank loam, he rejoiced,
On the riverbank, the shepherd on the riverbank rejoiced,
The shepherd, moreover, led the sheep on the riverbank.
To the shepherd walking to and fro on the riverbank,
To him who is a shepherd, the farmer approached,
The farmer Enkimdu approached.
Dumuzi . . . the farmer, the king of dike and ditch,
In his plain, the shepherd in his plain starts a quarrel with him,
The shepherd Dumuzi in his plain starts a quarrel with him.

But Enkimdu refuses to quarrel, and agrees to allow Dumuzi's flocks to pasture anywhere in his territory.

"I against you, shepherd, against you, shepherd, I against you
Why shall I strive?

Let your sheep eat the grass of the riverbank,
In my cultivated lands let your sheep walk about,
In the bright fields of Erech let them eat grain,
Let your kids and lambs drink the water of my Unun
     (*the name of a canal*)."

Dumuzi, thus appeased, invites the farmer to his wedding as one of his friends.

"*As for me who am a shepherd, at my marriage,*
Farmer, may you be counted as my friend,
Farmer Enkimdu, as my friend, farmer, as my friend,
May you be counted as my friend."

Whereupon Enkimdu offers to bring him and Inanna several selected farm products as a wedding gift:

"*I will bring you wheat, I will bring you beans,*
I will bring you lentils . . . . ,
You, maid, whatever is . . for you,
Maid, Inanna, I would bring you . . . . ."

The poet then ends the composition with these conventional literary notations:

In the dispute which took place between the shepherd and
     the farmer,
O maid Inanna, your praise is good.
It is a balbale (*poem*).

The reader of these pages has no doubt caught the faint sounds of more than one Biblical echo. The primeval sea, separation of heaven and earth, fashioning of man from clay, ethics, laws and law codes, suffering and submission, Cain-Abel-like disputes—all are reminiscent, at least to some small extent, of Old Testament themes and motifs. We now turn to a Sumerian poem revolving about a paradise myth that brings to mind several passages in the Book of Genesis. To be sure, this is a divine, not a human, paradise. And in it are no Adam and Eve to succumb to temptation. But the myth does have several motifs parallel to the Biblical paradise story, and it is barely possible that it provides a rather surprising explanation for the origin and background of the "rib" episode.

THE FIRST BIBLICAL
PARALLELS

Archaeological discoveries made in Egypt and in the Near
East in the past hundred years have opened our eyes to a
spiritual and cultural heritage undreamed of by earlier
generations. What with the unearthing of civilizations buried deep in dirt and dust, the deciphering of languages
dead for millenniums, and the recovery of literatures long
lost and forgotten, our historical horizon has been widened
by several millenniums. One of the major achievements of
all this archaeological activity in "Bible lands" is that a
bright and revealing light has been shed on the background
and origin of the Bible itself. We can now see that this
greatest of literary classics did not come upon the scene full-
blown, like an artificial flower in a vacuum; its roots reach
deep into the distant past and spread wide across the surrounding lands. Both in form and content, the Biblical
books bear no little resemblance to the literatures created
by earlier civilizations in the Near East. To say this is not
to detract in any way from the significance of the Biblical
writings, or from the genius of the Hebrew men of letters
who composed them. Indeed, one can only marvel at what
has been well termed "the Hebrew miracle," which trans-
formed the static motifs and conventionalized patterns of
their predecessors into what is perhaps the most vibrant and
dynamic literary creation known to man.

The literature created by the Sumerians left its deep impress on the Hebrews, and one of the thrilling aspects of

reconstructing and translating Sumerian belles-lettres consists in tracing resemblances and parallels between Sumerian and Biblical literary motifs. To be sure, the Sumerians could not have influenced the Hebrews directly, for they had ceased to exist long before the Hebrew people came into existence. But there is little doubt that the Sumerians had deeply influenced the Canaanites, who preceded the Hebrews in the land that later came to be known as Palestine, and their neighbors, such as the Assyrians, Babylonians, Hittites, Hurrians, and Arameans. A good illustration of Sumerian-Hebrew parallels is provided by the myth "Enki and Ninhursag." Its text was published in 1915, but its contents remained largely unintelligible until 1945, when I published a detailed edition of the text as *Supplementary Study No. 1 of the Bulletin of the American Schools of Oriental Research.* The poem consists of 278 lines inscribed on a six-column tablet now in the University Museum, with a small duplicate in the Louvre identified by Edward Chiera. Briefly sketched, the plot of this Sumerian paradise myth, which treats of gods rather than humans, runs thus:

Dilmun is a land that is "pure," "clean," and "bright" —a "land of the living," which knows neither sickness nor death. What is lacking, however, is the fresh water so essential to animal and plant life. The great Sumerian watergod Enki therefore orders Utu, the sun-god, to fill it with fresh water brought up from the earth. Dilmun is thus turned into a divine garden, green with fruit-laden fields and meadows. In this paradise of the gods eight plants are made to sprout by Ninhursag, the great mother-goddess of the Sumerians (probably originally Mother Earth). She succeeds in bringing these plants into being only after an intricate process involving three generations of goddesses, all begotten by the water-god and born—so the poem repeatedly underlines—without the slightest pain or travail. But perhaps because Enki wanted to taste them, his messenger, the two-faced god Isimud, plucks these precious plants one by one, and gives them to his master Enki, who proceeds to eat them each in turn. Whereupon the angered Ninhursag pronounces upon him the curse of death. Evidently to make sure that she will not change her mind and relent, she disappears from among the gods.

Enki's health begins to fail; eight of his organs become sick. As Enki is sinking fast, the great gods sit in the dust. Enlil, the air-god, the king of the Sumerian gods, seems unable to cope with the situation. Then the fox speaks up. If properly rewarded, he says to Enlil, he will bring Ninhursag back. As good as his word, the fox succeeds in some way (the relevant passage is unfortunately destroyed) in having the mother-goddess return to the gods and heal the dying water-god. She seats him by her side, and after inquiring which eight organs of his body ache him, she brings into existence eight corresponding healing deities, and Enki is brought back to life and health.

How does all this compare with the Biblical paradise story? First, there is some reason to believe that the very idea of a divine paradise, a garden of the gods, is of Sumerian origin. The Sumerian paradise was located, according to our poem, in the land of Dilmun, a land that was probably situated in southwestern Iran. It is in this same Dilmun that, later, the Babylonians, the Semitic people who conquered the Sumerians, located their "land of the living," the home of their immortals. There is good indication that the Biblical paradise, which is described as a garden planted *eastward* in Eden, from whose waters flow the four world rivers including the Tigris and Euphrates, may have been originally identical with Dilmun, the Sumerian paradise-land.

Again, the passage in our poem describing the watering of Dilmun by the sun-god with fresh water brought up from the earth, is suggestive of the Biblical, "But there went up a mist from the earth, and watered the whole face of the ground" (Genesis 2:6). The birth of the goddesses without pain or travail illuminates the background of the curse against Eve that it shall be her lot to conceive and bear children in sorrow. And Enki's eating of the eight plants and the curse uttered against him for this misdeed calls to mind the eating of the fruit of the tree of knowledge by Adam and Eve, and the curse pronounced against each of them for this sinful action.

But perhaps the most interesting result of our comparative analysis is the explanation provided by the Sumerian poem for one of the most puzzling motifs in the Biblical paradise story—the famous passage describing the fashioning of Eve, "the mother of all living," from the rib of Adam. Why a rib? Why did the Hebrew storyteller find it more fitting to choose a rib rather than any of the other organs of the body for the fashioning of the woman whose name, Eve, according to the Biblical notion, means approximately "she who makes live"? The reason becomes clear if we assume that a Sumerian literary background, such as that represented by the Dilmun poem, underlies the Biblical paradise tale. In the Sumerian poem, one of Enki's sick organs is the rib. The Sumerian word for "rib" is *ti* (pronounced *tee*). The goddess created for the healing of Enki's rib is called Nin-ti, "the lady of the rib." But the Sumerian word *ti* also means "to make live." The name Nin-ti may therefore mean "the lady who makes live," as well as "the lady of the rib." In Sumerian literature, therefore, "the lady of the rib" came to be identified with "the lady who makes live" through what may be termed a play on words. It was this, one of the most ancient of literary puns, which was carried over and perpetuated in the Biblical paradise story, although here, of course, it loses its validity, since the Hebrew word for "rib" and that for "who makes live" have nothing in common.

I came upon this possible Sumerian background for the explanation of the Biblical "rib" story quite independently in 1945, but it had already been suggested thirty years earlier by the eminent French cuneiformist Père Scheil, as the American Orientalist William Albright, who edited my publication, pointed out to me—which makes it all the more likely to be true.

To illustrate the mood and temper of the Sumerian poem, I shall quote several pertinent and characteristic extracts. Thus Dilmun, as a land of immortality where there is neither sickness nor death, is described in an obliquely phrased passage as follows:

In Dilmun the raven utters no cry,

The ittidu-*bird utters not the cry of the* ittidu-*bird,*
The lion kills not,
The wolf snatches not the lamb,
Unknown is the kid-devouring wild dog,
Unknown is the grain-devouring . . ,
Unknown is the widow,
The bird on high . .s not his . . ,
The dove droops not the head,
The sick-eyed says not "I am sick-eyed,"
The sick-headed says not "I am sick-headed,"
Its (Dilmun's) old woman says not "I am an old woman,"
Its old man says not "I am an old man,"
Unbathed is the maid, no sparkling water is poured in the city,
Who crosses the river (of death?) utters no . . ,
The wailing priests walk not round about him,
The singer utters no wail,
By the side of the city he utters no lament.

The passage concerned with the painless and effortless birth of the goddesses after only nine days, instead of nine months, of bearing, reads in part as follows:

The goddess Ninmu came out to the riverbank,
Enki in the marshlands looks about, looks about,
He says to his messenger Isimud:
"Shall I not kiss the young one, the fair?
Shall I not kiss Ninmu, the fair?"

His messenger Isimud answers:
"Kiss the young one, the fair,
Kiss Ninmu, the fair,
For my king I shall blow up a mighty wind."

Alone he set his foot in the boat,
A second time he set there . . . . ,
He embraced her, he kissed her,
Enki poured the seed into the womb,
She took the seed into the womb, the seed of Enki,
One day being her one month,
Two days being her two months,
Nine days being her nine months, the months of "woman-hood,"

Like . . -cream, like . . -cream, like good, princely cream,
Ninmu, like . . -cream, like . . -cream, like good, princely
  cream,
Gave birth to the goddess Ninkurra.

The eating of the eight plants is told in a passage revealing a typical Sumerian repetition pattern:

Enki in the marshlands looks about, looks about,
He says to his messenger Isimud:
"Of the plants their fate I would decree, their 'heart' I
  would know;
What, pray, is this (plant)? What, pray, is this (plant)?"
His messenger Isimud answers:
"My king, the tree-plant," he says to him;
He cuts it down for him, he (Enki) eats it.

"My king, the honey-plant," he says to him;
He plucks it for him, he eats it.

"My king, the roadweed (?)-plant," he says to him;
He cuts it down for him, he eats it.

"My king, the water-plant," he says to him;
He plucks it for him, he eats it.

"My king, the thorn-plant," he says to him;
He cuts it down for him, he eats it.

"My king, the caper-plant," he says to him;
He plucks it for him, he eats it.

"My king, the . . -plant," he says to him;
He cuts it down for him, he eats it.

"My king, the cassia-plant," he says to him;
He plucks it for him, he eats it.

Of the plants, Enki decreed their fate, knew (?) their
  heart.
Thereupon Ninhursag cursed the name of Enki:
"Until he is dead I shall not look upon him with the eye
  of life."

Ninhursag now disappears, but the fox in some way succeeds in bringing her back. Whereupon she proceeds to heal Enki's eight sick organs, including the rib, through the birth of eight deities, thus:

Ninhursag seated Enki by her pudendum,
"My brother, what hurts you?"
"My . . hurts me."
"To the god Abu I have given birth for you."

"My brother, what hurts you?"
"My jaw hurts me."
"To the god Nintulla I have given birth for you."

"My brother, what hurts you?"
"My tooth hurts me."
"To the goddess Ninsutu I have given birth for you."

"My brother, what hurts you?"
"My mouth hurts me."
"To the goddess Ninkasi I have given birth for you."

"My brother, what hurts you?"
"My . . hurts me."
"To the goddess Nazi I have given birth for you."

"My brother, what hurts you?"
"My arm hurts me."
"To the goddess Azimua I have given birth for you."

"My brother, what hurts you?"
"My rib hurts me."
*"To the goddess Ninti (that is, 'lady of the rib' or 'lady who
      makes live') I have given birth for you."*

"My brother, what hurts you?"
"My . . hurts me."
"To the god Enshag I have given birth for you."

Paradise, according to the Sumerian theologians, was for the immortal gods, and for them alone, not for mortal man. One mortal, however, and only one, according to the Sumerian mythmakers, did succeed in gaining admittance to this divine paradise. This brings us to the Sumerian "Noah" and the deluge myth, the closest and most striking Biblical parallel as yet uncovered in cuneiform literature.

20 A Flood

THE FIRST ''NOAH''

That the Biblical deluge story is not original with the Hebrew redactors of the Bible has been known from the time of the discovery and deciphering of the eleventh tablet of the Babylonian "Epic of Gilgamesh" by the British Museum's George Smith. The Babylonian deluge myth itself, however, is of Sumerian origin. In 1914 Arno Poebel published a fragment consisting of the lower third of a six-column Sumerian tablet in the Nippur collection of the University Museum, the contents of which are devoted in large part to the story of the flood. This fragment still remains unique and unduplicated, and although scholars have been "all eyes and ears" for new deluge tablets, not a single additional fragment has turned up in any museum, private collection, or excavation. The piece published by Poebel is still our only source, and the translation prepared by him is still basic and standard.

The contents of this lone tablet are noteworthy not only for the flood episode, although that is its main theme, but also for the passages preceding and introducing the deluge story. Badly broken as the text is, these passages are nevertheless of significance for Sumerian cosmogony and cosmology. They include a number of revealing statements concerning the creation of man, the origin of kingship, and the existence of at least five antediluvian cities. Here, then, is practically the entire extant text of the myth with all its tantalizing obscurities and uncertainties. It provides an apt example of what the cuneiformist is up against, and of the surprises the future holds in store for him.

Since it is the lower third of the tablet that is preserved, we start right off with a break of some 37 lines, and there is no way of knowing just how the myth began. We then find a deity addressing other deities, probably stating that he will save mankind from destruction and that as a result man will build the cities and temples of the gods. Following the address are three lines which are difficult to relate to the context; they seem to describe the actions performed by the deity to make his words effective. Then come four lines concerned with the creation of man, animals, and plants. This entire passage reads:

"My mankind, in its destruction I will . . ,
To Nintu I will return the . . . of my creatures,
I will return the people to their settlements,
Of the cities, they will build their places of the divine laws,
I will make restful their shade,
Of our houses, they will lay their bricks in pure places,
The places of our decisions they will found in pure places."

He directed the pure fire-quenching water,
Perfected the rites and the exalted divine laws,
On the earth he . . . d, placed the . . . there.

After An, Enlil, Enki, and Ninhursag
Had fashioned the blackheaded people,
Vegetation luxuriated from the earth,
Animals, four-legged (creatures) of the plain, were brought
*   artfully into existence.*

There follows another break of about 37 lines, after which we learn that kingship was lowered from heaven and that five cities were founded:

After the . . . of kingship had been lowered from heaven,
After the exalted tiara and the throne of kingship had been
*   lowered from heaven,*
He perfected the rites and the exalted divine laws . . . . ,
Founded the five cities in . . . pure places,
Called their names, apportioned them as cult centers.

The first of these cities, Eridu, he gave to Nudimmud, the
*   leader,*
The second, Badtibira, he gave to . . ,
The third, Larak, he gave to Endurbilhursag,
The fourth, Sippar, he gave to the hero Utu,
The fifth, Shuruppak, he gave to Sud.

When he had called the names of these cities, apportioned
*   them as cult centers,*
He brought . . . . ,
Established the cleaning of the small rivers as . . . . ."

A break of about 37 lines follows next; these must have
dealt largely with the decision of the gods to bring the
flood and destroy mankind. When the text becomes intelligible again, we find some of the gods dissatisfied and unhappy over the cruel decision. We are then introduced to
Ziusudra, the counterpart of the Biblical Noah. He is described as a pious, god-fearing king, who is constantly on
the lookout for divine revelations in dreams or incantations.
Ziusudra seems to station himself by a wall, where he hears
the voice of a deity informing him of the decision taken by
the assembly of the gods to send a flood and "to destroy
the seed of mankind." The longest passage reads:

The flood . . . .
. . . .
Thus was treated . . . . .
Then did Nintu weep like a . . . ,
The pure Inanna set up a lament for its people,
Enki took counsel with himself,
An, Enlil, Enki, and Ninhursag . . . . ,
The gods of heaven and earth uttered the name of An and
*   Enlil.*

Then did Ziusudra, the king, the pashishu of . . . . ,
Build a giant . . . . ;
Humbly, obedient, reverently he . . . . ,
Attending daily, constantly he . . . . ,
Bringing forth all kinds of dreams, he . . . . ,
Uttering the name of heaven and earth, he . . . . .
. . . . the gods a wall . . . . ,

Ziusudra, standing at its side, listened.

"Stand by the wall at my left side . . . . ,
By the wall I will say a word to you, take my word,
Give ear to my instructions:
By our . . a flood will sweep over the cult centers;
To destroy the seed of mankind . . . . ,
Is the decision, the word of the assembly of the gods.
By the word commanded by An and Enlil . . . . .
Its kingship, its rule (will be put to an end)."

The text must have continued with detailed instructions
to Ziusudra to build a giant boat and thus save himself from
destruction. But this is missing, since there is another break
of about 40 lines at this point. When the text becomes intelligible once again, we find that the flood in all its violence had already come upon the "land" and raged there
for seven days and nights. Then the sun-god Utu comes
forth again, bringing his precious light everywhere, and
Ziusudra prostrates himself before him and offers sacrifices.
The lines read:

All the windstorms, exceedingly powerful, attacked as one,
At the same time, the flood sweeps over the cult centers.

After, for seven days and seven nights,
The flood had swept over the land,
And the huge boat had been tossed about by the wind-
storms on the great waters,
Utu came forth, who sheds light on heaven and earth,
Ziusudra opened a window on the huge boat,
The hero Utu brought his rays into the giant boat.

Ziusudra, the king,
Prostrated himself before Utu,
The king kills an ox, slaughters a sheep.

Here, again, there follows a break of about 39 lines. The
last extant lines of our text describe the deification of
Ziusudra. After he had prostrated himself before An and
Enlil, he was given "life like a god" and breath eternal, and
translated to Dilmun, "the place where the sun rises."
Thus:

An and Enlil uttered "breath of heaven," "breath of earth,"
     by their . . it stretched itself,
Vegetation, coming up out of the earth, rises up.

Ziusudra, the king,
Prostrated himself before An and Enlil.
An and Enlil cherished Ziusudra,
Life like a god they give him:
Breath eternal like a god they bring down for him.
Then, Ziusudra the king,
The preserver of the name of vegetation and of the seed of
     mankind,
In the land of crossing, the land of Dilmun, the place where
     the sun rises, they caused to dwell.

The remainder of the tablet, containing about 39 lines of
the text, is destroyed, and so we know nothing of what may
have happened to the transfigured Ziusudra in the home of
the immortals.

From Paradise we now turn to Hades, from the "great
above" to the "great below," or, as the Sumerians themselves described it, "the land of no return." To this dark,
dread land of the dead a restive and unruly goddess descends to satisfy her unbounded ambitions. The story of
this "descent to the nether world," told in Chapter 21, is
one of the best preserved Sumerian myths thus far uncovered. It provides a rare parallel to one of the most significant New Testament motifs.

THE FIRST TALE OF
RESURRECTION

The Sumerian word for the Greek *Hades* and the Hebrew *Sheol* is *Kur*, which originally meant "mountain" and later came to mean "foreign land" because the mountainous countries bordering Sumer were a constant menace to its people. Cosmically considered, Kur is the empty space between the earth's crust and the primeval sea, and to it went all the shades of the dead. To reach it, a "man-devouring river" had to be crossed on a boat conducted by a special "man of the boat"—the Sumerian counterpart of the river Styx and the boatman Charon.

Though the nether world is the abode of the dead, "life" in it has its "lively" side. Isaiah 14:9–11, for example, describes the stirring of Sheol and the shades of former kings and chiefs at the approach of a king of Babylon. In the University Museum there is a tablet published by Stephen Langdon in 1919, inscribed with a poem which actually describes some of the experiences of a Sumerian king in the nether world. The extant part of the tablet runs as follows:

After his death, the great king Ur-Nammu comes to Kur. He first presents gifts and offerings to the seven underworld deities—to each in his own palace. He then brings gifts to two other deities, one of whom is the scribe of the nether world, to make sure of their support. Finally he arrives at the special spot which the priestly officials of Kur have pre-

pared as his habitation. Here he is greeted by certain of
the dead and made to feel at home. The dead hero Gilgamesh, who has become "the judge of the nether world,"
initiates him into the rules and regulations that govern the
infernal regions. But after "seven days," after "ten days,"
had passed, the "wail of Sumer" reaches him. The walls of
Ur which he had left unfinished, his newly built palace
which he had left unpurified, his wife whom he could no
longer press to his bosom, his child whom he could no
longer fondle on his knee—all these disturb his peace in the
nether world, and he sets up a long and bitter lament.

The shades of the dead could on special occasions be
"raised" to the earth temporarily. The First Book of Samuel
(Chapter 28) tells of the calling up of the shade of the
prophet from Sheol at the insistence of King Saul. This is
paralleled in the Sumerian poem "Gilgamesh, Enkidu, and
the Nether World" (see Chapter 23) which tells of the ascent of the shade of Enkidu from Kur to the waiting embrace of his master Gilgamesh, and reports the ensuing conversation between them.

Although Kur might be assumed to have been for mortals
only, quite a number of supposedly immortal deities were
found there. We even have the myths explaining the presence of several deities in the nether world.

According to the poem "The Begetting of the Moon-
God" (see Chapter 13), Enlil, the leading deity of the
Sumerian pantheon, is banished from Nippur to the nether
world by the other gods because he raped the goddess Ninlil. On the way he begets three underworld deities (two of
them at least are well known from other sources). But it is
in the case of the shepherd-god Dumuzi, the most renowned of the "dead" gods, that we can follow in considerable detail the events leading to his downfall, in a myth
which primarily concerns his wife, the goddess Inanna, a
high favorite with Sumerian myth-makers.

The goddess of love, whatever her name among ancient
peoples, sparked the imagination of men throughout the
ages. Venus to the Romans, Aphrodite to the Greeks, Ishtar
to the Babylonians, had minstrels and poets singing of their
deeds and misdeeds. The Sumerians worshiped the goddess

of love under the name of Inanna, "queen of heaven." Her husband was the shepherd-god Dumuzi, the Biblical Tammuz, the weeping for whose death was denounced as an abomination by the prophet Ezekiel as late as the second half of the first millennium B.C. His wooing and winning of Inanna is told in two versions. One, involving a rival, the farmer-god Enkimdu, was sketched in Chapter 18. In the other, Dumuzi is the sole suitor for Inanna's hand. According to this story, the shepherd Dumuzi comes to Inanna's house, milk and cream dripping from his hands and sides, and clamors for admittance. After consultation with her mother, Inanna bathes and anoints herself, puts on her queenly robes, adorns herself with precious stones, and opens the door for her groom-to-be. They embrace and probably cohabit, and he then carries her off to the "city of his god."

Little did Dumuzi dream, however, that the marriage which he so passionately desired would end in his own perdition and that he would be dragged down to hell. He failed to reckon with a woman's overwhelming ambition. This is told in "Inanna's Descent to the Nether World," a myth noteworthy for its resurrection motif. The plot runs as follows:

Though already mistress of heaven, the "Great Above," as her name indicates, Inanna longs for still greater power and sets her goal to rule the infernal regions, the "Great Below," as well. She therefore decides to descend to the nether world to see what can be done. Having collected all the appropriate divine laws and having adorned herself with her queenly robes and jewels, she is ready to enter the "land of no return."

The queen of the nether world is her older sister and bitter enemy, Ereshkigal, Sumerian goddess of death and gloom. Fearing, not without reason, lest her sister put her to death in the domain she rules, Inanna instructs her vizier Ninshubur, who is always at her beck and call, that if after three days she has failed to return, he is to set up a lament for her by the ruins, in the assembly hall of the gods. He is then to go to Nippur, the city of Enlil, the leading god of the Sumerian pantheon, and plead with him to save her and not let her be put to death in the nether world. If Enlil refuses, Ninshubur is to go to Ur, the city of the moon-god Nanna, and repeat his plea. If Nanna, too, refuses, he is to go to Eridu, the city of Enki, the god of wisdom, who "knows the food of life," who "knows the water of life," and he will surely come to her rescue.

Inanna then descends to the nether world and approaches Ereshkigal's temple of lapis lazuli. At the gate she is met by the chief gatekeeper, who demands to know who she is and why she has come. Inanna concocts a false excuse for her visit, and the gatekeeper, on instructions from his mistress, leads her through the seven gates of the nether world. As she passes through one gate after another, her garments and jewels are removed piece by piece in spite of her protests. Finally, after entering the last gate, she is brought stark naked and on bended knees before Ereshkigal and the Anunnaki, the seven dreaded judges of the nether world. They fasten upon her their eyes of death, and she is turned into a corpse, which is then hung from a stake.

Three days and three nights pass. On the fourth day, Ninshubur, seeing that his mistress has not returned, proceeds to make the rounds of the gods in accordance with her instructions. As Inanna had surmised, both Enlil and Nanna refuse all help. Enki, however, devises a plan to restore her to life. He fashions the *kurgarru* and the *kalaturru,* two sexless creatures, and entrusts to them the "food of life" and the "water of life," with instructions to proceed to the nether world and sprinkle this "food" and "water" on Inanna's impaled corpse. This they do, and Inanna revives.

Though Inanna is once again alive, her troubles are far from over, for it was an unbroken rule of the "land of no return" that no one who entered its gates might return to the world above unless he produced a substitute to take his place in the nether world. Inanna is no exception to the rule. She is indeed permitted to reascend to the earth, but is accompanied by a number of heartless demons with instructions to bring her back to the lower regions if she fails to provide another deity to take her place. Surrounded by these ghoulish constables, Inanna first proceeds to visit the two Sumerian cities Umma and Bad-tibira. The protecting gods of these cities, Shara and Latarak, terrified at the sight of the unearthly arrivals, clothe themselves in sackcloth and grovel in the dust before Inanna. Inanna seems to be gratified by their humility, and when the demons threaten to carry them off to the nether world she restrains the demons and thus saves the lives of the two gods.

Inanna and the demons, continuing their journey, arrive at the Sumerian city of Kullab. The guardian deity of this city is the shepherd-god Dumuzi, and since he is her husband, it is not surprising to find him refusing to wear sackcloth and grovel in the dust before his spouse. He dresses up instead in festive array and sits loftily upon his throne. Enraged, Inanna looks down upon him with "the eye of death" and hands him over to the eager and unmerciful demons to be carried off to the nether world. Dumuzi turns pale and weeps. He lifts his hands to the sky and pleads with the sun-god Utu, who is Inanna's brother and therefore his own brother-in-law. Dumuzi begs Utu to help him escape the clutches of the demons by changing his hand into the hand of a snake, and his foot into the foot of a snake.

Here, unfortunately, right in the middle of Dumuzi's prayer to Utu, our tablets come to an end. But since Dumuzi is well known from various sources as an underworld deity, the likelihood is that his plea to Utu was not heeded and that he was actually carried off to the nether world.

Here is the myth in the words of the ancient poet himself (a number of repetitious passages are omitted):

From the "great above" she set her mind toward the "great below,"
The goddess, from the "great above" she set her mind toward the "great below,"
Inanna, from the "great above" she set her mind toward the "great below."

My lady abandoned heaven, abandoned earth,
To the nether world she descended,
Inanna abandoned heaven, abandoned earth,
To the nether world she descended,

Abandoned lordship, abandoned ladyship,
        To the nether world she descended.

The seven divine laws she fastened at the side,
Gathered all the divine laws, placed them in her hand,
All the laws she set up at her waiting foot,
The shugurra, *the crown of the plain, she put upon her*
        head,
Locks of hair she fixed upon her forehead,
The measuring rod and line of lapis lazuli she gripped in
        her hand,
Small lapis lazuli stones she tied about her neck,
Twin nunuz-stones she fastened to her breast,
A gold ring she gripped in her hand,
The breastplate "Come, man, come" she bound about her
        breast,
With the pala-*garment of ladyship she covered her body,*
The ointment "Let him come, let him come" she daubed on
        her eyes.

Inanna walked toward the nether world,
Her vizier Ninshubur walked at her side,
The pure Inanna says to Ninshubur:
"O you who are my constant support,
My vizier of favorable words,
My knight of true words,
I am now descending to the nether world.

"When I shall have come to the nether world,
Set up a lament for me as (is done) by ruins,
In the assembly shrine beat the drum for me,
In the house of the gods wander about for me,
Lower your eyes for me, lower your mouth for me, ... ,
Like a pauper in a single garment dress for me,
To the Ekur, the house of Enlil, all alone direct thy step.

"Upon entering the Ekur, the house of Enlil,
Weep before Enlil:
'O Father Enlil, let not your daughter be put to death in the
        nether world,
Let not your good metal be covered with the dust of the
        nether world,

Let not your good lapis lazuli be broken up into the stone
   of the stoneworker,
Let not your boxwood be cut up into the wood of the
   woodworker,
Let not the maid Inanna be put to death in the nether
   world.'
If Enlil stands not by you in this matter, go to Ur.

"In Ur upon entering the . . -house of the land,
The Ekishnugal, the house of Nanna,
Weep before Nanna:
'O Father Nanna, let not your daughter . . . .' (Five lines
   repeated.)
If Nanna stands not by you in this matter, go to Eridu.

"In Eridu upon entering the house of Enki,
Weep before Enki:
'O Father Enki, let not your daughter . . . .' (Five lines
   repeated.)
Father Enki, the lord of wisdom,
Who knows the 'food of life,' who knows the 'water of life,'
He will surely bring me back to life."

Inanna walked toward the nether world,
To her messenger Ninshubur she says:
"Go, Ninshubur,
The word which I have commanded you do not neglect."

When Inanna had arrived at the palace, the lapis lazuli
   mountain,
At the door of the nether world she acted boldly,
In the palace of the nether world she spoke boldly,
"Open the house, gatekeeper, open the house,
Open the house, Neti, open the house, all alone I would
   enter."

Neti, the chief gatekeeper of the nether world,
Answers the pure Inanna:
"Who, pray, are you?"

"I am the queen of heaven, the place where the sun rises."

"If you are the queen of heaven, the place where the sun
   rises,

Why, pray, have you come to the land of no return?
On the road whose traveler returns not, how has your heart
    led you?"

The pure Inanna answers him:
"My elder sister Ereshkigal,
Because her husband, the lord Gugalanna, had been killed,
To witness the funeral rites,
. . . . ; so be it."

Neti, the chief gatekeeper of the nether world,
Answers the pure Inanna:
"Stay, Inanna, to my queen let me speak,
To my queen Ereshkigal let me speak, . . . let me speak."

Neti, the chief gatekeeper of the nether world,
Enters the house of his queen Ereshkigal and says to her:
"O my queen, it is a maid who like a god . . . . , ... ,
The seven divine laws . . . ." (The entire third stanza is
    here repeated.)

Then Ereshkigal bit her thigh, was filled with wrath,
Says to Neti, her chief gatekeeper:
"Come, Neti, chief gatekeeper of the nether world,
The word which I command you, neglect not.
Of the seven gates of the nether world, lift their bolts,
Of its one palace Ganzir, the 'face' of the nether world,
    press open its doors.
Upon her entering,
Bowed low, let her be brought naked before me."

Neti, the chief gatekeeper of the nether world,
Heeded the word of his queen.
Of the seven gates of the nether world, he lifted their bolts,
Of its one palace Ganzir, the "face" of the nether world, he
    pressed open its doors.
To the pure Inanna he says:
"Come, Inanna, enter."

Upon her entering,
The shugurra, *the crown of the plain of her head, was*
    removed.
"What, pray, is this?"

"Be silent, Inanna, the laws of the nether world are perfect,
O Inanna, do not deprecate the rites of the nether world."

Upon her entering the second gate,
The measuring rod and line of lapis lazuli was removed.
"What, pray, is this?"
"Be silent, Inanna, the laws of the nether world are perfect,
O Inanna, do not deprecate the rites of the nether world."

Upon her entering the third gate,
The small lapis lazuli stones of her neck were removed.
    (Inanna's question and the gatekeeper's answer are re-
        peated here, and in the following parallel passages.)
Upon her entering the fourth gate,
The twin nunuz-stones of her breast were removed.

Upon her entering the fifth gate,
The gold ring of her hand was removed.

Upon her entering the sixth gate,
The breastplate "Come, man, come" of her breast was re-
    moved.

Upon her entering the seventh gate,
The pala-garment of ladyship of her body was removed.
Bowed low, she was brought naked before her.

The pure Ereshkigal seated herself upon her throne,
The Anunnaki, the seven judges, pronounced judgment be-
    fore her,
She fastened her eye upon her, the eye of death,
Spoke the word against her, the word of wrath,
Uttered the cry against her, the cry of guilt,
The sick woman was turned into a corpse,
The corpse was hung from a nail.

After three days and three nights had passed,
Her vizier Ninshubur,
Her vizier of favorable words,
Her knight of true words,
Set up a lament for her as (is done) by ruins,
Beat the drum for her in the assembly shrine,
Wandered about for her in the house of the gods,

Lowered his eyes for her, lowered his mouth for her,

     . . . . ,

Like a pauper in a single garment dressed for her,

To the Ekur, the house of Enlil, all alone he directed his step.

Upon his entering the Ekur, the house of Enlil,

Before Enlil he weeps:

"O Father Enlil, let not your daughter be put to death in the nether world,

Let not your good metal be covered with the dust of the nether world,

Let not your good lapis lazuli be broken up into the stone of the stoneworker,

Let not your boxwood be cut up into the wood of the woodworker,

Let not the maid Inanna be put to death in the nether world."

. . . .

Father Enlil stood not by him in this matter, he went to Ur.

In Ur upon his entering the . . -house of the land,

The Ekishnugal, the house of Nanna,

Before Nanna he weeps:

"O Father Nanna, let not your daughter . . . ." (Five lines repeated.)

. . . .

Father Nanna stood not by him in this matter, he went to Eridu.

In Eridu upon his entering the house of Enki,

Before Enki he weeps:

"O Father Enki, let not your daughter . . . ." (Five lines repeated.)

Father Enki answers Ninshubur:

"What now has happened to my daughter! I am troubled,

What now has happened to Inanna! I am troubled,

What now has happened to the queen of all the lands! I am troubled,

*What now has happened to the hierodule of heaven! I am
    troubled."*
*He brought forth dirt from his fingernail and fashioned the
    kurgarru,*
*He brought forth dirt from the red-painted fingernail and
    fashioned the kalaturru,*
To the kurgarru he gave the 'food of life,'
To the kalaturru he gave the 'water of life,'
Father Enki says to the kalaturru and kurgarru:

"· · · ·

Only the last part of Enki's speech is preserved. It reads:

*"They (the nether world gods) will offer you the water of
    the river, do not accept it,*
They will offer you the grain of the field, do not accept it,
*'Give us the corpse hung from the nail,' say to her (Eresh-
    kigal),*
*One of you sprinkle upon her the 'food of life,' the other
    the 'water of life,'*
Then will Inanna arise."

The *kurgarru* and *kalaturru* carry out Enki's instruction,
but only the last part of this passage is preserved. It reads:

They offer them the water of the river, they accept it not,
They offer them the grain of the field, they accept it not,
"Give us the corpse hung from the nail," they said to her.

The pure Ereshkigal answers the kalaturru and kurgarru:
"The corpse, it is your queen's."

*"The corpse, though it is our queen's, give to us," they said
    to her.*

They give them the corpse hung from the nail,
*One sprinkled upon her the "food of life," the other, the
    "water of life."*
Inanna arose.

Inanna is about to ascend from the nether world,
The Anunnaki seized her (saying):
*"Who of those who have descended to the nether world
    ever ascends unharmed from the nether world!*

If Inanna would ascend from the nether world,
Let her give someone as her substitute."

Inanna ascends from the nether world,
The small demons like shukur-*reeds,*
The large demons like dubban-*reeds,*
Held on to her side.
Who was in front of her, though not a vizier, held a scepter
*   in his hand,*
Who was at her side, though not a knight, had a weapon
*   fastened about the loin.*
They who accompanied her,
They who accompanied Inanna,
Were beings who know not food, who know not water,
Eat not sprinkled flour,
Drink not libated water,
Take away the wife from the man's lap,
Take away the child from the nursemaid's breast.

Inanna proceeds to the two Sumerian cities Umma and
Bad-tibira, whose two deities prostrate themselves before
her and are thus saved from the clutches of the demons.
Then she arrives at the city Kullab, whose tutelary deity
is Dumuzi. The poem continues:

Dumuzi put on a noble robe, he sat high on (his) seat.
The demons seized him by his thighs . . . . ,
The seven (demons) rush at him as at the side of a sick
*   man,*
The shepherds play not the flute and pipe before him.

She (Inanna) fastened the eye upon him, the eye of death,
Spoke the word against him, the word of wrath,
Uttered the cry against him, the cry of guilt:
"As for him, carry him off."
The pure Inanna gave the shepherd Dumuzi into their
*   hands.*

They who accompanied him,
They who accompanied Dumuzi,
Were beings who know not food, know not water,
Eat not sprinkled flour,

Drink not libated water,
Sate not with pleasure the wife's lap,
Kiss not the well-fed children,
Take away the man's son from his knee,
Carry off the daughter-in-law from the house of the father-
in-law.

Dumuzi wept, his face turned green,
Toward heaven to (the sun-god) Utu he lifted his hand:
"O Utu, you are my wife's brother, I am your sister's hus-
band,
I am one who brings cream to your mother's house,
I am one who brings milk to Ningal's house,
Turn my hand into the hand of a snake,
Turn my foot into the foot of a snake,
Let me escape my demons, let them not seize me."

The reconstruction and translation of "Inanna's Descent to the Nether World" has been a slow and gradual process, in which a number of scholars played an active role. It began in 1914, when Arno Poebel first published three small pieces belonging to this myth in the University Museum at Philadelphia. In the same year, the late Stephen Langdon published two pieces which he had uncovered in the Museum of the Ancient Orient at Istanbul. One of these was the upper half of a large four-column tablet which proved to be of major importance for the reconstruction of the text of the myth. Edward Chiera uncovered three additional pieces in the University Museum. These were published in his two posthumous volumes consisting of copies of Sumerian literary texts. I prepared these volumes for publication for the Oriental Institute in 1934.

By 1934 we had eight pieces, all more or less fragmentary, dealing with the myth. Nevertheless, the contents remained obscure, for the breaks in the tablets were so numerous and came at such crucial points in the story that an intelligent reconstruction of the extant parts of the myth remained impossible. It was a fortunate and remarkable discovery of Chiera's that saved the situation. He identified in the University Museum at Philadelphia the *lower* half of the same four-column tablet whose *upper* half had been

found and copied by Langdon years before in the Museum
of the Ancient Orient at Istanbul. The tablet had evidently
been broken before or during the excavation, and the two
halves had become separated. One had been retained in Istanbul, and the other had come to Philadelphia. Chiera died
before he was in a position to utilize its contents.

It was Chiera's recognition of the lower half of the "Inanna's Descent" tablet that enabled me to publish the first
edition of the myth in 1937 in the *Revue d'Assyriologie,*
for, when the lower was joined to the upper half, the combined text furnished an excellent framework in which all
the other extant fragments could be properly arranged.
There were still numerous gaps and breaks in the text
which made its translation and interpretation no easy matter, and the meaning of several significant passages in the
story remained obscure. In 1937, while working in the Istanbul Museum of the Ancient Orient as a Guggenheim
Fellow, I was fortunate enough to discover in Istanbul
three additional pieces belonging to the myth, and upon returning to the United States in 1939 I located another large
piece in the University Museum at Philadelphia and yet another in 1940. These five fragments helped to fill in some
of the most serious lacunae in the first reconstruction and
translation, and it was now possible to prepare a considerably fuller edition of the text. This appeared in the *Pro-
ceedings of the American Philosophical Society* in 1942.

But matters did not rest there. Some time afterward, I
was privileged to examine and help identify the hundred-
odd Sumerian literary tablets in the Yale Babylonian Collection, which contains one of the most important tablet collections in the world. In the course of this work, I came
upon an excellently preserved tablet, already identified by
Edward Chiera as early as 1924 in a note which had es-
caped my attention, inscribed with ninety-two lines of text.
The last thirty lines contain an entirely new passage which
carries on the story from where it had broken off in pre-
viously known texts.

This new material turned out to have an unexpected significance. It cleared up a misconception concerning the god
Dumuzi which students of Mesopotamian mythology and

religion had held for more than half a century. Almost ever since the Semitic version of our myth, commonly known as "Ishtar's Descent to the Nether World," was first published, and long before its Sumerian counterpart came to be known to any extent, it had been generally supposed that the god Dumuzi was carried off to the nether world, for some unknown reason, *before* Inanna's descent. It had been assumed that Inanna descended to the lower regions in order to free her husband Dumuzi and bring him back to earth. The new Yale text, however, proved these assumptions to be groundless. Inanna did not save her husband Dumuzi from the nether world. Rather, it was she who, angered by his contemptuous attitude, actually handed him over to the demons to be carried off to the land of no return. The addition of the Yale tablet (Ferris Stephens, Curator of the Yale Babylonian Collection, prepared an excellent copy) made it necessary to publish a third edition of the myth. This up-to-date revision, which includes many constructive suggestions by my Sumerological colleagues Adam Falkenstein, Benno Landsberger, and Thorkild Jacobsen, was published in 1951 in Volume V of the *Journal of Cuneiform Studies.*

In the first part of the present chapter, the word Kur was explained as the cosmic space separating the earth's crust from the violent primeval sea (the Biblical Tehom) below. But Kur also seems to have stood for a monstrous dragon who held Tehom's destructive waters in check. The slaying of dragons by gods and heroes, a favorite motif in Sumerian mythology, is discussed in Chapter 22.

22 *Slaying of the Dragon*

THE FIRST "ST. GEORGE"

The dragon-slaying motif is a high favorite with the mythographers of almost all peoples and ages. In Greece especially, where tales involving gods and heroes were legion,
there was hardly a hero who did not slay his dragon. Perhaps Heracles and Perseus are the best-known of the Greek
killers of monsters. With the rise of Christianity, the heroic
feat was transferred to the saints; witness the story of St.
George and the Dragon, and its ubiquitous parallels. The
names and the details vary from place to place and story
to story. But what is the original source of the incidents?
Since the dragon-slaying theme was an important motif in
the Sumerian mythology of the third millennium B.C., it is
reasonable to assume that many a thread in the texture of
the Greek and early Christian dragon tales winds back to
Sumerian sources.

At present we have at least three versions of the dragon-
slaying motif as it was current in Sumer more than thirty-
five hundred years ago. In two of these versions the heroes
are deities—the water-god Enki, the closest Sumerian
counterpart of the Greek Poseidon, and Ninurta, the god
in charge of the South Wind. The third version introduces
a mortal dragon-killer—the hero Gilgamesh—who may well
be the original "St. George."

In the myth involving Enki, it is the monster Kur who
seems to be the villain of the piece. The struggle probably
took place not long after the separation of heaven and

earth, and (if the fragmentary lines are correctly interpreted) Kur's wrongdoing consisted in the abducting of a
sky-goddess, which calls to mind the Greek story of the
rape of Persephone. Unfortunately we have only a dozen
laconic lines from which to reconstruct the story, for none
of the tablets on which the details of the myth were inscribed have as yet been excavated. The story is told in
a brief passage which is part of the prologue to the epic
tale "Gilgamesh, Enkidu, and the Nether World." The passage comes immediately after the "creation" lines. The contents are as follows:

After heaven and earth had been separated, An, the
heaven-god, carried off heaven, while Enlil, the air-god,
carried off the earth. It was then that the foul deed was
committed. The goddess Ereshkigal was probably carried
off violently as the prize of the Kur (it is not stated who
committed the deed, but it is not unlikely that it was the
Kur itself). Thereupon Enki set out in a boat to the Kur.
His purpose is not stated but it was probably to avenge
the abduction of the goddess Ereshkigal. The Kur fought
savagely with all kinds of stones, and it attacked Enki's
boat, front and rear, with the primeval waters which it
controlled. Here the brief prologue passage ends, since the
author of "Gilgamesh, Enkidu, and the Nether World" was
not interested in the dragon story primarily, but was anxious to proceed with his Gilgamesh tale. And so we are left
in the dark concerning the outcome of the battle. There is
little doubt, however, that Enki was victorious. And it is
not unlikely that the myth was invented for the purpose
of explaining why, in historical times, Enki, like the Greek
Poseidon, was conceived as a sea-god and why his temple
in Eridu was designated as the Abzu, a Sumerian word for
"sea."

Here, in full, is the prologue passage from which this
particular dragon-slaying myth is adduced:

After An had carried off the heaven,
After Enlil had carried off the earth,
After Ereshkigal had been carried off to Kur as its prize,

After he had set sail, after he had set sail,

After the father had set sail against Kur,
After Enki had set sail against Kur,
Against the king, the small ones it (Kur) hurled;
Against Enki, the large ones it hurled.

Its small ones, stones of the hand,
Its large ones, stones of "dancing" reeds,
The keel of the boat of Enki
In battle, like the attacking storm, overwhelm.

Against the king, the water at the head of the boat
Like a wolf devours,
Against Enki, the water at the rear of the boat
Like a lion strikes down.

The second version of the dragon-slaying motif forms part of a poem of more than six hundred lines, which may be titled "The Deeds and Exploits of the God Ninurta." Its contents are reconstructed from several scores of tablets and fragments, many of which are still unpublished.

The villain of the piece is not Kur but Asag, the demon of sickness and disease, whose abode is in the Kur—that is, the nether world. The hero is Ninurta, the god of the South Wind, who was regarded as the son of Enlil, the air-god. Following a hymnal introduction, the poem begins the story with an address to Ninurta by Sharur, his personified weapon. For some unstated reason the Sharur has set his mind against the Asag-demon, and therefore his address is full of phrases extolling the heroic qualities and deeds of Ninurta, whom he urges to attack and destroy the monster. Ninurta sets out to do as bidden. At first he seems to have met more than his match, and he "flees like a bird." However, the Sharur addresses him once again with reassuring words. Ninurta now attacks the Asag fiercely with all the weapons at his command, and the demon is destroyed.

With the destruction of the Asag, a serious calamity overtakes Sumer. The primeval waters of the Kur rise to the surface, and as a result of their violence no fresh waters can reach the fields and gardens. The gods of Sumer who "carried its pickax and basket"—that is, who had charge of irrigating Sumer and preparing it for cultivation—are desperate. The Tigris does not rise; it has no "good" water in its channel.

Famine was severe, nothing was produced,
At the small rivers, there was no "washing of the hands,"
    The waters rose not high.

The fields were not watered,
    There was no digging of (irrigation) ditches.
In all the lands there was no vegetation,
    Only weeds grew.

Thereupon the lord put his lofty mind to it.
Ninurta, the son of Enlil, brought great things into being.

Ninurta sets up stones over the Kur, heaping them like a great wall in front of Sumer. These stones hold back the "mighty waters," and as a result the waters of the Kur no longer rise to (the surface of the) earth. As for the waters which have already flooded the land, Ninurta gathers them and leads them into the Tigris, which is now in a position to water the fields with its overflow. In the language of the poet:

What had been scattered, he gathered,
What of the Kur had been scattered,
He guided and hurled into the Tigris,
The high waters it pours over the fields.
Behold, now, everything on earth,
Rejoiced afar at Ninurta, the king of the land.
The fields produced abundant grain,
The vineyard and orchard bore their fruit,
(The harvest) was heaped up in granaries and hills,
The Lord made mourning to disappear from the land,
He made happy the spirit of the gods.

Hearing of her son's great and heroic deeds, his mother, Ninmah, is filled with compassion for him; she becomes so restless that she is unable to sleep in her bedchamber. She therefore addresses Ninurta from afar with a prayer for permission to visit him and gaze upon him. He looks at her with the "eye of life," saying:

"O lady, because you would come to the Kur,

O Ninmah, because for my sake you would enter the inimi-
*   cal land,*
Because you have no fear of the terror of the battle sur-
*   rounding me,*
Therefore, of the hill which I, the hero, have heaped up,
Let its name be Hursag (Mountain) and you be its queen."

Ninurta then blesses the Hursag that it may produce all
kinds of herbs; wine and honey; various kinds of trees; gold,
silver, and bronze; cattle, sheep, and all "four-legged creatures." Following this blessing, he turns to the stones, cursing those which had been his enemies in his battle with
the Asag-demon, and blessing those which had been his
friends. This passage, in style and tone, brings to mind the
blessing and cursing of Jacob's sons in the Book of Genesis.
The poem then closes with a long hymnal passage in exaltation of Ninurta.

In the third version of the dragon-slaying tales, a man,
not a god, is the protagonist. He is Gilgamesh, the most
renowned of all Sumerian heroes. The monster whom he
kills is Huwawa, the guardian of the "Land of the Living,"
particularly its holy cedars. The story is told in a poem
which I have titled "Gilgamesh and the Land of the Living,"
pieced together from fourteen tablets and fragments, and
last published in 1950 in *Ancient Near Eastern Texts* (edited by James Pritchard; second edition, 1955). As yet only
the first 174 lines of the poem have been recovered. Even so,
the poem is recognizable as a literary creation which must
have had a profound emotional and aesthetic appeal to its
highly credulous Sumerian audience. Its motivating theme,
man's anxiety about death and its sublimation in the notion
of an immortal name, has a universal significance that lends
it high poetic value. Its plot structure reveals a careful and
imaginative selection of such details as are essential to its
predominantly poignant mood. Stylistically, the poet obtains a fitting rhythmic effect by his skillful use of varied
patterns of repetition and parallelism. All in all, this poem is
one of the finest Sumerian literary works as yet uncovered.
Its contents may be summarized as follows:

The "lord" Gilgamesh, realizing that, like all mortals, he

must die sooner or later, is determined at least to "raise up a name" for himself before he meets his destined end. He therefore sets his heart on journeying to the far-distant "Land of the Living," with the probable intention of felling its cedars and bringing them to Erech. He informs his loyal servant and constant companion, Enkidu, of his proposed undertaking. Enkidu advises him first to acquaint the sun-god Utu with his plan, for it is Utu who has charge of the cedar land.

Acting on this advice, Gilgamesh brings offerings to Utu and pleads for his support of the contemplated journey to the "Land of the Living." At first Utu seems skeptical of Gilgamesh's qualifications, but Gilgamesh repeats his plea in more persuasive language. Utu takes pity on him and decides to help him—probably by immobilizing the seven vicious demons personifying the destructive weather phenomena that might menace Gilgamesh in his journey across the mountains between Erech and the "Land of the Living." Overjoyed, Gilgamesh gathers fifty volunteers from Erech —unattached men who have neither "house" nor "mother" and who are ready to follow him in whatever he does. After he has had weapons of bronze and wood prepared for himself and his companions, they cross the seven mountains with the help of Utu.

Just what happens immediately after the crossing of the last of the seven mountains is not clear, since the relevant passage is poorly preserved. When the text becomes intelligible again, we find that Gilgamesh has fallen into a heavy sleep from which he is awakened only after considerable time and effort. Thoroughly aroused by this delay, he swears by his mother Ninsun and his father Lugalbanda that he will enter the "Land of the Living" and will brook no interference from either man or god. Enkidu pleads with him to turn back, for the guardian of the cedars is the fearful monster Huwawa, whose destructive attack none may withstand. But Gilgamesh will have none of this caution. Convinced that with Enkidu's help no harm can befall either of them, he bids his servant to put away fear and go forward with him.

The monster Huwawa, spying them from his cedar house,

makes frantic but apparently vain efforts to drive off Gilgamesh and his adventurous band. Following a break of some
lines, we learn that Gilgamesh, after cutting down seven
trees, has probably come to Huwawa's inner chamber.
Strangely enough, at the very first, and seemingly very
light, attack by Gilgamesh, Huwawa is overcome with
fright. He utters a prayer to the sun-god Utu, and adjures
Gilgamesh not to kill him. Gilgamesh would like to act the
generous victor, and, in riddle-like phrases, suggests to
Enkidu that Huwawa be set free. But Enkidu is fearful of
the consequences and advises against such unwise action.
Following Huwawa's indignant criticism of Enkidu's ungen-
erous attitude, our two heroes cut off Huwawa's neck. They
then seem to bring his corpse before Enlil and Ninlil. But
what follows is altogether uncertain, for after several fragmentary lines, the available material comes to an end.

Here is the literal translation of the more intelligible portions of the poem:

The lord, toward the Land of the Living set his mind,
The lord, Gilgamesh, toward the Land of the Living set
*   his mind,*
He says to his servant Enkidu:
"O Enkidu, not (yet) have brick and stamp brought forth
*   the fated end,*
I would enter the 'land,' I would set up my name,
In its places where the names have been raised up, I would
*   raise up my name,*
In its places where the names have not been raised up, I
*   would raise up the names of the gods."*

His servant Enkidu answers him:
"O my master, if you would enter the 'land,' inform Utu,
Inform Utu, the hero Utu—
The 'land,' it is Utu's charge,
The land of the cut-down cedar, it is the hero Utu's charge
*   —inform Utu."*

Gilgamesh laid his hands on an all-white kid,
A brown kid, an offering, he pressed to his breast,
In his hand he placed the silver staff of his . . . ,

He says to Utu of heaven:
"O Utu, I would enter the 'land,' be my ally,
I would enter the land of the cut-down cedar, be my ally."

Utu of heaven answers him:
"True you are . . . , but what are you to the 'land'?"

"O Utu, a word I would speak to you, to my word your
    ear,
I would have it reach you, give ear to it.
In my city man dies, oppressed is the heart,
Man perishes, heavy is the heart,
I peered over the wall,
Saw the dead bodies . . . floating in the river;
As for me, I too will be served thus; verily 'tis so.
Man, the tallest, cannot reach to heaven,
Man, the widest, cannot cover the earth.
Not (yet) have brick and stamp brought forth the fated
    end,
I would enter the 'land,' I would set up my name,
In its places where the names have been raised up, I would
    raise up my name,
In its places where the names have not been raised up, I
    would raise up the names of the gods."

Utu accepted his tears as an offering,
Like a man of mercy, he showed him mercy,
The seven heroes, the sons of one mother, ... ,
He brings into the mountain caves.

Who felled the cedar, acted joyfully,
The lord Gilgamesh acted joyfully,
In his city, as one man, he . . . . . ,
As two companions, he . . . . . ,
"Who has a house, to his house! Who has a mother, to his
    mother!
Let single males who would do as I (do), fifty, stand at
    my side."

Who had a house, to his house; who had a mother, to his
    mother,
Single males who would do as he (did), fifty, stood at his
    side.

To the house of the smiths he directed his step,
The . . , the . . -ax, his "Might of Heroism" he caused to
*   be cast there.*
To the . . garden of the plain he directed his step,
The . . -tree, the willow, the apple-tree, the box-tree, the
*   . . -tree he felled there.*
The "sons" of his city who accompanied him placed them
*   in their hands.*

The next fifteen lines are fragmentary, but we learn that
Gilgamesh, after crossing the seven mountains, has fallen
asleep, and someone is waking him, thus:

He touches him, he rises not,
He speaks to him, he answers not.
"Who are lying, who are lying,
O Gilgamesh, lord, son of Kullab, how long will you lie?
The 'land' has become dark, the shadows have spread over
*   it,*
Dusk has brought forth its light,
Utu has gone with lifted head to the bosom of his mother,
*   Ningal,*
O Gilgamesh, how long will you lie?
Let not the sons of your city who have accompanied you,
Stand waiting for you at the foot of the mountain,
Let not your mother who gave birth to you be driven off
*   to the 'square' of the city."*

He gave heed,
With his "word of heroism" he covered himself like a gar-
*   ment,*
His garment of thirty shekels which he carried in his hand
*   he wrapped about his breast,*
Like a bull he stood on the "great earth,"
He put his mouth to the ground, his teeth shook.
"By the life of Ninsun, my mother who gave birth to me,
*   of pure Lugalbanda, my father,*
May I become as one who sits to be wondered at on the
*   knee of Ninsun, my mother who gave birth to me."*
A second time moreover he says to him:
"By the life of Ninsun, my mother who gave birth to me,
*   of pure Lugalbanda, my father,*

Until I will have killed that 'man,' if he be a man, until I
will have killed him, if he be a god,
My step directed to the 'land,' I shall not direct to the city."

The faithful servant pleaded, . . d life,
He answers his master:
"O my master, you who have not seen that 'man,' are not
terror-stricken,
I who have seen that 'man' am terror-stricken.
The warrior, his teeth are the teeth of a dragon,
His face is the face of a lion,
His . . is the onrushing floodwater,
From his forehead which devours trees and reeds, none
escape.
O my master, journey you to the 'land,' I will journey to
the city,
I will tell your mother of your glory, let her laugh,
I will tell her of your ensuing death, let her shed bitter
tears."

"For me another will not die, the loaded boat will not sink,
The three-ply cloth will not be cut,
The . . . will not be overwhelmed,
House and hut, fire will not destroy.
Do you help me (and) I will help you, what can happen
to us? . . . .
Come, let us go forward, we will cast eyes upon him,
If we go forward,
(And) there be fear, there be fear, turn it back,
There be terror, there be terror, turn it back,
In your . . . , come, let us go forward."

When they had not yet come within a distance of 1200
feet,
Huwawa . . d his cedar house,
Fastened his eye upon him, the eye of death,
Nodded his head to him, shook his head at him, ...
He (Gilgamesh) himself uprooted the first tree,
The "sons" of his city who accompanied him
Cut down its crown, bundle it,
Lay it at the foot of the mountain.

*After he himself had finished off the seventh, he approached
    his chamber,
Turned upon the "snake of the wine-quay" in his wall,
Like one pressing a kiss he slapped his cheek.*

*Huwawa, (his) teeth shook, . . . his hand trembled,
"I would say a word to you . . . ,
(O Utu), a mother who gave birth to me I know not, a
    father who reared me I know not,
In the 'land' you gave birth to me, you raised me."
He adjured Gilgamesh by the life of heaven, life of earth,
    life of the nether world,
Took him by the hand, brought him to . . . .*

*Then did the heart of Gilgamesh take pity on the . . . ,
He says to his servant Enkidu:
"O Enkidu, let the caught bird go (back) to its place,
Let the caught man return to the bosom of his mother."*

*Enkidu answers Gilgamesh:
"The tallest who has not judgment,
Namtar (demon of death) will devour, Namtar who knows
    no distinctions.
If the caught bird goes (back) to its place,
If the caught man returns to the bosom of his mother,
You will not return to the city of the mother who gave birth
    to you."*

*Huwawa says to Enkidu:
"Against me, O Enkidu, you have spoken evil to him,
O hired man . . . . you have spoken evil to him."*

*When he had thus spoken,
They cut off his neck;
Placed upon him . . . . . ,
Brought him before Enlil and Ninlil . . .*

Gilgamesh is the most celebrated of all Sumerian heroes
and a favorite with ancient poets and minstrels. However,
modern Orientalists first came to know of him and his heroic exploits not from Sumerian but from Semitic sources.
He is the protagonist in the Babylonian epic now generally
admitted to be the most significant literary creation of the

whole of ancient Mesopotamia. But a comparative analysis of this Babylonian epic and its Sumerian forerunners shows that the Babylonian authors and redactors utilized, modified, and molded Sumerian epics for their own purposes. In Chapter 23 an effort is made to distinguish the Sumerian warp from the Semitic woof.

THE FIRST CASE OF

LITERARY BORROWING

George Smith, an Englishman who had been studying the thousands of clay tablets and fragments brought to the British Museum from the mounds covering ancient Nineveh, read a paper, on December 3, 1862, before the then recently organized Society of Biblical Archaeology. His paper proved to be a milestone for Biblical studies, particularly in their comparative aspects.

In this paper Smith announced that, on one of the clay tablets dug up from the long-buried library of King Ashurbanipal, who reigned in the seventh century B.C., he had discovered and deciphered a version of the deluge myth which showed marked resemblances to the flood story in the Book of Genesis. The announcement caused no small sensation in scholarly circles and even aroused the enthusiasm of the general public the world over. The *Daily Telegraph*, a London newspaper of the period, immediately volunteered funds for a new expedition to Nineveh. George Smith himself undertook the excavations, but his health and temperament were unsuited to the Near East. He died in the field at the early age of thirty-six.

Not long after he had announced the discovery of the Babylonian flood story, Smith realized, on further study of the tablets and fragments from the Ashurbanipal library, that this deluge myth formed but a small part of a long poem, and that the ancient Babylonians themselves referred to it as the "Gilgamesh Cycle." According to the ancient scribes, it consisted of twelve songs or cantos of about three hundred lines each. Each canto was inscribed on a separate tablet in the Ashurbanipal library. The deluge story formed the major part of the eleventh tablet.

Since the days of George Smith, numerous new pieces of this Semitic "Gilgamesh Cycle," or "Epic of Gilgamesh" as it is now generally called, have been excavated in Iraq. Some of these were inscribed in the Old Babylonian period —that is, as early as the seventeenth or eighteenth century B.C. Ancient translations of parts of the poem into Hurrian, as well as the Indo-European Hittite language, have been found on clay tablets excavated in Asia Minor, from the second half of the second millennium B.C. It is thus evident that the Babylonian "Epic of Gilgamesh" was studied, translated, and imitated in ancient times all over the Near East. Today about half of its approximately 3,500 lines of text have been recovered. A superb edition of practically all the available material was published in 1930 by another Englishman, the late archaeologist and humanist R. Campbell Thompson. Since then two new and more up-to-date English translations have appeared: Alexander Heidel's *The Gilgamesh Epic and Old Testament Parallels* and Ephraim Speiser's in *Ancient Near Eastern Texts* (edited by James Pritchard).

There is good reason for this popularity, both ancient and modern, for, from the point of view of human interest and dramatic impact, the "Epic of Gilgamesh" is unique in Babylonian literature. In most Babylonian literary works, it is the gods who hold the center of the stage—gods who tend to represent abstractions rather than personalities, personified intellectualizations rather than profound spiritual forces. Even in Babylonian tales where the protagonists seem to be mortal men, the role they play is mechanical, impersonal, and lacking in dramatic impact. The characters are bloodless, colorless creatures whose puppetlike movements serve the purpose of the highly stylized etiological myth.

The situation is different in the "Epic of Gilgamesh." In

this poem it is man who holds the center of the stage—the man Gilgamesh, who loves and hates, weeps and rejoices, strives and wearies, hopes and despairs. True, the gods are not absent; indeed, Gilgamesh himself, in the mythological patter and pattern of the times, is two-thirds divine and one-third mortal. But it is Gilgamesh as man who dominates the action of the poem. The gods and their activities serve only as background and setting for the dramatic episodes in the hero's life. What gives these episodes lasting significance and universal appeal is their *human* quality. They revolve about forces and problems common to man everywhere through the ages—the need for friendship, the instinct for loyalty, the impelling urge for fame and name, the love of adventure and achievement, the all-absorbing fear of death, and the all-compelling longing for immortality. It is the varied interplay of these emotional and spiritual drives in man that constitutes the drama of the "Epic of Gilgamesh"—drama which transcends the confines of time and space. Little wonder that the influence of this poem on ancient epic literatures was as wide as it was deep. Even the reader of today is moved by the universal sweep of its action, the elemental power of its tragedy.

The poem begins with a short introductory passage in praise of Gilgamesh and his city, Erech. We then read that Gilgamesh, the king of Erech, is a restless hero, unrivaled and undisciplined, who tyrannizes over the dwellers of his city. Especially oppressive are his demands for the satisfaction of his Rabelaisian sex appetite. The Erechites cry out in anguish to the gods, who, realizing that Gilgamesh acts the tyrant and bully because he has still to find his match among his fellow humans, direct the great mother-goddess Aruru to put an end to the intolerable situation. She proceeds to fashion from clay the powerful Enkidu, who, naked and long-haired, and innocent of all human relations, spends his days and nights with the wild beasts of the plains. It is Enkidu, more brute than man, who is to subdue Gilgamesh's arrogance and discipline his spirit. First, however, Enkidu must be "humanized," a process which turns out to be largely woman's task. An Erechite courtesan arouses and satisfies his sex instincts. As a result he loses in physical stature and brute strength but gains in mental and spiritual stature. This sex experience makes Enkidu wise, and the wild beasts no longer recognize him as their own. Patiently the courtesan guides him in the civilized arts of eating, drinking, and dressing.

The humanized Enkidu is now ready to meet Gilgamesh, whose arrogant and tyrannical spirit he is destined to subdue. Gilgamesh has already learned in his dreams of the coming of Enkidu. Eager to display his unrivaled position in Erech, he arranges a nocturnal orgy and invites Enkidu to attend. Enkidu, however, is repelled by Gilgamesh's sexual cravings, and blocks his way in an effort to prevent him from entering the house appointed for the unseemly gathering. Thereupon the two titans join in combat—Gilgamesh, the sophisticated townsman, and Enkidu, the simple plainsman. Enkidu seems to be getting the better of his rival, when (for some unstated reason) Gilgamesh's wrath leaves him, and the two kiss and embrace. Out of this bitter struggle is born the friendship of the two heroes—a friendship destined to become proverbial in world lore as loyal and lasting, and rich in heroic achievement.

But Enkidu is not happy in Erech. Its gay, sensuous life is making a weakling of him. And so Gilgamesh reveals to his friend his adventurous plan to journey to the far-distant cedar forest, kill its fearful guardian, the mighty Huwawa, fell the cedar tree, and "destroy all that is evil from the land." Enkidu, who in his early savage days had wandered freely through the cedar forest, warns Gilgamesh of the mortal danger of the undertaking. But Gilgamesh only mocks his fears; it is enduring fame and name that he longs for, not a prolonged but unheroic existence. He confers with the elders of Erech, obtains the approval of the sun-god Shamash, the patron of all travelers, and has the craftsmen of Erech cast gigantic weapons for himself and Enkidu. Thus prepared, they set out on their adventure. After a long, wearisome journey, they arrive at the dazzlingly beautiful cedar forest, kill Huwawa, and fell the cedar.

Adventure leads to adventure. Upon their return to Erech, Ishtar, the goddess of love and lust, becomes infatuated with the well-formed Gilgamesh. With the prom-

ise of many rich favors, she tries to induce Gilgamesh to
satisfy her desires. But Gilgamesh is no longer the undisciplined tyrant of former days. Well aware of her promiscuity
and faithlessness, he mocks at her offer and spurns it. Thereupon Ishtar, bitterly disappointed and deeply offended, tries
to persuade Anu, the heaven-god, to send the Bull of
Heaven against Erech to destroy Gilgamesh and his city.
Anu at first refuses, but when Ishtar threatens to bring up
the dead from the nether world, he is forced to consent.
The Bull of Heaven descends and begins to lay waste the
city of Erech, slaughtering its warriors by the hundreds.
Gilgamesh and Enkidu together take up the struggle against
the beast, and in a mighty concerted effort succeed in killing
him.

The two heroes have now reached the pinnacle of their
career, and the city of Erech rings out with the song of
their exalted deeds. But inexorable fate brings a sudden
and cruel end to their happiness. Because of his part in
killing Huwawa and the Bull of Heaven, Enkidu is sen-
tenced to an early death by the gods. After a twelve-day
illness, Enkidu breathes his last, while his friend Gilgamesh
looks on helplessly, stunned with grief. His anguished spirit
is now obsessed with one doubly bitter thought: Enkidu is
dead, and sooner or later he will meet the same fate. He
finds little comfort in the fame and glory of his past heroic
deeds. It is tangible, physical immortality which his tor-
mented spirit now craves. He must seek and find the secret
of eternal life.

As Gilgamesh well knew, there was but one individual
in history who had succeeded in obtaining immortality—
Utanapishtim, the wise and pious king of ancient Shuruppak, one of the five royal cities that had existed before the
flood. (The mound which covers this city was excavated
by German and American expeditions, and a large group
of tablets from the first half of the third millennium were
discovered.)

Gilgamesh decides to make his way at all costs to the
distant dwelling place of Utanapishtim. Perhaps that im-
mortalized hero would reveal his precious secret. He wan-
ders long and far, over mountain and plain, ever exposed

to wild beasts and famine. He crosses the primeval sea and "the waters of death." Finally, weary and emaciated, his hair long and shaggy, his filthy body covered with raw animal hides, the once-proud ruler of Erech stands before Utanapishtim, eager to learn the mystery of eternal life.

But Utanapishtim's words are far from encouraging. The king of Shuruppak narrates at great length the story of the destructive deluge that the gods had once brought against the earth in order to exterminate all living creatures. He, too, would surely have perished, had it not been for the sheltering boat he had built on the advice of the great Ea, the god of wisdom. As for the gift of eternal life, it was the gods who willed its bestowal upon him; where, however, was the god who willed Gilgamesh's immortality? Despairing of his fate, Gilgamesh is ready to return empty-handed to Erech, when a ray of hope appears. Utanapishtim, at the urging of his wife, reveals to Gilgamesh the whereabouts of the plant of eternal youth that lies at the bottom of the sea. Gilgamesh dives to the bottom, brings up the plant, and proceeds joyfully to Erech. But the gods willed otherwise. While Gilgamesh goes bathing in a well, a snake carries off the plant. Weary and bitterly disappointed, the hero returns to Erech, to find what comfort he can in its enduring walls.

So much for the contents of the first eleven tablets of the Babylonian "Epic of Gilgamesh." (The so-called twelfth tablet, which actually does not belong to the epic at all, is treated at the end of the present chapter.) As to the date of the composition of the poem, a comparison of the text of the Old Babylonian version with that of the much later Assyrian, shows that the poem was current, in substantially the form in which we know it, as early as the first half of the second millennium B.C. As to its origins, even a superficial examination, restricted mainly to onomastic considerations, shows that much of its contents must go back to Sumerian rather than Semitic sources, in spite of the antiquity of the Babylonian poem. The names of the two protagonists, Gilgamesh and Enkidu, are in all likelihood of Sumerian origin. The parents of Gilgamesh bear the Sumerian names Lugalbanda and Ninsun. The goddess Aruru, who fashioned Enkidu, is the all-important Sumerian mother-goddess more commonly known under the names Ninmah, Ninhursag, and Nintu (see Chapter 13). The Sumerian god An, who fashioned the Bull of Heaven for the vengeful Ishtar, was taken over in Babylonian as Anu. It is the Sumerian god Enlil who decreed Enkidu's death. In the deluge episode, it is the Sumerian gods who played the predominant roles.

But there is no need to rely on logical deduction alone for the conclusion that much of the "Epic of Gilgamesh" is of Sumerian origin. We actually have the Sumerian forerunners of several of the episodes narrated in the poem. From 1911 to 1935, twenty-six Sumerian tablets and fragments inscribed with Gilgamesh poems were published by such well-known cuneiformists as Radau, Zimmern, Poebel, Langdon, Chiera, De Genouillac, Gadd, and Fish. Fourteen of these texts came from the hand of Edward Chiera alone. Since 1935 I have identified in Istanbul and Philadelphia more than sixty additional Gilgamesh pieces and have copied a goodly portion of them.

Thus we now have a relatively large group of Sumerian Gilgamesh texts. A comparative analysis of their contents with those of the "Epic of Gilgamesh" will reveal in what manner and to what extent the creators of the Babylonian epic utilized Sumerian sources. However, the problem of the Sumerian origin of the "Epic of Gilgamesh" is not as simple as it may seem at first glance, and unless the underlying complexities are clearly grasped, they could lead to the wrong solution. Therefore it is advisable to restate the problem in the form of an outline of questions:

1. Is there a Sumerian original for the "Epic of Gilgamesh" as a whole? That is, can we expect to find a Sumerian poem which, in spite of differences in form and content, so closely resembles the Babylonian epic that it can be readily recognized and accepted as its Sumerian precursor?

2. If it becomes clear from the material on hand that there is no Sumerian original for the Babylonian epic as a whole, and that only some of its episodes go back to Su-

merian prototypes, are we in a position to identify these episodes with reasonable certainty?

3. In the case of those episodes for which no Sumerian version is as yet available, are we justified in assuming a Semitic origin, or is there reason to believe that these, too, go back to Sumerian sources?

With these questions in mind, we are ready to make a comparative analysis of the contents of the relevant available Sumerian material. This material consists of six poems which may be titled as follows:

"Gilgamesh and the Land of the Living"
"Gilgamesh and the Bull of Heaven"
"The Deluge"
"The Death of Gilgamesh"
"Gilgamesh and Agga of Kish"
"Gilgamesh, Enkidu, and the Nether World"

It should be understood that the text of most of these poems is still fragmentary and that the translation is often difficult and uncertain even where the text is complete. Nevertheless, the available Sumerian material does provide sufficient data to answer with certainty Nos. 1 and 2 in our outline of questions. And while the question in No. 3 cannot be answered with equal certainty, we can arrive at some reasonably safe conclusions.

Before the three questions can be answered, it is necessary to examine the contents of each of the six poems:

1. The contents of the poem "Gilgamesh and the Land of the Living" were sketched in Chapter 22. This tale is obviously the counterpart of the cedar-forest episode of the Babylonian "Epic of Gilgamesh." But when the two versions are put side by side for a comparison, they are found to have only the bare skeleton of the story in common. In both versions Gilgamesh decides to journey to the cedar forest; he is accompanied by Enkidu; he seeks and obtains the protection of the sun-god; they arrive at their destination; the cedar is felled; Huwawa is killed. But the two versions vary greatly in detail, arrangement, and emphasis. For example, in the Sumerian poem, Gilgamesh is accompanied not only by Enkidu but also by a party of fifty

Erechites, while in the Babylonian version he is accompanied by Enkidu alone. Again, in the Sumerian poem, no reference is made to the council of elders of the city of Erech, which plays so prominent a role in the Semitic version.

2. The Sumerian poem "Gilgamesh and the Bull of Heaven" is still unpublished. Its contents, poorly preserved as they are, may be sketched as follows: After a lacuna of some twenty lines, the poem continues with an address to Gilgamesh by the goddess Inanna (the Sumerian counterpart of the Babylonian Ishtar), in which she describes the gifts and favors she is prepared to shower upon him. It is reasonable to assume that the preceding missing portion of the text contained Inanna's love proposals. Another break in the text follows, which must have contained Gilgamesh's rejection of Inanna's offers. When the text becomes intelligible once again, we find Inanna before An, the heaven-god, asking to be presented with the Bull of Heaven. An at first refuses, but Inanna threatens to take up the matter with all the great gods of the universe. Terrified, An grants her request. Inanna then sends the Bull of Heaven down against Erech, and it ravages the city. From here on, the available text, which concludes with an address by Enkidu to Gilgamesh, becomes unintelligible. The end of the poem, which probably described Gilgamesh's victorious struggle with the Bull of Heaven, is missing altogether.

When the contents of this Sumerian poem are compared with those of its Babylonian counterpart in the "Epic of Gilgamesh," they show a close and unmistakable resemblance in the broad outlines of the plot. In both poems Inanna (Ishtar) offers her love and tempting gifts to Gilgamesh; the offer is rejected; with the unwilling consent of An (Anu), the Bull of Heaven is sent to attack Erech; the beast ravages the city, but is finally killed. As for the details, the two versions vary almost beyond the point of recognition. The gifts offered by Inanna (Ishtar) to tempt Gilgamesh are quite different in the two versions. Gilgamesh's rejection speech, which, in the Babylonian epic, consists of 56 lines and is filled with learned allusions to Babylonian mythology and proverbs, is much briefer in the

Sumerian version. The conversations between Inanna (Ishtar) and An (Anu) bear little similarity in the two versions. Nor is there any reason to doubt that the concluding details of the Sumerian poem, when these are recovered, will have but little in common with those of the Babylonian epic.

3. The Sumerian poem known as "The Deluge" is described in Chapter 20, which gives a translation of the poem's entire flood-episode passage. The flood episode also constitutes the major part of the eleventh tablet of the Babylonian "Epic of Gilgamesh." The fact that the Sumerian account of the flood is not in any way connected with the Sumerian Gilgamesh tales provides us with a clue for determining some of the procedures employed in ancient literary borrowing.

The Sumerian flood episode is part of a poem devoted primarily to the myth of the immortalization of Ziusudra, and this myth was artfully utilized by the Babylonian poets for their own purposes. Thus, when the weary Gilgamesh comes before Utanapishtim (the Babylonian Ziusudra) and questions him concerning the secret of eternal life, the Babylonian poets did not let him answer briefly and to the point; instead, they took advantage of this opening to insert their version of the deluge myth. The first (the creation) part of the Sumerian myth, they omitted altogether as unnecessary to their theme. They retained only the deluge episode ending with Ziusudra's immortalization. And by making Utanapishtim (Ziusudra) the narrator, and putting the narration into the first person instead of the third, they changed the Sumerian form, in which the narrator was a nameless poet.

In addition we find variation in details. Ziusudra is described as a pious, humble, god-fearing king, but Utanapishtim is not thus described. On the other hand, the Babylonian version is much more lavish with details concerning the building of the boat, and the nature and violence of the flood. In the Sumerian myth the flood lasts seven days and seven nights; in the Babylonian version it lasts six days and seven nights. Finally, the sending of the birds to test the degree of water abatement is found only in the Babylonian epic.

4. The text of the poem designated tentatively as "The Death of Gilgamesh," is still quite fragmentary (see *Ancient Near Eastern Texts,* pages 50–52). From its meager extant portions, only the following contents are recognizable: Gilgamesh still seems to be on his quest for immortality. He is informed, however, that eternal life is impossible to obtain. Kingship, prominence, heroism in battle—all these have been decreed for him, but not immortality. Fragmentary as it is, the available text of our poem shows an indubitable source relationship to portions of the ninth, tenth, and eleventh tablets of the "Epic of Gilgamesh." These tablets contain Gilgamesh's plea for eternal life, and the rejoinder that it is death, not immortality, which is man's fate. As for the Sumerian description of the death of Gilgamesh, strangely enough it has no counterpart in the extant versions of the Babylonian "Epic of Gilgamesh."

5. There is no trace of the Sumerian poem "Gilgamesh and Agga" (see Chapter 5) in the Babylonian epic. This is one of the shortest of all Sumerian epic tales; it consists of no more than 115 lines of text. Nevertheless, it is of significance from several points of view. In the first place, its plot deals with humans only; unlike other Sumerian epic tales, it introduces no mythological motifs involving the Sumerian deities. Secondly, it is of considerable historical importance, for it provides a number of hitherto unknown facts concerning the early struggles of the Sumerian city-states. Finally, it is of special significance for the history of political thought and practice, since it reveals the existence of what were to some extent democratic institutions as early as 2800 B.C. Perhaps these are the very factors which induced the Babylonian redactors to omit this epic tale altogether from the "Epic of Gilgamesh." The Sumerian tale lacks those superhuman qualities and supernatural heroics so characteristic of epic poetry.

6. For comments on Babylonian borrowings from the Sumerian poem "Gilgamesh, Enkidu, and the Nether World," see the end of the present chapter.

This brings to an end the comparative analysis of the contents of the relevant Sumerian Gilgamesh material at our disposal, and it is now possible to answer the questions formulated earlier.

1. Is there a Sumerian original of the Babylonian "Epic of Gilgamesh" as a single organic unit? Obviously not. The Sumerian poems vary considerably in length, and they consist of individual, disconnected tales. The plot sequence of the Babylonian epic, in which the several episodes are modified and connected to form a reasonably integrated whole, is a Babylonian innovation and achievement.

2. Are we in a position to identify those episodes in the Babylonian epic which go back to Sumerian prototypes? Yes, at least to some extent. The cedar-forest episode (Tablets III–V of the epic); the "Bull of Heaven" (Tablet VI); portions of the "quest for immortality" episode (Tablets IX, X, XI); the "deluge" story (Tablet XI)—all have their Sumerian counterparts. The Babylonian versions, however, are no slavish reproductions of their Sumerian originals. It is only the broad outlines of the plot that they have in common.

3. But what of those portions of the "Epic of Gilgamesh" for which no Sumerian prototypes have been found? These include the introduction at the beginning of the epic; the series of incidents culminating in the forging of the bond of friendship between Gilgamesh and Enkidu (Tablets I and II); the death and burial of Enkidu (Tablets VII, VIII). Are these of Babylonian origin, or do they, too, go back to Sumerian sources? The answer to these questions must be hypothetical. Nevertheless, an analysis of this Babylonian material in the light of extant Sumerian epics and myths permits a number of suggestive, if tentative, conclusions.

First, there is the introductory passage of the Babylonian epic. After portraying the hero as an all-seeing, all-knowing wanderer who had built the walls of Erech, the poet continues with a rhapsodic description of these walls, largely in the form of a rhetorical address to the reader. In none of the known Sumerian epic material do we find a parallel stylistic feature. We may therefore conclude that the introduction to the epic was a Babylonian innovation. The chain of events leading to the friendship between

the two heroes, which follows the introduction and constitutes the major part of Tablets I and II of the Babylonian
epic, consists of the following episodes: the tyranny of Gilgamesh; the creation of Enkidu; the "fall" of Enkidu; the
dreams of Gilgamesh; the civilizing of Enkidu; the struggle
between the heroes. These incidents form a well-knit plot
progression, culminating in the friendship of the two heroes.
In all probability, this friendship motif was then utilized
by the poet to help motivate the journey to the cedar forest.
No such motivation is to be found in the Sumerian version
of the journey to the cedar forest, and we may assume that
we will find no Sumerian counterpart of the chain of incidents as linked in the Babylonian epic. It would not surprise
us, however, to find Sumerian prototypes for several of the
individual incidents comprising the plot chain, although
these prototypes need not always consist of Gilgamesh tales.
The mythological motifs in the episodes concerned with the
creation of Enkidu, the dreams of Gilgamesh, and the struggle between the heroes, certainly reflect Sumerian sources.
As for the "fall" and civilizing of Enkidu, the criteria for a
reasonably safe conclusion are lacking at the moment, and
we must leave undecided the interesting question whether
the concept that sex experience is responsible for man's wisdom is of Semitic or Sumerian origin.

Finally, the story of the death of Enkidu and his burial
is in all likelihood of Babylonian rather than Sumerian origin. According to the Sumerian poem "Gilgamesh, Enkidu,
and the Nether World," Enkidu did not die at all in the
ordinary sense of the word but was seized and held fast
by Kur, a dragon-like demon in charge of the nether world,
after he had knowingly broken the taboos of the nether
world. The incident of the death of Enkidu was invented
by the Babylonian authors of the "Epic of Gilgamesh" in
order to motivate dramatically Gilgamesh's quest for immortality, which climaxes the poem.

To sum up: Of the various episodes comprising the "Epic
of Gilgamesh," several go back to Sumerian prototypes actually involving the hero Gilgamesh. Even in those episodes
which lack Sumerian counterparts, most of the individual
motifs reflect Sumerian mythic and epic sources. In no case,

however, did the Babylonian poets slavishly copy the Sumerian material. They so modified its content and molded its form, in accordance with their own temper and heritage, that only the bare nucleus of the Sumerian original remains recognizable. As for the plot structure of the epic as a whole—the forceful and fateful episodic drama of the restless, adventurous hero and his inevitable disillusionment—it is definitely a Babylonian, rather than Sumerian, development and achievement. In a very deep sense, therefore, the "Epic of Gilgamesh" may be truly described as a Semitic creation.

But it is only the first eleven tablets of the "Epic of Gilgamesh" which can be described as a Semitic literary creation (in spite of obvious borrowings from Sumerian sources). Tablet XII (the last tablet of the epic) is nothing more than a practically verbatim translation into the Semitic Akkadian—also known as Babylonian or Assyrian—of the second half of a Sumerian poem. The Babylonian scribes tacked this on to the first eleven tablets in total disregard of the sense and continuity of the epic as a whole.

It had long been suspected that the twelfth tablet was nothing more than an appendage to the first eleven tablets, which constitute a reasonably well-integrated unit, but the proof was not available until the text of the Sumerian poem "Gilgamesh, Enkidu, and the Nether World" was pieced together and translated. However, as early as 1930, in connection with his publication of a Sumerian tablet from Ur inscribed with part of the poem, C. J. Gadd, formerly of the British Museum, recognized the close relationship between its contents and those of the twelfth tablet of the Semitic epic.

The full text of the poem "Gilgamesh, Enkidu, and the Nether World" is still unpublished. (See "Gilgamesh and the *Huluppu*-Tree," *Assyriological Study No. 8* of the Oriental Institute of the University of Chicago; and *Sumerian Mythology*, pages 30 ff.) Here is a brief sketch:

The poem begins with an introduction of twenty-seven lines, the contents of which have nothing to do with the story itself. The first thirteen lines of this passage contain some of the basic data for the analysis of the Sumerian concepts of the creation of the universe (see Chapter 13),

while the remaining fourteen lines describe the struggle between Enki and Kur (see Chapter 22). Then follows the
story:

Once upon a time a *huluppu*-tree (perhaps a willow),
planted on the bank of the Euphrates and nurtured by its
waters, was violently attacked by the South Wind and
flooded by the waters of the Euphrates. The goddess
Inanna, walking by, took the tree in her hand and brought
it to her city, Erech, where she planted it in her holy garden. There she tended it most carefully, for she planned
that when the tree had grown big she would make of its
wood a chair for herself and a couch.

Years passed. The tree matured and grew big. But
Inanna found herself unable to cut it down, for at its base
the snake who "knows no charm" had built its nest; in its
crown, the *Imdugud*-bird had placed its young; in its middle, Lilith had built her house. And so Inanna, the light-
hearted and ever joyful maid, shed bitter tears.

As dawn broke, and her brother, the sun-god Utu, came
forth from his sleeping chamber, Inanna tearfully repeated
to him all that had befallen her *huluppu*-tree. Thereupon
Gilgamesh, who presumably heard her plaint, chivalrously
came to her aid. He donned his armor, weighing fifty
minas; and with his ax of the road, seven talents and seven
minas in weight, he slew the snake who "knows no charm"
at the base of the tree. Seeing this, the *Imdugud*-bird fled
with its young to the mountain, while Lilith tore down her
house and fled to the desolate places. Gilgamesh and the
men of Erech who accompanied him then cut down the
tree, and gave it to Inanna for her chair and couch.

What did Inanna do? From the base of the tree she fashioned a *pukku* (perhaps a drum); and from its crown, a
mikku (drumstick). There follows a passage of twelve lines
describing Gilgamesh's activity in Erech with this *pukku*
and *mikku*, or "drum" and "drumstick." Despite the fact
that the text is in perfect condition, it is still impossible to
penetrate its meaning. It is probable that it describes certain tyrannical acts which brought woe to the inhabitants
of Erech. When the story becomes intelligible once again,
it continues with the statement that "because of the outcry

of the young maidens," the *pukku* and the *mikku* fell into
the nether world. Gilgamesh put in his hand and his foot
to retrieve them, but was unable to reach them. He then
seated himself at the gate of the nether world and lamented:

"*O my* pukku, *O my* mikku,
My pukku *with lustiness irresistible,*
My mikku *with dance-rhythm unrivaled,*
My pukku *which was with me formerly in the house of the
      carpenter—*
*The wife of the carpenter was with me then like the mother
      who gave birth to me,*
*The daughter of the carpenter was with me then like my
      younger sister—*
My pukku, *who will bring it up from the nether world,*
My mikku, *who will bring it up from the 'face' of the nether
      world?"*

Gilgamesh's servant Enkidu thereupon volunteered to
descend to the nether world and bring them up for him,
saying:

"*O my master, why do you cry, why is your heart sick?*
Your pukku, *lo, I will now bring it up from the nether
      world,*
Your mikku, *I will bring it up from the 'face' of the nether
      world."*

Hearing his servant's generous offer, Gilgamesh warned
him of a number of nether-world taboos which he must
guard against. The passage runs as follows:

Gilgamesh says to Enkidu:
"*If now you will descend to the nether world,*
A word I speak to you, take my word,
Instruction I offer you, take my instruction.
Do not put on clean clothes,
*Lest like an enemy the (nether world) stewards will come
      forth,*
Do not anoint yourself with the good oil of the bur-*vessel,*
Lest at its smell they will crowd about you.

"*Do not throw the throw-stick in the nether world,*

*Lest they who were struck by the throw-stick will surround
    you,
Do not carry a staff in your hand,
Lest the shades will flutter all about you.*

*"Do not put sandals on your feet,
In the nether world make no cry;
Kiss not your beloved wife,
Strike not your hated wife,
Kiss not your beloved son,
Strike not your hated son,
Lest the outcry of Kur will seize you,
(The outcry) for her who is lying, for her who is lying,
To the mother of Ninazu who is lying,
Whose holy body no garment covers,
Whose holy breast no cloth wraps."*

The mother of Ninazu in these lines may refer to the
goddess Ninlil, who, according to the myth concerning the
birth of the moon-god Sin (see Chapter 13), accompanied
the god Enlil to the nether world.

Enkidu did not heed the instructions of his master, but
committed those very acts against which Gilgamesh had
warned him. And so he was seized by Kur and was unable
to ascend again to the earth. Thereupon Gilgamesh proceeded to Nippur and wept before Enlil:

*"O Father Enlil, my pukku fell into the nether world,
My mikku fell into the 'face' of the nether world,
I sent Enkidu to bring them up, Kur has seized him.
Namtar (the demon of death) has not seized him, Asag
    (the demon of disease) has not seized him,
Kur has seized him.
Nergal's ambusher (that is Death), who spares no one, has
    not seized him,
Kur has seized him.
In battle, the place of manliness, he has not fallen,
Kur has seized him."*

But Enlil refused to stand by Gilgamesh, who then proceeded to Eridu and repeated his plea before Enki. The
latter ordered the sun-god Utu to open a hole in the nether

world and to allow the shade of Enkidu to ascend to the earth. Utu did as bidden, and the shade of Enkidu appeared before Gilgamesh. Master and servant embraced, and Gilgamesh questioned Enkidu about what he saw in the nether world. The first seven questions concern the treatment in the nether world of those who were fathers of from one to seven sons. The remaining text of the poem is poorly preserved, but we have parts of the Gilgamesh-Enkidu colloquy concerning the treatment, in the nether world, of the palace servant, of the birth-giving woman, of him who falls in battle, of him whose shade has no one to care for it, and of him whose body lies unburied in the plain.

It is the second half of the poem which the Babylonian scribes translated practically verbatim and appended to the "Epic of Gilgamesh" as its twelfth tablet. For the modern scholar this was no mean boon, since, with the aid of the Sumerian version, it was possible to restore numerous broken words, phrases, and whole lines in the Akkadian text, and thus to clarify, at long last, the contents of the twelfth tablet, which had remained unintelligible in spite of the efforts of a number of distinguished cuneiformists.

Gilgamesh was not the only Sumerian hero. His two predecessors, Enmerkar and Lugalbanda, were also favorites with Sumerian poets. As a matter of fact, the Sumerians, to judge from their epic literature, had developed a so-called Heroic Age. This Heroic Age is discussed in Chapter 24.

MAN'S FIRST HEROIC AGE

Historians now generally realize (and this is largely to the credit of the English scholar H. Munro Chadwick) that the so-called Heroic Ages, which are come upon from time to time and from place to place in the history of civilization, represent not mere literary imagination but very real and significant social phenomena. Thus, to take only three of the better-known examples, there is the Greek Heroic Age, which flourished on the mainland of Greece toward the very end of the second millennium B.C.; the Heroic Age of India, which probably dates only a century or so later than that of Greece; and the Teutonic Heroic Age, which dominated much of northern Europe from the fourth to the sixth centuries A.D. All three of these Heroic Ages reveal a marked resemblance in social structure, governmental organization, religious concepts, and aesthetic expression. It is obvious that they owe their origin and being to similar social, political, and psychic factors.

The Sumerian heroic narrative poems sketched in this and the foregoing chapters constitute an epic literature which introduces a new Heroic Age to world history and literature—the Sumerian Heroic Age. Although it probably had its *floruit* toward the end of the first quarter of the third millennium B.C., and thus precedes by more than 1,500 years even the oldest of the three Indo-European Heroic Ages (that of the Greeks), its culture pattern is remarkably close to the culture pattern typical of the long-known Heroic Ages.

The Greek, Indian, and Teutonic Heroic Ages, as Chadwick concludes from relevant literary records, are essentially barbaric periods which show a number of salient characteristics in common. The political unit consists of a petty kingdom ruled by a king or prince who obtains and holds his rule through military prowess. His mainstay in power consists of the *comitatus*, a retinue of armed loyal followers who are prepared to do his bidding without question, no matter how foolhardy and dangerous the undertaking. There may be an assembly, but it is convened at the ruler's pleasure and serves only in an advisory and confirmatory capacity. The ruling kings and princes of the separate principalities carry on among themselves a lively, and at times friendly and even intimate, intercourse. They thus tend to develop into what may be termed an international aristocratic caste whose thoughts and acts have little in common with those of their subjects.

On the religious side, the three Indo-European Heroic Ages are characterized by a worship of anthropomorphic deities, which to a large extent seem to be recognized throughout the various states and principalities. These gods form organized communities in a chosen locality, though, in addition, each god has a special abode of his own. There are few traces of a chthonic or spirit cult. At death the soul travels to some distant locality that is regarded as a universal home and is not reserved for members of any particular community. Some of the heroes are conceived as springing from the gods, but there is no trace of heroic worship or hero cults. All these features common to the Heroic Ages of Greece, India, and Northern Europe, are shared by the Heroic Age of Sumer.

But the parallelism extends even further. Indeed, it is particularly apparent on the aesthetic plane, especially in literature. One of the notable achievements of all four of these Heroic Ages was the creation of heroic narrative tales—in *poetic form*—that were to be spoken or sung. They reflect and illuminate the spirit of the age and its temper. Impelled by the thirst for fame and name so characteristic of the ruling caste during a Heroic Age, the bards and minstrels attached to the court were moved to improvise nar-

rative poems or lays celebrating the adventures and achievements of kings and princes. These epic lays, with the
primary object of providing entertainment at the frequent
courtly banquets and feasts, were probably recited to the
accompaniment of the harp or lyre.

None of these early heroic lays have come down to us
in their original form, since they were composed when writing was either altogether unknown or, if known, of little
concern to the illiterate minstrel. The written epics of the
Greek, Indian, and Teutonic Heroic Ages date from much
later days, and consist of highly complex literary redac-
tions in which only a selected number of the earlier lays
are imbedded, and these in a highly modified and expanded form. In Sumer, there is good reason to believe,
some of the early heroic lays were first inscribed on clay
five to six hundred years following the close of the Heroic
Age, and then only after they had undergone considerable
transformation at the hands of priests and scribes. However,
it should be carefully noted that the copies of the Sumerian epic texts which we have at present date almost entirely from the first half of the second millennium B.C.

The written epics of the three Indo-European Heroic
Ages show a number of striking similarities in form and
content. In the first place, all the poems are concerned primarily with individuals. It is the deeds and exploits of the
individual hero that are the prime concern of the poet, not
the fate or glory of the state or community. Moreover, while
there is little doubt that some of the adventures celebrated
in the poems have a historical basis, the poet does not hesitate to introduce unhistorical motifs and conventions, such
as exaggerated notions of the hero's powers, ominous
dreams, and the presence of divine beings. Stylistically, the
epic poems abound in static epithets, lengthy repetitions,
and recurrent formulas, and in descriptions that tend to
be overleisurely and unusually detailed. Particularly noteworthy is the fact that all the epics devote considerable
space to speeches.

In all these respects, the pattern of Sumerian heroic poetry is similar to the pattern of Greek, Indian, and Teutonic
epic material. Since it is hardly likely that a literary genre

so individual in style and technique as narrative poetry was created and developed independently, at different time intervals, in Sumer, Greece, India, and Northern Europe, and since the narrative poetry of the Sumerians is by all odds the oldest of the four, it seems reasonable to conclude that in Sumer may be found the origin of epic poetry.

To be sure, there are a number of outstanding differences between the Sumerian epic material and that of the Greeks, Indians, and Teutons. For example, the Sumerian epic poems consist of individual, disconnected tales of varying length, each of which is restricted to a single episode. There is no attempt to articulate and integrate these episodes into a larger unit. As shown in Chapter 23, this was first achieved by the Babylonian poets, who borrowed, modified, and molded the relatively brief and episodic Sumerian tales—particularly in their "Epic of Gilgamesh"—with the view of fashioning an epic of considerable length and complexity. There is relatively little characterization and psychological penetration in the Sumerian material. The heroes tend to be broad types, more or less undifferentiated, rather than highly personalized individuals. Moreover, the incidents and plot motifs are related in a rather static and conventionalized style; there is little of that plastic, expressive movement which characterizes such poems as Homer's *Iliad* and *Odyssey*. Another interesting difference: Mortal women play hardly any role in Sumerian epic literature, while they have a very prominent part in Indo-European epic literature. Finally, in the matter of technique, the Sumerian poet gets his rhythmic effects primarily from variations in the repetition patterns. He makes no use whatever of the meters or uniform line so characteristic of Indo-European epics.

Let us turn now to the contents of the extant Sumerian epic poems. At present we can identify nine epic tales varying in length from one hundred to more than six hundred lines. Two of these revolve about the hero Enmerkar; two revolve about the hero Lugalbanda (in one of these Enmerkar, too, plays a considerable role); and five revolve about the most famous of the three heroes, Gilgamesh. All three are known from the Sumerian king list, a historical

document which, like our epic material, has been found inscribed on tablets dating from the first half of the second
millennium B.C. The list was probably composed in the last
quarter of the third millennium B.C. In the king list, these
three heroes are stated to be the second, third, and fifth
rulers of the first dynasty of Erech, which, according to the
Sumerian sages, followed the first dynasty of Kish, which
in turn followed immediately upon the flood. The contents
of one of the Enmerkar tales and of all five Gilgamesh
poems have been discussed in Chapters 4, 5, 22 and 23.
This leaves only three tales—one of Enmerkar and two of
Lugalbanda—to complete the sketch of the extant Sumerian
epic literature.

The second Enmerkar tale, like the tale treated in Chapter 4, is concerned with the submission of a lord of Aratta
to Enmerkar. However, in this poem it is not Enmerkar
who makes the first demands on his rival, the lord of
Aratta. It is, rather, the lord of Aratta himself who first
issues the challenge that leads to his own discomfiture.
Throughout the second Enmerkar poem, the lord of Aratta
is referred to by his actual name, Ensukushsiranna, and it
is therefore not certain whether he is identical with the lord
of Aratta who remains unnamed in the first Enmerkar poem.
As for the available contents of this second Enmerkar tale,
until 1952 only approximately one hundred well-preserved
lines, at the beginning of the poem, and some twenty-five
well-preserved lines toward the end, were identifiable. But
in the 1951–52 excavations of Nippur under the joint auspices of the Oriental Institute and the University Museum,
two excellently preserved tablets, which fill in much of the
missing text, were unearthed. As a result, the plot can now
be tentatively reconstructed as follows:

In the days when Ennamibaragga-Utu was (perhaps)
king of Sumer as a whole, Ensukushsiranna, the lord of
Aratta, whose vizier had the name Ansiggaria, issued a
challenge via a herald to Enmerkar, the lord of Erech,
whose vizier was Namennaduma. The gist of the message
was that Enmerkar should recognize Ensukushsiranna as his
overlord, and that the goddess Inanna should be brought
to Aratta.

Enmerkar is contemptuous of the challenge and, in a long address in which he depicts himself as the favorite of the gods, declares that Inanna will remain in Erech and demands that Ensukushsiranna should be his vassal. Thereupon Ensukushsiranna gathers in the members of his council and asks them what to do. They seem to advise him to submit, but he refuses indignantly. Then the *mashmash*-priest of Aratta, probably Urgirnunna by name, comes to his aid, and boasts (unfortunately it is uncertain from the text just who the speaker is) that he will cross "the river of Erech," subdue all the lands "above and below, from the sea to the cedar mountain," and return with heavily laden boats (sic!) to Aratta. Ensukushsiranna is delighted, and gives him five minas of gold and five minas of silver, as well as the necessary supplies.

When the *mashmash* reaches Erech (the poem does not state how he got there) he steps up to the holy stable and sheepfold of the goddess Nidaba and induces her cow and goat to withhold their cream and milk from her dining halls. The flavor of the passage may be felt from the following tentative rendering:

He (the mashmash) *speaks with the cow, converses with*
*   her like a human,*
"Cow, who eats your cream, who drinks your milk?"

"Nidaba eats my cream,
Nidaba drinks my milk,
My milk and cheese . . . . ,
Is placed as fitting in the large (dining) halls, the halls of
*   Nidaba.*
I would bring my cream . . from the holy stable,
I would bring my milk . . from the sheepfold,
The steadfast cow, Nidaba, Enlil's foremost child . . . . ."

"Cow, . . your cream to your . . , . . your milk to
*   your . . . . ."*

The cow . . d her cream to her . . , . . d her milk to
*   her . . , ...*

(These lines are then repeated for the goat.)

As a result of this withholding act on the part of Nidaba's
cow and goat, the stables and sheepfolds of Erech become
desolate. The shepherds mourn and wail while their helpers
take to the road. Thereupon Nidaba's two shepherds, Mashgula and Uredinna, "sons born of one mother," intervene
and, probably on the advice of the sun-god Utu (the relevant passage is poorly preserved), they succeed in outwit-
ting the *mashmash* with the help of Mother Sagburru. The
passage follows:

*The two of them (Mashgula and Uredinna) threw the
  prince into the river,*
The mashmash *brought forth the great* suhur-*fish out of
  the water,*
*Mother Sagburru brought forth the . . -bird out of the
  water,*
The . . -bird snatched the suhur-*fish, brought him to the
  mountain.*

A second time they threw the prince into the river,
The mashmash *brought forth a ewe and its lamb out of the
  water,*
Mother Sagburru brought forth the wolf out of the water,
*The wolf snatched the ewe and its lamb, brought them to
  the wide plain.*

A third time they threw the prince into the river,
The mashmash *brought forth a cow and its calf out of the
  water,*
Mother Sagburru brought forth the lion out of the water,
*The lion snatched the cow and its calf, brought them to the
  canebrake.*

A fourth time they threw the prince into the river,
The mashmash *brought forth the wild sheep out of the
  water,*
*Mother Sagburru brought forth the mountain leopard out
  of the water,*
*The mountain leopard snatched the wild sheep, brought
  him to the mountain.*

A fifth time they threw the prince into the river,

The mashmash *brought forth the young gazelle out of the
     water,*
Mother Sagburru brought forth the gug-beast *out of the
     water,*
The gug-beast *snatched the young gazelle, brought him to
     the forests.*

Having thus been outwitted again and again, the *mashmash's* "face turns black, his counsel is dissipated." When
Mother Sagburru begins to taunt him for his stupidity, he
pleads with her to let him return to Aratta in peace, and
promises to sing her praises there. But Sagburru will have
none of this. Instead she kills him and throws his dead body
into the Euphrates.

When Ensukushsiranna hears of what has happened to
the *mashmash*, he hurriedly sends a messenger to Enmerkar
and completely capitulates:

*"You are the beloved of Inanna, you alone are exalted,
Inanna has truly chosen you for her holy lap;
From the lower (lands) to the upper (lands) you are their
     lord, I am second to you,
From (the moment of) conception, I was not your equal,
     you are the 'big brother,'
I cannot compare with you ever."*

The poem ends with lines characteristic of a "disputation" composition (see Chapter 18):

*"In the dispute between Enmerkar and Ensukushsiranna,
After (?) victory of Enmerkar over Ensukushsiranna; O
     Nidaba, praise."*

We turn now to the epic tales in which the hero Lugalbanda plays the leading role. The first, which may be titled
"Lugalbanda and Enmerkar," is a poem of more than four
hundred lines, the majority of which are excellently preserved. In spite of the relatively few breaks in the text, the
sense of many passages is far from clear, and the following
sketch of the intelligible parts of its contents, based on repeated efforts to get at the meaning of the poem, must still
be considered highly tentative.

The hero Lugalbanda, who seems to find himself against his will in the far-distant land of Zabu, is eager to get back to his city, Erech. He is determined first to win the friendship of the *Imdugud*-bird who decrees the fates and utters the word which none may transgress. While the *Imdugud*-bird is away, therefore, he goes to his nest and presents his young with fat, honey, and bread, paints their faces, and places the *shugurra* crown upon their heads. The *Imdugud*-bird, upon returning to his nest, is most gratified with this godlike treatment of his young, and proclaims himself ready to bestow friendship and favor upon whatever god or man has done this gracious deed.

Lugalbanda steps up to receive his reward, and the *Imdugud*-bird, in a eulogistic passage replete with blessings, bids him go, head high, to his city. Upon Lugalbanda's request, he decrees for him a favorable journey, and adds some pertinent advice which he is to repeat to no one, not even his closest followers. The *Imdugud*-bird re-enters his nest, while Lugalbanda returns to his friends and tells them of his imminent journey. They try to dissuade him, for it is a journey from which none return, since it involves the crossing of high mountains and of the dreaded river of Kur. However, Lugalbanda is adamant, and the outcome is the successful journey to Erech.

In Erech, Lugalbanda's lord and liege, Enmerkar, son of the sun-god Utu, is in great distress. For many years past, the Semitic Martu had been ravaging both Sumer and Akkad. Now they were laying siege to Erech itself. Enmerkar finds that he must get through a call for help to his sister, the goddess Inanna of Aratta. But he can find no one to undertake the dangerous journey to Aratta to deliver his message. Whereupon Lugalbanda steps up to his king and bravely volunteers for the task. Upon Enmerkar's insistence on secrecy, he swears he will make the journey alone, unaccompanied by his followers. After receiving from Enmerkar the exact words of his message to Inanna of Aratta, Lugalbanda hastens to his friends and followers and informs them of his imminent journey. They try to dissuade him, but to no avail. He takes up his weapons, crosses the seven mountains that reach from one end of Anshan to the other, and finally arrives with joyful step at his destination.

There in Aratta, Lugalbanda is given a warm welcome by Inanna. On her asking what brought him all alone from Erech to Aratta, he repeats verbatim Enmerkar's message and call for help. Inanna's answer, which marks the end of the poem, is obscure. It seems to involve a river and its unusual fish, which Enmerkar is to catch; also certain water vessels that he is to fashion; and finally, workers of metal and stone whom he is to settle in his city. But just how all this will remove the threat of the Martu from Sumer and Akkad, or lift the siege from Erech, is far from clear.

The second Lugalbanda tale, which may tentatively be titled "Lugalbanda and Mount Hurrum," probably runs well over six hundred lines. At present, however, with the end of the poem missing, we can account only for close to five hundred lines of text, of which about two-thirds are in excellent condition. The available contents of this difficult text, may be sketched as follows:

Enmerkar, the lord of ancient Erech, has decided to journey to Aratta, probably for the purpose of conquest. Accompanied by a huge host of Erechites under the command of seven unnamed heroes—who are described as "true sons of Kullab," "born of the goddess Urash," "fed by the milk of the stall"—and of Lugalbanda, who was "their eighth," he arrives at Mount Hurrum. But then and there Lugalbanda falls ill. His brothers and friends seem to do all they can to revive him, but to no avail: "When they raised his neck, there was no breath (of life)." Terrified, they take counsel together and decide that, since he is already "dead," they will leave him on Mount Hurrum, proceed on their journey, "and when we return from Aratta, we will bring our brother's corpse to Kullab (a city in the district of Erech)."

Abandoned and forsaken, the still living but sick-to-death Lugalbanda, after two days and a half—or, as our author puts it, "after to two days half a day had been added"—lifted his head to the rising sun, the god Utu, and "as unto his father who gave birth to him, he uttered a prayer to

him," the burden of which is that he should not let him
perish on Mount Hurrum,

*"A place where there is no mother to stand by, no father to
        stand by,*
No friend to stand by, no dear one to stand by,
Where my mother will not say: 'O my son,'
Where my brother will not say: 'O my brother!'"

And sure enough, our poet tells us:

Utu accepted his prayer,
Brings down to him, to Mount Hurrum, his "breath of life."

Thereupon Lugalbanda lifts his eyes to the planet Venus
and utters a prayer to the goddess Inanna, "the whore going
forth to the brothel, who makes sweet the bed-chambers,"
and "as unto his father (*sic!*) who gave birth to him, he
uttered a prayer to her" that she should not let him perish
on Mount Hurrum, "the mountain of the *hashur*-tree."
Inanna, too, accepts his prayer, gives him breath of life,
and "covers him like a garment with joyous heart."

Lugalbanda then lifts his face to the moon and utters a
prayer to the god Sin, "the star who lights up the sky when
the sun sets, who brightens the night with bright light,"
"whose bright countenance illuminates Mount Hurrum,"
which reads in part:

> *"King, untouchable in the distant sky,*
> *O Sin, untouchable in the distant sky,*
> *King, who loves straightforwardness, hates evil,*
> *O Sin, who loves straightforwardness, hates evil,*
> *Wipe out (?) evil like a snake . . . ."*

The god Sin, too, hearkens of course to Lugalbanda's
prayer and "gave him life." Once again now Lugalbanda
lifts his eyes to the sun and utters a prayer of glorification,
which reads in part:

*"O Utu, shepherd of the Land, father of the black-headed
        people,*
When you go to sleep, the people too go to sleep with you;
Mighty Utu, when you rise, the people too rise with you;
Utu, without you

The prince travels not . . . the slave travels not to . . .
Of him who travels alone, you are his twin-brother,
Utu, of the man on a journey you are his "third,"
Of the . . . you are his twin eye;
The poor, the helpless, the naked,
The "breast" of your light clothes like a garment of long
     wool,
The needy you cover with a garment of white wool . . . .
Hero, son of the goddess Ningal, I sing your glory!"

Lugalbanda, his health restored with the help of the "food of life" and the "water of life," now seems to wander all alone over the highland steppe, living by hunting its wild life and gathering its uncultivated plants. Once, having fallen asleep, he dreams that he is commanded, perhaps by the sun-god Utu, to take up his weapons, hunt and kill a wild ox, and present its fat to the rising Utu; also to slaughter a kid and pour out its blood in a ditch and its fat on the plain. Upon awaking, Lugalbanda not only carries out the commands he had heard in his dream but also prepares food and strong drink for An, Enlil, Enki, and Ninhursag, the four leading deities of the Sumerian pantheon. The available text of the poem ends with what seems to be a eulogy of the seven heavenly lights which help the moon-god Nanna, the sun-god Utu, and the goddess of the planet Venus, Inanna, to illuminate the cosmos.

So much for our survey of the extant Sumerian epic literature and the Heroic Age which it reveals. Unlike narrative and hymnal poetry, the lyric is rather rare in Sumerian literature—particularly the love lyric. To date, only two love poems have been recovered among hundreds and thousands of Sumerian tablets. These two poems, as is apparent from the translations in Chapter 25, are not love poems in the secular sense. Both are probably rhapsodic songs of love uttered by a royal bride to her king. They call to mind the Biblical "Song of Songs."

THE FIRST LOVE SONG

While working in the Istanbul Museum of the Ancient Orient as Fulbright Research Professor—it was toward the end of 1951—I came upon a little tablet with the museum number 2461. For weeks I had been studying, more or less cursorily, drawerful after drawerful of still uncopied and unpublished Sumerian literary tablets, in order to identify each piece and, if possible, assign it to the composition to which it belonged. All this was spadework preparatory to the selection, for copying, of those pieces which were most significant—since it was clear that there would be no time that year to copy all of them. The little tablet numbered 2461 was lying in one of the drawers, surrounded by a number of other pieces.

When I first laid eyes on it, its most attractive feature was its state of preservation. I soon realized that I was reading a poem, divided into a number of stanzas, which celebrated beauty and love, a joyous bride and a king named Shu-Sin (who ruled over the land of Sumer close to four thousand years ago). As I read it again and yet again, there was no mistaking its content. What I held in my hand was one of the oldest love songs written down by the hand of man.

It soon became clear that this was not a secular poem, not a song of love between just "a man and a maid." It involved a king and his selected bride, and was no doubt intended to be recited in the course of the most hallowed of ancient rites, the rite of the "sacred marriage." Once a year, according to Sumerian belief, it was the sacred duty of the ruler to marry a priestess and votary of Inanna, the goddess of love and procreation, in order to ensure fertility to the soil and fecundity to the womb. The time-honored ceremony was celebrated on New Year's day and was preceded by feasts and banquets accompanied by music, song, and dance. The poem inscribed on the little Istanbul clay tablet was in all probability recited by the chosen bride of King Shu-Sin in the course of one of these New Year celebrations.

The poem was copied by Muazzez Cig, one of the Turkish curators of the Istanbul tablet collection. An edition of the poem consisting of copy, text, transliteration, translation, and commentary was published jointly with Cig in the *Belleten* of the Turkish Historical Commission, Volume 16 (pages 345 ff.). Here is a tentative translation:

Bridegroom, dear to my heart,
Goodly is your beauty, honeysweet,
Lion, dear to my heart,
Goodly is your beauty, honeysweet.

You have captivated me, let me stand tremblingly before
    you,
Bridegroom, I would be taken by you to the bedchamber,
You have captivated me, let me stand tremblingly before
    you,
Lion, I would be taken by you to the bedchamber.

Bridegroom, let me caress you,
My precious caress is more savory than honey,
In the bedchamber, honey filled,
Let us enjoy your goodly beauty,
Lion, let me caress you,
My precious caress is more savory than honey.

Bridegroom, you have taken your pleasure of me,
Tell my mother, she will give you delicacies,
My father, he will give you gifts.

Your spirit, I know where to cheer your spirit,

Bridegroom, sleep in our house until dawn,
Your heart, I know where to gladden your heart,
Lion, sleep in our house until dawn.

You, because you love me,
Give me pray of your caresses,
My lord god, my lord protector,
My Shu-Sin who gladdens Enlil's heart,
Give me pray of your caresses.

Your place goodly as honey, pray lay (your) hand on it,
Bring (your) hand over it like a gishban-*garment,*
Cup (your) hand over it like a gishban-sikin-*garment,*

It is a balbale-*song of Inanna.*

The only other known Sumerian love song is also inscribed on an Istanbul tablet. Although it was published
by Edward Chiera in 1924, it was not translated until 1947,
when Adam Falkenstein's excellent and detailed edition of
the text appeared in *Die Welt des Orients* (pages 43–50).
This poem, too, consists of the loving words of an unnamed
votary to her king, but its structure is not too clear and its
meaning is obscure in spots. It seems to consist of six
strophes: two of four lines each, one of six lines, two more
of four lines, and one of six lines. The logical relationship
between the various strophes is not too clear. The first
strophe sings of the birth of Shu-Sin, while the second seems
to consist of exclamatory lines exalting Shu-Sin, his mother
Abisimti, and his wife Kubatum. In the third and longer
strophe, the poetess tells of the gifts presented her by the
king as a reward for her joyous *allari*-songs. Of the last
three strophes, the first and third consist of exclamatory
lines exalting the king, while the second sings temptingly
of the poetess' own charms. Here is the tentative translation
of the entire poem:

She gave birth to him who is pure, she gave birth to him
     who is pure,
The queen gave birth to him who is pure,
Abisimti gave birth to him who is pure,
The queen gave birth to him who is pure.

O my (queen) who is favored of limb,
O my (queen) who is . . d of head, my queen Kubatum,
O my (lord) who is . . d of hair, my lord Shu-Sin,
O my (lord) who is . . d of word, my son of Shulgi!

Because I uttered it, because I uttered it, the lord gave me
    a gift,
Because I uttered the allari-*song, the lord gave me a gift,*
A pendant of gold, a seal of lapis lazuli, the lord gave me
    as a gift,
A ring of gold, a ring of silver, the lord gave me as a gift,
Lord, your gift is brimful of . . , lift your face unto me,
Shu-Sin, your gift is brimful of . . , lift your face unto me.

. . . . lord . . . . lord . . . . ,
. . . . like a weapon . . . . ,
The city lifts its hand like a dragon, my lord Shu-Sin,
It lies at your feet like a lion-cub, son of Shulgi.

My god, of the wine-maid, sweet is her drink,
Like her drink sweet is her vulva, sweet is her drink,
Like her lips sweet is her vulva, sweet is her drink,
Sweet is her mixed drink, her drink.

My Shu-Sin who favored me,
O my (Shu-Sin) who favored me, who fondled me,
My Shu-Sin who favored me,
My beloved of Enlil, (my) Shu-Sin,
My king, the god of his land!

It is a balbale *of Bau.*

The Sumerian poems and essays that are analyzed in
the present volume represent only a small fraction of the
available Sumerian literary remains—not to mention the innumerable tablets still underground. By the first half of the
second millennium B.C. a large number of Sumerian literary
works of all types were current in Sumerian schools. They
were inscribed on clay tablets, prisms, and cylinders of as-
sorted sizes and shapes, which had to be handled, stored,
and cared for. *A priori* it seemed reasonable to suppose that
some of the Sumerian faculty personnel would find it convenient to list the names of groups of literary works for

purposes of reference and filing. In 1942 two such book lists were identified. One is in the Louvre, and the other in the University Museum. These, the first "library catalogues," are discussed in Chapter 26.

THE FIRST LIBRARY
CATALOGUE

The University Museum has a tablet catalogued as No.
29-15-166. It is an ancient Sumerian "book list." It is small,
only 2½ inches in length by 1½ inches in width, and in
practically perfect condition. The scribe, by dividing each
side into two columns, and by using a minute script, succeeded in cataloguing the titles of sixty-two literary works
on this small tablet. The first forty titles he divided into
groups of ten by ruling a dividing line between numbers
10 and 11, 20 and 21, 30 and 31, 40 and 41. The remaining twenty-two he separated into two groups, the first consisting of nine titles and the second of thirteen. At least
twenty-four of the titles which this scribe listed in his catalogue can be identified as belonging to compositions for
which we now have the texts themselves, in full or in large
part. We may have considerable portions of the texts of
many more of the listed works. But since the title of a Sumerian composition consisted of part—and usually the *first*
part—of its first line, there is no way of identifying the titles
of those poems or essays in which the first lines were broken
away or seriously damaged.

The recognition of the contents of the little tablet in the
University Museum as a "book list" did not come about
simply and at first glance. When I first took the little tablet
from its place in the cupboard to study it, I had no inkling

of the true nature of its contents. Blithely assuming that it was but another Sumerian poem, I tried to translate it as a connected text. To be sure, I was troubled by the extreme brevity of the individual lines, and by the inexplicable division of the text into various groupings by means of ruled lines. But the thought that it was a "book list" would probably never have entered my mind, had I not grown familiar with the initial lines of a number of the Sumerian literary works in my efforts, over the years, to piece together their available texts. As I read and reread, again and again, the individual phrases on the little tablet, the similarity between them and the first lines of a number of the poems and essays struck me as unusual. From there on it was relatively simple, and a detailed comparison led to the conclusion that the lines inscribed on the tiny document contained not a connected text, but a disjointed list of titles of a number of Sumerian literary works.

Once the contents of the catalogue tablet had been recognized and deciphered, it seemed advisable to look through all the Sumerian material published by the various museums during the past decades to see if a similar document, the nature of its contents unrecognized, had already been published. Sure enough, in searching through the Louvre publication *Textes Religieux Sumériens,* I found that the Louvre tablet AO 5393, described as a hymn by its copyist, the French scholar Henri de Genouillac, is really a catalogue corresponding in large part to our University Museum tablet. Indeed, to judge from the script, it may have been written by the very same scribe. The Louvre tablet is also divided into four columns. It catalogues sixty-eight titles, six more than the University Museum tablet. Forty-three of the titles are identical on the two tablets, although the order frequently varies. The Louvre tablet therefore has twenty-five titles that are not in the University Museum tablet, while the latter has nineteen titles that are not in the former. Altogether, the two catalogues list the titles of eighty-seven literary compositions. Among the twenty-five listed only on the Louvre tablet, eight titles are of compositions whose texts we now have in large part. This brings the total identifiable compositions to thirty-two.

As for the principles which guided the scribe in the arrangement of his catalogue, these are by no means clear. In the first place, since the forty-three titles common to both catalogues differ considerably in the order of their arrangement, it is obvious that the guiding principles were not identical for the two catalogues. *A priori* one might have expected the nature of the contents of the compositions to have been the determining criterion. Actually, this is rarely the case. The only very convincing example of arrangement according to content is that of the last thirteen titles of the University Museum tablet, which are all "wisdom" compositions. Interestingly enough, none of these are found on the Louvre tablet.

At present we are ignorant of the practical purposes which the catalogue was intended to serve and can only guess at the actual factors that impelled the scribe to a particular choice. To mention some of the more obvious possibilities, he may have written the titles as he stored the literary tablets in a container, or as he arranged them on the shelves of the library room of the "tablet house." In any case, the size of the tablet may have played a considerable role in the order of selection. Until additional data comes to light, the problem of the catalogue arrangement must remain obscure.

For purposes of illustration, here is a list of those titles in the two documents which can be identified with the poems and essays discussed throughout this book:

1. *Ene nigdue* ("The Lord, That Which Is Appropriate"), listed as No. 3 in the University Museum tablet (and probably also in the Louvre document, which is broken at this point), begins the myth "The Creation of the Pickax," the first lines of which were utilized for deducing the Sumerian concepts of the creation of the universe (see Chapter 13).

2. *Enlil Sudushe* ("Enlil Far-reaching"), listed as No. 5 in both documents, begins the Enlil hymn quoted in large part in Chapter 13.

3. *Uria* ("The Days of Creation"), listed as No. 7 in both catalogues, begins the epic tale "Gilgamesh, Enkidu, and the Nether World" (see Chapter 23). The title

Uria appears two more times in the catalogues, which indicates that the cataloguer must have had two additional works beginning with this phrase. Nevertheless, he did not seem to feel it necessary to distinguish between these three identical titles.

4. *Ene kurlutilashe* ("The Lord toward the Land of the Living"), listed as No. 10 in both catalogues, begins the dragon-slaying tale "Gilgamesh and the Land of the Living" (see Chapter 22).

5. *Lukingia Ag* ("The Heralds of Ag(ga)"), listed as No. 11 in the University Museum tablet but omitted in the Louvre piece, begins the politically significant epic tale, "Gilgamesh and Agga" (see Chapter 5). The Sumerian title stops with the syllable *Ag*, although this is only the first part of the name.

6. *Hursag ankibida* ("On the Mountain of Heaven and Earth"), listed as No. 17 in the University Museum tablet but omitted in the Louvre document, begins the disputation "Cattle and Grain" (see Chapter 14), which is important for the Sumerian ideas concerning the creation of man.

7. *Uru nanam* ("Lo, the City"), listed as No. 22 in the University Museum tablet but omitted in the Louvre piece, begins the *Nanshe* hymn (see Chapter 14), which is important for the history of Sumerian ethics and morals.

8. *Lugalbanda* ("Lugalbanda"), listed as No. 39 in the University Museum tablet but omitted in the Louvre piece, begins the epic tale "Lugalbanda and Enmerkar" (see Chapter 24).

9. *Angalta kigalshe* ("From the Great Above to the Great Below"), listed as No. 41 in the University Museum document but as No. 34 in the Louvre tablet, begins the myth "Inanna's Descent to the Nether World" (see Chapter 21).

10. *Mesheam iduden* ("Where Did You Go?"), listed as No. 50 in the University Museum tablet but omitted in the Louvre document, is the end of the first line of the "schooldays" composition discussed in Chapter 2. The entire first line of this essay reads *Dumu edubba*

uulam meshe iduden ("Schoolboy, where did you go
from earliest days?"). But the ancient scribe chose the
last rather than the first part of this line for his catalogue, perhaps because there were a number of essays
beginning with the word *Dumu edubba* ("Schoolboy"), and he wished to distinguish between them.

11. *Uul engarra* ("In Days of Yore the Farmer"), listed
as No. 53 in the University Museum tablet but omitted
in the Louvre piece, begins the essay containing the
instructions of a farmer to his son, and described as
the first "Farmer's Almanac" in Chapter 11.

12. *Lugal u melambi nirgal,* listed as No. 18 in the Louvre
tablet but omitted in the University Museum document, begins the dragon-slaying myth "The Deeds and
Exploits of the God Ninurta" (see Chapter 22).

13. *Lulu nammah dingirre* ("Man, the Exaltedness of the
Gods"), listed as No. 46 in the Louvre piece and omitted in the University Museum tablet, begins the poetic
essay on human suffering and submission discussed in
Chapter 15.

The Sumerians held out no comforting hopes for man
and his future. To be sure, they longed for security and
at least three of the four freedoms that we espouse today
—freedom from fear, want, and war. But it never occurred
to them to project these longings and wishes into the future.
Instead, they thought of them in retrospect and relegated
them to the long-gone past. The first recorded ideas concerning a Golden Age are presented in Chapter 27.

27 *World Peace and Harmony*

MAN'S FIRST GOLDEN AGE

In classical mythology, the Golden Age is represented as an age of perfect happiness, when men lived without toil or strife. In Sumerian literature, we have, preserved for us on a tablet, man's first conception of the Golden Age. The Sumerian view of the Golden Age is found in the epic tale "Enmerkar and the Land of Aratta" (see Chapter 4). In this tale there is a passage of twenty-one lines that describes a once-upon-a-time state of peace and security, and ends with man's fall from this blissful state. Here is the passage:

*Once upon a time, there was no snake, there was no
        scorpion,
There was no hyena, there was no lion,
There was no wild dog, no wolf,
There was no fear, no terror,
Man had no rival.*

*Once upon a time, the lands Shubur and Hamazi,
Many (?)-tongued Sumer, the great land of princeships' di-
        vine laws,
Uri, the land having all that is appropriate,
The land Martu, resting in security,
The whole universe, the people in unison (?),
To Enlil in one tongue gave praise.*

*(But) then, the father-lord, the father-prince, the father-
        king,*

Enki, the father-lord, the father-prince, the father-king,
The irate (?) father-lord, the irate (?) father-prince, the
*   irate (?) father-king,*
. . . . abundance . . . .
. . . . (5 lines destroyed)
. . man . . . .

The first eleven lines, which are excellently preserved, describe those happy "long ago" days when man, fearless and unrivaled, lived in a world of peace and plenty, and all the peoples of the universe worshiped the same deity, Enlil. Indeed, if "in one tongue" is to be taken literally, and not as a figurative expression for a phrase such as "with one heart," the words would indicate that the Sumerians, like the Hebrews of later times, believed in the existence of a universal speech prior to the period of the confusion of languages.

As for the ten lines that constitute the next part of the passage, they are so fragmentary that we can only guess at their content. To judge from the context, it seems safe to surmise that Enki, displeased with, or jealous of, the sway of Enlil, took some action to disrupt it, and thus put an end to man's Golden Age by bringing about conflicts and wars among the peoples of the world. Perhaps (on the assumption that lines 10 and 11 are to be taken literally), Enki even brought about a confusion of languages. If so, we may have here the first inkling of a Sumerian parallel to the Biblical "Tower of Babel" story (Genesis 11:1–9), except that the Sumerians attributed man's fall to the jealousy between the gods while the Hebrews believed it resulted from Elohim's jealousy of man's ambition to be like a god.

The poet of the Golden Age passage designated it as the "Spell of Enki." Enmerkar, the lord of Erech and a favorite of the god Enki—so runs the story—is determined to make a vassal state of the mineral-rich Aratta. He therefore sends a herald to the lord of Aratta with a message threatening Aratta's destruction unless he and his people bring down precious metal and stone, and build and decorate Enki's temple, the Abzu. It was to further impress the lord of

Aratta that Enki instructed the herald to repeat the "Spell of Enki," which relates how Enki had put an end to Enlil's sway over the earth and its inhabitants.

Besides shedding light on the Sumerian ideas of man's blissful past, the passage of twenty-one lines is of importance for another reason: It gives some idea of the size and

Fig. 3. Ancient Sites. Map of southern Iraq locating important excavated sites.

geography of the physical world known to the Sumerians. To judge from lines 6 to 9, the poet conceived of the universe as four major land divisions. His own country, *Sumer*, formed the southern boundary of this universe and consisted (roughly estimated) of the territory between the Tigris and Euphrates Rivers from a line somewhat south of the thirty-third parallel down to the Persian Gulf. Directly north of Sumer was *Uri*, which probably consisted of the territory between the Tigris and Euphrates north of the thirty-third parallel, and included the later Akkad and Assyria. East of Sumer and Uri was *Shubur-Hamazi*, which no doubt included much of western Iran. To the west and southwest of Sumer was *Martu*, which included the territory between the Euphrates River and the Mediterranean Sea, as well as Arabia. In short, the universe as conceived by the Sumerian poets, extended at least from the Armenian highlands on the north to the Persian Gulf, and from the Iranian highlands on the east to the Mediterranean Sea.

Appendix A

A CURSE AND A MAP: NEW
GLEANINGS FROM THE
TABLETS OF SUMER

This appendix was written largely in the city of Jena, where I spent ten weeks, in the fall of 1955, studying and trans-literating the Sumerian literary tablets and fragments in the Hilprecht Sammlung ("Hilprecht Collection") of the Friedrich-Schiller University. These documents, all of which were excavated more than fifty years ago by the University of Pennsylvania (see Introduction), formed part of the private collection of antiquities of Hermann Hilprecht, the first to hold the chair of Clark Research Professor of Assyriology at the University of Pennsylvania—the very chair which I now hold. On Hilprecht's death in 1925, the entire collection was bequeathed to the University of Jena, now officially known as the Friedrich-Schiller University.

The Hilprecht Collection has some 2,500 tablets and fragments, but only 150 of these are inscribed with Sumerian literary works. For fifteen years I had been trying to go to Jena to study these tablets, the existence of which was known from a brief note in one of the German scholarly journals. But first came the Nazis, then the war, and then the "Iron Curtain." With the relaxation of international tensions in 1955, the time seemed ripe for another trial. I was granted permission to work in the Hilprecht Collection for several months, and while there received the fullest co-operation of the Friedrich-Schiller University and its Department of Research. The Assistant Keeper of the Hilprecht Collection, Dr. Inez Bernhardt, who is in charge of the tablets, was most helpful.

Here are some of the more important results of this study:

There are 150 Sumerian literary pieces in the Hilprecht Collection. About one hundred are very small pieces, with only a few broken lines preserved. But the rest are fairly well-preserved tablets, thirteen of which are inscribed with from four to eight columns. It is important to bear in mind, however, that at the present stage of the restoration process of the Sumerian literary works, fragments containing new text, no matter what their size, are more valuable from the scientific point of view than well-preserved tablets with texts already available.

The 150 tablets and fragments represent practically all the known Sumerian literary categories: myths and epic tales, hymns and lamentations, historiographic documents and letters, and wisdom and gnomic compositions, such as proverbs, essays, debates, and "catalogues." Relatively few new compositions are represented. Among the more interesting of the new compositions are a hymn to the god Hendursagga as the vizier of the goddess Nanshe, who supervised man's moral behavior; a love-dialogue between Innana and Dumuzi; a myth involving the underworld deity Ningishzida and the goddess Ninazimua; an extract of a myth, telling how two brother gods brought down barley to Sumer "which knew no barley" from the mountain where it had been stored by the god Enlil; a pleading letter by one Gudea to his personal deity; and finally two precious "book lists," or catalogues, of the type treated in Chapter 26.

However, the major significance of the Sumerian literary tablets in the Hilprecht Collection lies in the fact that they help to fill innumerable gaps and breaks in compositions already known and pieced together, in large part, in the past two decades from the tablets and fragments found in various museums the world over, particularly in the Istanbul Museum of the Ancient Orient and the University Museum in Philadelphia. The text of almost all these compositions will benefit in some degree. But in the case of several of the documents, the relevant pieces in the Hilprecht Collection are of crucial importance.

One of these important documents is analyzed here to illustrate the significance of the newly studied material. It is a composition of close to 300 lines which may be best titled "The Curse of Agade: The Ekur Avenged." Though more than a score of published and unpublished pieces inscribed with parts of this work had been identified, its real character eluded us, particularly since the second half of the document was still restorable in part only. Because much of its text spoke of the destruction, devastation, and desolation of Agade, it was taken to be a lamentation over the destruction of Agade, although its formal structure differed markedly from such comparable works as "Lamentation over the Destruction of Ur" and "Lamentation over the Destruction of Nippur." The Hilprecht Collection has seven pieces inscribed with parts of this myth, and one of these (H. S. 1514) is a well-preserved four-column tablet inscribed with the last 138 lines. With the help of this additional text, it has become clear that this composition is not a lamentation at all but a historiographic document written in a highly poetic prose. In it a Sumerian writer and sage presents his interpretation of the causes behind a memorable historical event which had proved to be catastrophic for Sumer as a whole, and particularly for the mighty city of Agade.

The century beginning with approximately 2300 B.C.—to use the so-called "low chronology"—witnessed the rise in Mesopotamia of a Semitic conqueror and ruler named Sargon. After vanquishing the Sumerian capital cities of Kish in the north and Erech in the south, Sargon made himself master of practically the entire Near East, including Egypt and Ethiopia. His capital was the city of Agade, in northern Sumer, but its exact location is still uncertain. Under the rule of Sargon and his immediate followers, Agade became the richest and most powerful city in Sumer. Gifts and tribute from all the surrounding lands were brought to it. But less than a century after its phenomenal rise came its precipitate fall. It was attacked and destroyed by the

Guti, a barbaric, ruthless horde from the mountains to the east, who then proceeded to ravage Sumer as a whole.

This humiliating and disastrous event must have preyed on the hearts and minds of many thinking Sumerians, and some at least were moved to seek an explanation of the cause behind it. One of those who sought an explanation was the author of our historiographic document. He found what, from his point of view (no doubt most of the Sumerians, and in particular the Nippurites, agreed with him) was the only true answer: Naram-Sin, the fourth ruler of the Agade Dynasty, had sacked Nippur and committed all sorts of desecrating acts against the Ekur, Enlil's great sanctuary. Enlil therefore turned to the Guti and brought them down from their mountainous abode, to destroy Agade and avenge his beloved temple. Moreover, eight of the more important deities of the Sumerian pantheon, in order to soothe the spirit of their ruler Enlil, laid a curse upon Agade that it should forever remain desolate and uninhabited. And this, adds the author at the end of his work, was indeed the case: Agade actually has remained desolate and uninhabited.

Our historiographer begins his work with an introduction contrasting the glory and power of Agade which marked its rise, and the ruin and desolation which engulfed it after its fall. The first several lines of the composition read: "After, with frowning forehead, Enlil had put the people of Kish to death like the Bull of Heaven, and like a lofty ox had crushed the house of Erech into dust; after in due time, Enlil had given to Sargon, the king of Agade, the lordship and kingship from the lands above to the lands below," then (to paraphrase some of the more intelligible passages) did the city of Agade become prosperous and powerful under the tender and constant guidance of its tutelary deity, Inanna. Its buildings were filled with gold, silver, copper, tin, and lapis lazuli; its old men and women gave wise counsel; its young children were full of joy; music and song resounded everywhere; all the surrounding lands lived in peace and security. Naram-Sin, moreover, made glorious its shrines, raised its walls mountain-high, while its gates remained wide open. To it came the nomadic Martu, the people who "know not grain," from the west, bringing choice oxen and sheep; to it came Meluhhaites, "the people of the black land," bringing their exotic ware; to it came the Elamite and Subarean from the east and north carrying loads like "load-carrying asses"; to it came all the princes, chieftains and sheiks of the plain, bringing gifts monthly and on the New Year.

But then came the catastrophe, or as the author puts it: "The gates of Agade, how they lay prostrate; . . . . , the holy Inanna leaves untouched their gifts; the Ulmash (Inanna's temple) is fear-ridden (since) she has gone from the city, left it; like a maid who forsakes her chamber, the holy Inanna has forsaken her Agade shrine; like a warrior with raised weapons she attacked the city in fierce battle, made it turn its breast to the enemy." And so in a very short time, "in not five days, not ten days," lordship and kingship departed from Agade; the gods turned against her, and Agade lay desolate and waste; Naram-Sin sulked by himself, dressed in sackcloth; his chariots and boats lay unused and neglected.

How did this come to be? Our author's version is that Naram-Sin, during the seven years in which his rule was firmly established, had acted contrary to Enlil's word; had permitted his soldiers to attack and ravage the Ekur and its groves; had demolished the buildings of the Ekur with copper axes and hatchets, so that "the house lay prostrate like a dead youth"; indeed, "all the lands lay prostrate." Moreover, at the Gate called "Gate of No Grain-Cutting" he cut grain; "the 'Gate of Peace' he demolished with the pickax"; he desecrated the holy vessels, cut down the Ekur's groves, ground up its gold, silver, and copper vessels into dust; loaded up all the possessions of the destroyed Nippur on boats docked right by Enlil's sanctuary, and carried them off to Agade.

But no sooner had he done this than "counsel left Agade," and "the good sense of Agade turned to folly." Then "Enlil, the raging flood which has no rival, because of his beloved house which has been attacked, what destruction wrought": He lifted his eyes to the mountains and brought down the Guti, "a people which brooks no controls"; "it covered the earth like the locust," so that none could escape its power.

Communication, whether by land or sea, became impossible throughout Sumer. "The herald could not proceed on his journey; the sea-rider could not sail his boat . . . . ; brigands dwelt on the roads; the doors of the gates of the land turned to clay; all the surrounding lands were planning evil in their city walls." As a result, dire famine came upon Sumer. "The great fields and meadows produced no grain; the fisheries produced no fish; and the watered gardens produced neither honey nor wine." Because of the famine, prices were inflated sky-high, so that one lamb brought only half a *sila* of oil, or half a *sila* of grain, or half a mina of wool.

With misery, want, death, and desolation thus threatening to overwhelm practically all "mankind fashioned by Enlil," eight of the more important deities of the Sumerian pantheon—namely, Sin, Enki, Inanna, Ninurta, Ishkur, Utu, Nusku and Nidaba—decide that it is high time to soothe Enlil's rage. In a prayer to Enlil they vow that Agade, the city which destroyed Nippur, will itself be destroyed like Nippur. And so these eight deities "turn their faces to the city, pronounce (a curse of) destruction upon Agade":

"City, you who dared assault the Ekur, who (defied) Enlil,
Agade, you who dared assault the Ekur, who (defied) Enlil,
May your groves be heaped up like dust, ...
May your clay (bricks) return to their abyss,
May they become clay (bricks) cursed by Enki,
May your trees return to their forests,
May they become trees cursed by Ninildu.
Your slaughtered oxen—may you slaughter your wives instead,
Your butchered sheep—may you butcher your children instead,
Your poor—may they be forced to drown their precious (?) children, ... ,
Agade, may your palace built with joyful heart, be turned into a depressing ruin . . . . ,
Over the places where your rites and rituals were conducted,

*May the fox (who haunts) the ruined mounds, glide his
    tail . . ,*
May your canal-boat towpaths grow nothing but weeds,
*May your chariot-roads grow nothing but the 'wailing
    plant,'*
Moreover, on your canal-boat towpaths and landings,
*May no human being walk because of the wild-goats, ver-
    min (?), snakes, and mountain scorpions,*
May your plains where grew the heart-soothing plants,
Grow nothing but the 'reed of tears,'
*Agade, instead of your sweet-flowing water, may bitter
    water flow,*
*Who says 'I would dwell in that city' will not find a good
    dwelling place,*
*Who says 'I would lie down in Agade' will not find a good
    sleeping place."*

And, the historian concludes, that is exactly what happened:

Its canal-boat towpaths grew nothing but weeds,
Its chariot-roads grew nothing but the 'wailing plant,'
Moreover, on its canal-boat towpaths and landings
*No human being walks because of the wild-goats, vermin
    (?), snakes, and mountain-scorpions,*
*The plains where grew the heart-soothing plants, grew
    nothing but the 'reed of tears,'*
*Agade, instead of its sweet-flowing water, there flowed
    bitter water,*
*Who said 'I would dwell in that city' found not a good
    dwelling place,*
*Who said 'I would lie down in Agade' found not a good
    sleeping place.*

Probably the most important document in the Hilprecht
Collection is not a Sumerian literary work at all, but a map—
by all odds the oldest known city map in history. Inscribed
in a fairly well-preserved clay-tablet, now 21 by 18 centi-
meters in size, it consists of a plan of Nippur, the ancient
cultural center of Sumer, showing several of its more important temples and buildings, its "Central Park," its rivers

and canals, and particularly its walls and gates. It gives more than a score of detailed measurements, which, after due checking, show that the map was drawn carefully to scale. In short, though this particular cartographer lived perhaps about 1500 B.C.—that is, some 3,500 years ago—he drew up the plan with the care and accuracy required of his modern counterpart. (*See Fig. 4.*)

The writing on the map, which includes primarily the names of buildings, rivers, and gates, is a mixture of Sumerian and Akkadian. In most cases the names are still written with their early Sumerian ideographs, although at the time the map was prepared, Sumerian had long been a "dead" language. Only a few of the words are written in Akkadian, the language of the Semitic people who conquered the Sumerians and made themselves the masters in the land in the first quarter of the second millennium B.C.

The map was oriented not due north-south, but more or less at a 45-degree angle, thus:

In the center is the name of the city *Nippur* (No. 1), written with its ancient Sumerian ideograph *EN-LIL-KI*, "the place of Enlil"—that is, the city where dwelt the air-god Enlil, the leading deity of the Sumerian pantheon.

The buildings shown on the map are the *Ekur* (No. 2), "Mountain House," Sumer's most renowned temple; the *Kiur* (No. 3), a temple adjacent to the *Ekur* which seems to have played an important role in connection with the Sumerian beliefs concerning the nether world; the *Anniginna* (No. 4), an unknown enclosure of some sort (the reading of the name itself is uncertain); and far out on the outskirts of the city, the *Eshmah* (No. 6), "Lofty Shrine." In the corner formed by the Southeast and Southwest Walls is Nippur's "Central Park" (No. 5), the *Kirishauru*, which means literally "Park of the Center of the City."

Forming the southwest boundary of the city is the Euphrates River (No. 7), written in its ancient Sumerian form, *Buranun*. On the northwest, the city was bounded by the *Nunbirdu* Canal (No. 8), where, according to the ancient Sumerian myth of the birth of the moon-god (see Chapter 13), the god Enlil first saw his future spouse bathing and fell instantly in love with her. Right through the center of the city flows the *Idshauru* (No. 9), literally "Midcity Canal," now known as the *Shatt-en-Nil*.

But it is the walls and gates to with the ancient mapmaker pays particular attention, which makes it seem not improbable that the plan was prepared in connection with the defense of the city against an expected attack. The Southwest Wall is shown breached by three gates: the *Kagal Musukkatim* (No. 10), "Gate of the Sexually Impure" (the reading and meaning of this name were suggested to me verbally by Adam Falkenstein); the *Kagal Mah* (No. 11), "Lofty Gate"; and the *Kagal Gula* (No. 12), "Great Gate."

The Southeast Wall, too, is breached by three gates: the *Kagal Nanna* (No. 13), "Nanna Gate" (Nanna is the Sumerian moon-god); *Kagal Uruk* (No. 14), "Erech Gate" (the Biblical Erech, a city to the southeast of Nippur); and *Kagal Igibiurishe* (No. 15), "Ur-facing Gate" (Ur is the Biblical Ur of the Chaldees). The two last-named gates "gave away," in a sense, the orientation of the map, since Erech and Ur were cities located southeast of Nippur.

The Northwest Wall is breached by only one gate, the *Kagal Nergal* (No. 16), "Nergal Gate." Nergal is the god who was king of the nether world and husband of the goddess Ereshkigal, who plays an important role in the myth "Inanna's Descent to the Nether World" (see Chapter 21).

Finally, there is a moat running parallel to the Northwest Wall (No. 17), and another running parallel to the Southeast Wall (No. 18). Both are labeled *Hiritum,* the Akkadian (not Sumerian) word meaning "moat," by the ancient cartographer.

One of the most interesting features of this map is the detail of the measurements, for, as my assistant, Dr. Edmund Gordon, informed me after careful study, most of them are actually drawn to scale. The measure used was in all probability the Sumerian *gar,* although this is never actually written on the map. The *gar* was composed of 12 cubits and measured approximately 20 feet. Thus the width of the Anniginna (No. 4) measures 30 (written as three "tens") *gar*—that is, about 600 feet. Or, to take the Midcity Canal (No. 9), its width is given as 4 (three units on top and one unit at the bottom)—that is, about 80 feet, which corresponds to the width of the present Shatt-en-Nil. The distance between the *Kagal Musukkatim* (No. 10) and the *Kagal Mah* (No. 11) is given as 16 (*gar*)—that is, about 320 feet, while that between the *Kagal Mah* (No. 11) and the *Kagal Gula* (No. 12), which is practically three times as great, is given correctly as 47 (*gar*), or about 940 feet.

Fig. 4. Map of Nippur. Copy by Dr. Inez Bernhardt, Assistant Keeper of the Hilprecht Collection, Freidrich-Schiller University, Jena.

The lay reader can read and test the measurements for himself, if he bears in mind that a vertical wedge may stand for either 60 or 1, and a cornerlike wedge for 10. The two measurements that are off scale to a considerable extent are the 7½ (that is, 7,30 = 7 + 30/60) at the lower right corner of "Central Park" (No 5); and the 24½ (that is, 24,30 = 24 + 30/60) of the third section of the Northwest Wall. In the latter case it is not improbable that the scribe inadvertently omitted a cornerlike wedge at the beginning, and that the number should have read 34½, which would make it to scale.

The tablet on which this map is inscribed was excavated at Nippur in the fall of 1899 by the University of Pennsylvania. It was found in a terra-cotta jar, together with a score of other inscribed pieces, which ranged in date from about 2300 to about 600 B.C. This jar, to judge from its contents, was, as the excavators described it, a veritable "little museum." In 1903, Hermann Hilprecht published a very small photograph of the tablet in his *Explorations in Bible Lands* (page 518). But this photograph was largely illegible and practically useless for the translation and interpretation of the document (several scholars have tried their hand at it). Since then the tablet has lain in the Hilprecht Collection uncopied and unpublished all these years. Now at last it has been carefully and painstakingly copied by Dr. Inez Bernhardt, under my guidance, and the resulting study will appear under joint authorship in the *Wissenschaftliche Zeitschrift* of the Friedrich-Schiller University.

Appendix B

THE ORIGIN AND DEVELOPMENT OF THE CUNEIFORM SYSTEM OF WRITING AND OTHER COMMENTS ON THE ILLUSTRATIONS

Fig. 1, p. xxi. *The Origin and Development of the Cuneiform System of Writing.* The cuneiform system of writing was probably originated by the Sumerians. The oldest inscriptions unearthed to date—more than one thousand tablets and fragments from about 3000 B.C.—are in all likelihood written in the Sumerian language. Whether it was the Sumerians who invented the script or not, it was certainly they who, in the third millennium B.C., fashioned it into an effective writing tool. Its practical value was gradually recognized by the surrounding peoples, who borrowed it from the Sumerians and adapted it to their own languages. By the second millennium B.C., it was current throughout the Near East.

The cuneiform script began as pictographic writing. Each sign was a picture of one or more concrete objects and represented a word whose meaning was identical with, or closely related to, the object pictured. The defects of a system of this type are twofold: the complicated form of the signs and the fact that the great number of signs required render it too unwieldly for practical use. The Sumerian scribes overcame the first difficulty by gradually simplifying and conventionalizing the form of the signs until their pictographic originals were no longer apparent. As for the second difficulty, they reduced the number of signs and kept them within limits by resorting to various helpful devices. The most significant device was substituting phonetic for ideographic values. The accompanying table was prepared to illustrate this development. It proceeds from top to bottom:

No. 1 is the picture of a star. It represents primarily the Sumerian word *an*, "heaven." The same sign is used to represent the word *dingir*, "god."

No. 2 represents the word *ki*, "earth." It is obviously intended to be a picture of the earth, although the interpretation of the sign is still uncertain.

No. 3 is probably a stylized picture of the upper part of a man's body. It represents the word *lu*, "man."

No. 4 is a picture of the pudendum. It represents the word *sal*, "pudendum." The same sign is used to represent the word *munus*, "woman."

No. 5 is the picture of a mountain. It represents the word *kur*, whose primary meaning is "mountain."

No. 6 illustrates the ingenious device developed early by the inventors of the Sumerian system of writing whereby they were enabled to represent pictorially words for which the ordinary pictographic representation entailed a certain amount of difficulty. The sign for the word *geme*, "slave-girl," is actually a combination of two signs—that for *munus*, "woman," and that for *kur*, "mountain" (signs 4 and 5 on our table). Literally, therefore, this compound sign expresses the idea "mountain-woman." But since the Sumerians obtained their slave-girls largely from the mountainous regions about them, this compound sign adequately represented the Sumerian word for "slave-girl," *geme.*

No. 7 is the picture of a head. It represents the Sumerian word *sag,* "head."

No. 8 is also the picture of a head. The vertical strokes underline the particular part of the head which is intended—that is, the mouth. The sign therefore represents the Sumerian word *ka,* "mouth." The same sign represents the word *dug,* "to speak."

No. 9 is probably the picture of a bowl used primarily as a food container. It represents the word *ninda,* "food."

No. 10 is a compound sign consisting of the signs for mouth and food (Nos. 8 and 9 on our table). It represents the word *ku,* "to eat."

No. 11 is a picture of a water stream. It represents the word *a,* "water." This sign furnishes an excellent illustration of the process by which the Sumerian script gradually lost its unwieldy pictographic character and became a phonetic system of writing. Though the Sumerian word *a* represented by sign No. 11 was used primarily for "water," it also had the meaning "in." This word "in" is a word denoting relationship and stands for a concept which is difficult to express pictographically. To the originators of the Sumerian script came the ingenious idea that, instead of trying to invent a complicated picture-sign to represent the word "in," they could use the sign for *a,* "water," since the words sounded exactly alike. The early Sumerian scribes came to realize that a sign belonging to a given word could be used for another word with an altogether unrelated meaning, if the *sound* of the two words was identical. With the gradual spreading of this practice, the Sumerian script lost its pictographic character and tended more and more to become a purely phonetic script.

No. 12 is a combination of the signs for "mouth" and "water" (Nos. 8 and 11). It represents the word *nag,* "to drink."

No. 13 is a picture of the lower part of the leg and foot
in a walking position. It represents the word *du,*
"to go," and also the word *gub,* "to stand."

No. 14 is a picture of a bird. It represents the word
mushen, "bird."

No. 15 is a picture of a fish. It represents the word *ha,*
"fish." This sign furnishes another example of the
phonetic development of the Sumerian script. The
Sumerian word *ha* means not only "fish" but also
"may"—that is, the Sumerians had two words *ha,*
which were identical in pronunciation but quite
unrelated in meaning. And so, early in the development of the script, the Sumerian scribes began
to use the sign for *ha,* "fish," to represent also the
phonetically sounded *ha,* "may."

No. 16 is a picture of the head and horns of an ox. It
represents the word *gud,* "ox."

No. 17 is a picture of the head of a cow. It represents the
word *ab,* "cow."

No. 18 is the picture of an ear of barley. It represents the
word *she,* "barley."

The signs in the first column are from the earliest known
period in the development of Sumerian writing. Not long
after the invention of the pictographic script, the Sumerian
scribes found it convenient to turn the tablet in such a way
that the pictographs lay on their backs. As the writing developed, this practice became standard, and the signs were
regularly turned 90 degrees. The second column in the
table gives the pictographic signs in this turned position.
The next two columns represent the "archaic" script current
from approximately 2500 to 2350 B.C.: column III shows the
wedgelike signs written on clay, while column IV shows the
linear form of the signs as inscribed upon stone or metal.
Columns V and VI show the signs current from about 2350
to 2000 B.C. In column VII the signs resemble those current
during the first half of the second millennium B.C., the
period in which most of the tablets treated in this book were
actually written. The more simplified forms depicted in the

last column were the signs used by the royal scribes of Assyria in the first millennium B.C.

Fig. 2, p. 68. *Plowing Scene*. Albert Clay's reconstruction of the plowing scene depicted in the seal impression on a tablet published by him in 1912 in *Documents from the Temple Archives of Nippur Dated in the Reigns of Cassite Rulers* (No. 20). Note in particular the seeder plow, the very implement mentioned in the "Farmer's Almanac."

Fig. 3, p. 224. *Ancient Sites. Map of Southern Iraq*. Starting with Nippur in the approximate center of Sumer and proceeding in a southerly direction, some of the most important excavated sites are: Fara, the ruins covering ancient Shuruppak, the city in which Ziusudra, the Babylonian Noah reigned (Chapter 20); Tello, the ruins covering ancient Lagash (Chapters 6 and 7); Warka, the Erech of the Bible, the city of the heroes Enmerkar, Lugalbanda, and Gilgamesh (Chapters 4, 5, 22, 23, and 24), to which the goddess Inanna brought the *me*'s from Eridu (Chapter 13); Ur, the seat of three Sumerian dynasties, particularly the one founded by the lawgiver Ur-Nammu (Chapter 8; his grandson was the Shu-Sin of the love poems in Chapter 25); and finally Eridu, the seat of Enki, the Sumerian god of wisdom (Chapter 13). To the north of Nippur is Babylon, from which comes the name Babylonia later given to Sumer (in Sumerian times, however, it was a town of minor importance); Kish, the city of the first postdiluvian dynasty, one of whose kings was the Agga of the epic tale "Gilgamesh and Agga" (Chapter 5); Uqair, the ruins where the Iraqi Department of Antiquities excavated the "Painted Temple" (Plate 12); and finally Baghdad, modern capital of Iraq. On the outskirts of Baghdad is Tell Harmal (not indicated on the map), where Taha Baqir of the Iraqi Directorate of Antiquities excavated a number of public buildings and a number of school "textbooks" (Plate 4).

Fig. 4, p. 235. *Map of Nippur*. Copy by Dr. Inez Bernhardt, Assistant Keeper of the Hilprecht Collection, Friedrich-Schiller University, Jena.

Halftone Plates

Plate 1. *Nippur Scribal Quarter—Old Excavations.* The city of Nippur, about one hundred miles south of modern Baghdad in Iraq, was the spiritual and cultural center of ancient Sumer. Between 1889 and 1900, the University of Pennsylvania sent out four expeditions, which excavated thousands of tablets. Among them were the several thousand tablets and fragments with Sumerian literary inscriptions which constitute the basic source material for this book. The ruins shown on this old Nippur expedition photograph are of houses on "Tablet Hill," which covers Nippur's scribal quarter. Many of the Sumerian literary tablets were found in this area. Some of the ruins may be of schoolhouses or houses of professors who taught the pupils in their homes.

Plate 2. *Nippur Scribal Quarter—New Excavations.* Expedition photograph of ruins of houses on Tablet Hill, which was carefully excavated and recorded by the joint Oriental Institute-University Museum expedition to Nippur, under the direction of Donald McCown. About one thousand Sumerian literary pieces, mostly fragments, were unearthed in three excavating seasons between 1948 and 1952.

Plate 3. *Stairs of the Ziggurat of Tchoga-Zanbil, in Western Persia.* Though dating from several centuries after the Sumerian era—about 1300 B.C.—this ziggurat serves as one of the best preserved examples of those famous "Towers of Babel" which formed a bond between heaven and earth. The ziggurat of Tchoga-Zanbil, which is approximately 147 feet in height, was uncovered only recently (1952–56) by a French expedition under the direction of the noted archaeologist, Roman Ghirshman.

Plate 4. *Tell Harmal: Temple, Palace, and School* (?). Tell Harmal is a small mound six miles due east of Baghdad. The site was probably first settled in the middle of the third millennium B.C., but the most important discoveries made here were from the early part of the second millennium B.C. The most noteworthy building was a temple (right center on the photograph) consisting of an entrance vestibule, courtyard, antecella, and cella, all arranged with communicating doors on a single axis, so that the niche in the cella, on which the statue of the deity probably rested, was visible from the street when all doors were open. Among the other buildings were a palace, smaller temples, and what was perhaps a school building, where a number of "textbooks" were excavated, as well as the Semitic Bilalama law code mentioned in Chapter 8. The smooth brick walls surrounding parts of the excavation as a kind of façade are modern. They were built to help conserve the building, at least for a reasonable time. Otherwise they would be turned into ruins—by wind, rain, and storm—almost immediately after excavation. Harmal was excavated by the Iraqi, who now have a flourishing, capable, and productive Directorate of Antiquities under the dynamic directorship of Dr. Naji al Asil, a man of archaeological vision. Members of its staff like Taha Baqir, Fuad Safar, and Mohammed Ali have become world-famous excavators. Further details on the Harmal excavations can be found in *Sumer*, Vols. 2–6.

Plate 5. *War and Peace: The "Standard" from Ur*. Depicted on this University Museum photograph are two scenes of the type that may have been present in the minds and hearts of the Erech "Congress" as its members were pondering fateful decisions. One scene shows the Sumerian king in his chariot, triumphant in battle over an enemy whose soldiers are shown either led away as captives or trampled to death under the chargers' merciless hooves. The other scene depicts a rich royal banquet, probably in celebration of the victory. Note in particular the lyre-carrying minstrel in the upper right corner of the top register. He is no doubt one of the minstrels who were the prototypes of the poets who composed the myths and epic tales treated in the present volume. For details on the "standard" from Ur, and on other epoch-making discoveries, see Leonard Woolley's *Ur Excavations: The Royal Cemetery* (1934).

Plate 6. *"Netting" the Enemy*. Mythological scene on a limestone monument, commonly known as the "Stele of the Vultures" (a little over six feet in height), which was excavated in Lagash and is now in the Louvre. It depicts the

imprisonment of the defeated Ummaites by Ningirsu, the
tutelary deity of Lagash, in his "great net"—the mace and
the eagle over two lions are Ningirsu's emblems. The stele
was erected by Eannatum, the great conquering ruler of the
Lagash dynasty, who lived about 2400 B.C. Full details of
the stele and its inscription are given in Heuzey and
Thureau-Dangin's exemplary work, *Restitution matérielle
de la Stèle des Vautours,* and in André Parrot's *Tello.*

Plate 7. *Gudea, the "Architect."* Diorite statue of Gudea
(about three and a half feet in height) with a plan of a
temple; it was excavated in Lagash and is now in the
Louvre. Gudea ruled in Lagash about 2100 B.C. and is
noted for his numerous inscriptions commemorating his
various building enterprises. He was an older contemporary
of Namhani, the ruler of Lagash who was defeated by Ur-
Nammu, the world's first known lawgiver (see Chapter 8).

Plate 8. *Idi-Narum, an Official of Mari.* Pink stone statuette, about eight inches in height, excavated at Mari and
now in the Aleppo Museum. The name of the official is inscribed on the back of the statuette; so, too, is his title, but
unfortunately the meaning of the Sumerian words describing it is still obscure. Mari was a Semitic city on the central
Euphrates, considerably to the west of Sumer proper, but
its culture was predominantly Sumerian. Throughout the
third millennium it was largely under Sumerian control.
For one brief period, sometime about 2500 B.C., it produced
a dynasty which reigned over Sumer as a whole. The statuette, too, probably dates from about the middle of the third
millennium B.C.

Plate 9. *Lion Attacking Bull.* The scene, a common motif
in Sumerian iconography, is carved on a shell excavated at
Lagash and now in the Louvre. It dates from the middle
of the third millennium.

Plate 10. *Man's Oldest Prescriptions.* Reverse of the
"medical" tablet from Nippur in the University Museum.
The two marked-off sections are two prescriptions which
read as follows:

(1) *gish-hashhur-babbar* (white pear (?) -tree); *e-ri-na
u-gish-nanna* (the root (?) of the "moon"-plant); *u-gaz*

(pulverize); *kash-e u-tu* (dissolve in beer); *lu al-nag-nag* (let the man drink); and

(2) *numun-nig-nagar-sar* (the seed of the "carpenter"-plant); *shim-mar-ka-zi* (gum resin of *markazi*); *u-ha-shu-an-um* (thyme); *u-gaz* (pulverize); *kash-e u-tu* (dissolve in beer); *lu al-nag-nag* (let the man drink). For details, see *Illustrated London News*, February 26, 1955, pp. 370–71.

Plate 11. *Hymn to the "Great Physician of the Black-headed People."* Obverse of an excellently preserved four-column tablet from Nippur in the Museum of the Ancient Orient, dating from about 1750 B.C. The tablet is inscribed with a hymn to the goddess Ninisinna, who is here called the "great doctor of the blackheaded people (the Sumerians)." According to the author of this hymn, Ninisinna had charge of the *me*'s, or divine laws, set up for the healing arts before creation. She had been presented with them by Enki, the god in charge of all the *me*'s (see Chapter 13), and taught them to her son Damu, one of the names sometimes given to the god Dumuzi (Tammuz). In this hymn the diseases are attributed to demons, and the cure consists primarily of incantations. The text has been copied and published by Edward Chiera in his *Sumerian Religious Texts* (No. 6).

Plate 12. *Sumerian "Painted Temple."* An attempted reconstruction of a temple of the early third millennium B.C., excavated by the Iraqi Directorate of Antiquities in 1940–41 under the direction of Seton Lloyd and Fuad Safar at Tell Uqair, a mound about fifty miles south of Baghdad. The plan can be restored with a fair degree of certainty. The roofing is the most doubtful part of the reconstruction. The temple probably consisted of a long central hall with an altar at one end and an offering table in the center. Two ranges of four subsidiary rooms each surrounded the central hall. The temple was built on a terrace, which in turn rested on a tall D-shaped platform. One stairway led from the platform to the terrace, and two symmetrically arranged stairways descended from the terrace to the bottom of the platform. The outer walls of the building consisted of alter-

nating rows of buttresses and recesses and were painted
white with a coat of gypsum paint. The inside walls of the
temple were found covered with frescoes, of which little
could be recovered because they tended to cling to the
solid brickwork with which later builders filled the inside
of the temple. For details of the Uqair excavations, see
Journal of Near Eastern Studies, Vol. 2, No. 2.

Plate 13. *Ur-Nammu, the First "Moses."* Part of one of
the panels of a stele excavated by Leonard Woolley at Ur
and now in the University Museum. It depicts the king Ur-
Nammu making a libation before the Moon God Nanna
(seated), who was the tutelary deity of Ur. In the god's
right hand are the "line" and the "rod," surveying implements essential to the building of a temple, which is the
main theme of the stele. Ur-Nammu is noted as the Sumerian ruler who promulgated the first law code known to
date. For details see Chapter 8.

Plate 14. *Ebih-il, the Steward.* Alabaster statuette, a
little over twenty inches high, excavated at Mari and now
in the Louvre. The name and the title are inscribed on the
back of the statuette, which, to judge from the rather
archaic script, may be a little earlier than that of Idi-Narum.

Plate 15. *Ur-Nanshe, the Singer.* Limestone statuette
from about 2500 B.C., a little over eight inches in height,
excavated at Mari and now in the Damascus Museum.
There is some doubt about the sex of the individual represented by the statue. The excavators took it to be a
woman, but the name Ur-Nanshe is a name given to males
only and indicates that the figure is that of a man.

Plate 16. *Woman with a "Stole."* Diorite statue just under
seven inches in height, excavated in Lagash and now in
the Louvre. It dates from about 2000 B.C. and represents a
lady of Lagash with unusually heavy eyebrows, a rather
firm chin, and warm lips. A richly embroidered stole-like
dress covers practically her entire body.

Plate 17. *A Semitic King of Sumer.* Remarkably realistic
bronze head, three-quarters life size, excavated in Nineveh
and now in the Iraq Museum in Baghdad. There is no
inscription by which the head could be identified. But it

probably represents one of the kings of the Semitic dynasty known as the "Dynasty of Agade," which ruled over Sumer in the twenty-third century B.C., or thereabouts (see Appendix A for details).

ANCHOR BOOKS

HISTORY

FROM THE STONE AGE TO CHRISTIANITY—W. F. Albright, A100

GATEWAY TO HISTORY—Allan Nevins, New, revised edition, A314

HISTORY BEGINS AT SUMER—Samuel Noah Kramer, A175

A HISTORY OF BOLSHEVISM—From Marx to the First Five Years' Plan, Arthur Rosenberg; translated from the German by Ian F. D. Morrow, A588

HISTORY OF ENGLAND, Vol. I—G. M. Trevelyan, A22a

HISTORY OF ENGLAND, Vol. II—G. M. Trevelyan, A22b

HISTORY OF ENGLAND, Vol. III—G. M. Trevelyan, A22c

A HISTORY OF EUROPE, Vol. 1—Henri Pirenne, A156a

A HISTORY OF EUROPE, Vol. 2—Henri Pirenne, A156b

A HISTORY OF ISLAMIC SPAIN—W. Montgomery Watt and Pierre Cachia, A601

A HISTORY OF THE ITALIAN REPUBLICS—J. C. L. Sismondi; Introduction by Wallace K. Ferguson, A520

A HISTORY OF ROME—Moses Hadas, ed., A78

A HISTORY OF WEST AFRICA—Basil Davidson, A550

HITLER'S SOCIAL REVOLUTION—Class and Status in Nazi Germany, 1933–1939—David Schoenbaum, A590

THE HOUSE OF HABSBURG—Adam Wandruszka, A453

IMPERIALISM AND SOCIAL REFORM: English Social-Imperial Thought, 1895–1914—Bernard Semmel, A618

THE INTELLECTUAL HISTORY OF EUROPE, Vol. I: The Beginnings of Western Civilization to Luther—Friedrich Heer, A610a

THE INTELLECTUAL HISTORY OF EUROPE, Vol. II: The Counter-Reformation to the 20th Century—Friedrich Heer, A610b

JOURNEYS TO ENGLAND AND IRELAND—Alexis de Tocqueville; J. P. Mayer, ed., A611

LABOURING MEN—Studies in the History of Labour—E. J. Hobsbawm, A552

MARTYRDOM AND PERSECUTION IN THE EARLY CHURCH—W. H. C. Frend, A546

MEDIEVAL CITIES—Henri Pirenne, A82

MONT-SAINT-MICHEL AND CHARTRES—Henry Adams, A166

A NEW HISTORY OF THE COLD WAR: Third edition, expanded, of A History of the Cold War—John A. Lukacs, A533

THE OLD REGIME AND THE FRENCH REVOLUTION—Alexis de Tocqueville, A60

THE PATH TO DICTATORSHIP, 1918–1933: Ten Essays by German Historians—trans. by John Conway, with an introduction by Fritz Stern, A547

THE PHILOSOPHY OF HISTORY IN OUR TIME—Hans Meyerhoff, ed., A164

THE POLITICS OF CULTURAL DESPAIR: A Study in the Rise of Germanic Ideology—Fritz Stern, A436